Sports Starters

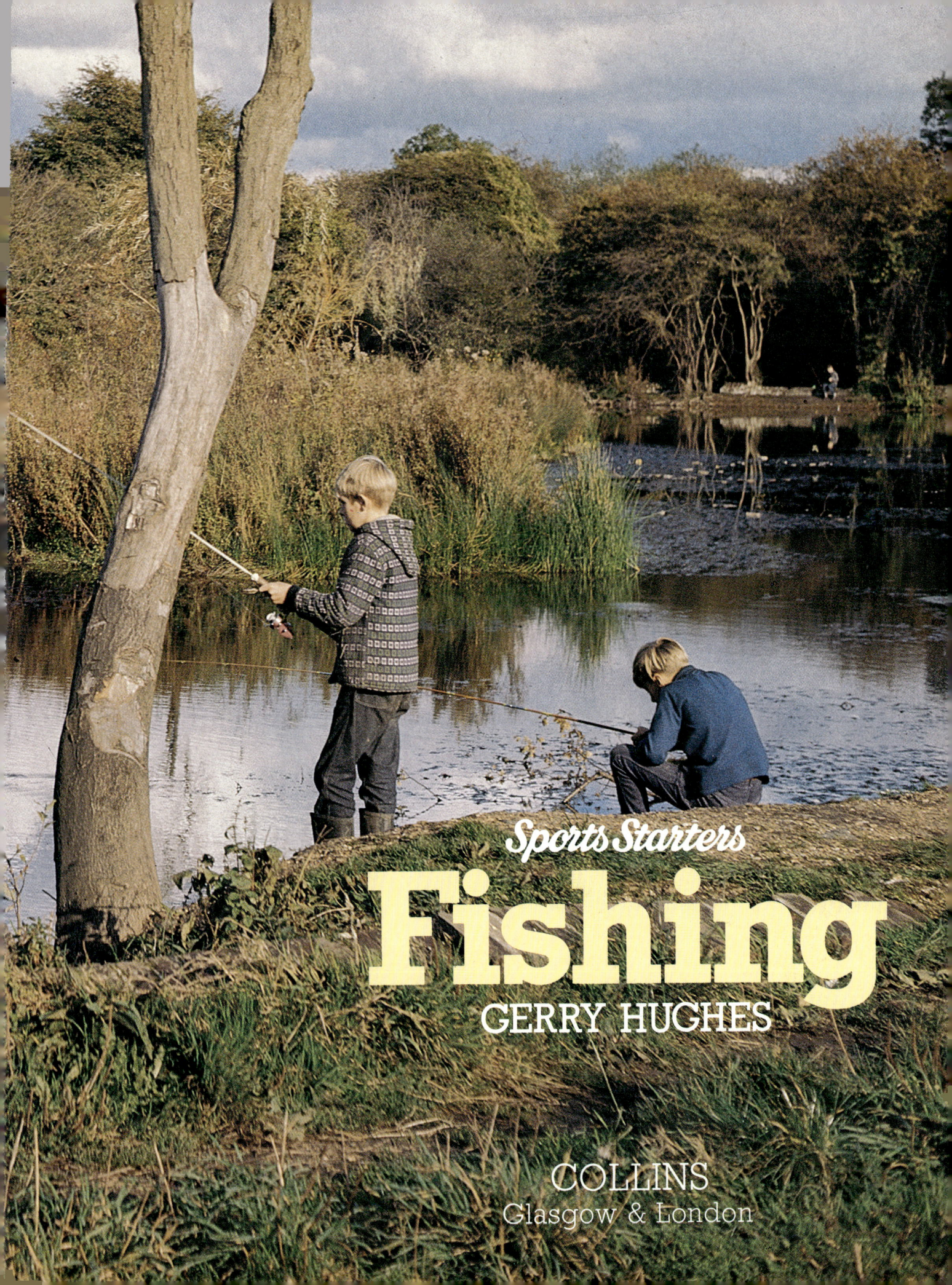

Fishing

GERRY HUGHES

COLLINS
Glasgow & London

First published 1979
by William Collins Sons and Company Limited,
Glasgow and London
© 1979 William Collins Sons and Company Limited

Devised, edited and designed by Youé and Spooner Limited

Illustrations by Ted Andrews
Filmset by Photocomp Limited
Colour processing by Medway Reprographic Limited

ISBN 0 00 411609 7

Printed in Great Britain

Contents

8 Introduction

10 Coarse fishing
tackle · tackling up · terminal float tackle
floats and shotting · ledgering · bite indicators · spinning
locating a swim · finding the fish · recognize the species
bait · casting · striking and landing · clothing
fishing in all weathers · at night · basic knots

58 The best on the bank

60 Trout fishing
fly-fishing tackle · choice of stillwaters
trout in rivers · on the bank · casting
recognize the species

76 The fascination of fly-tying

78 Salmon and sea trout

80 Battling with the big ones

82 Sea fishing
tackle · natural bait · artificial bait · understanding the sea
pier and harbour fishing · beach casting · rock fishing
recognize the saltwater species · some British sea fish records
boat fishing · boat tackle

110 Catch a conger

112 The mighty sharks

114 Safety and courtesy

116 Do-it-yourself rods

118 Trout waters

121 Useful addresses

122 Glossary of terms

124 Bibliography

125 Acknowledgments

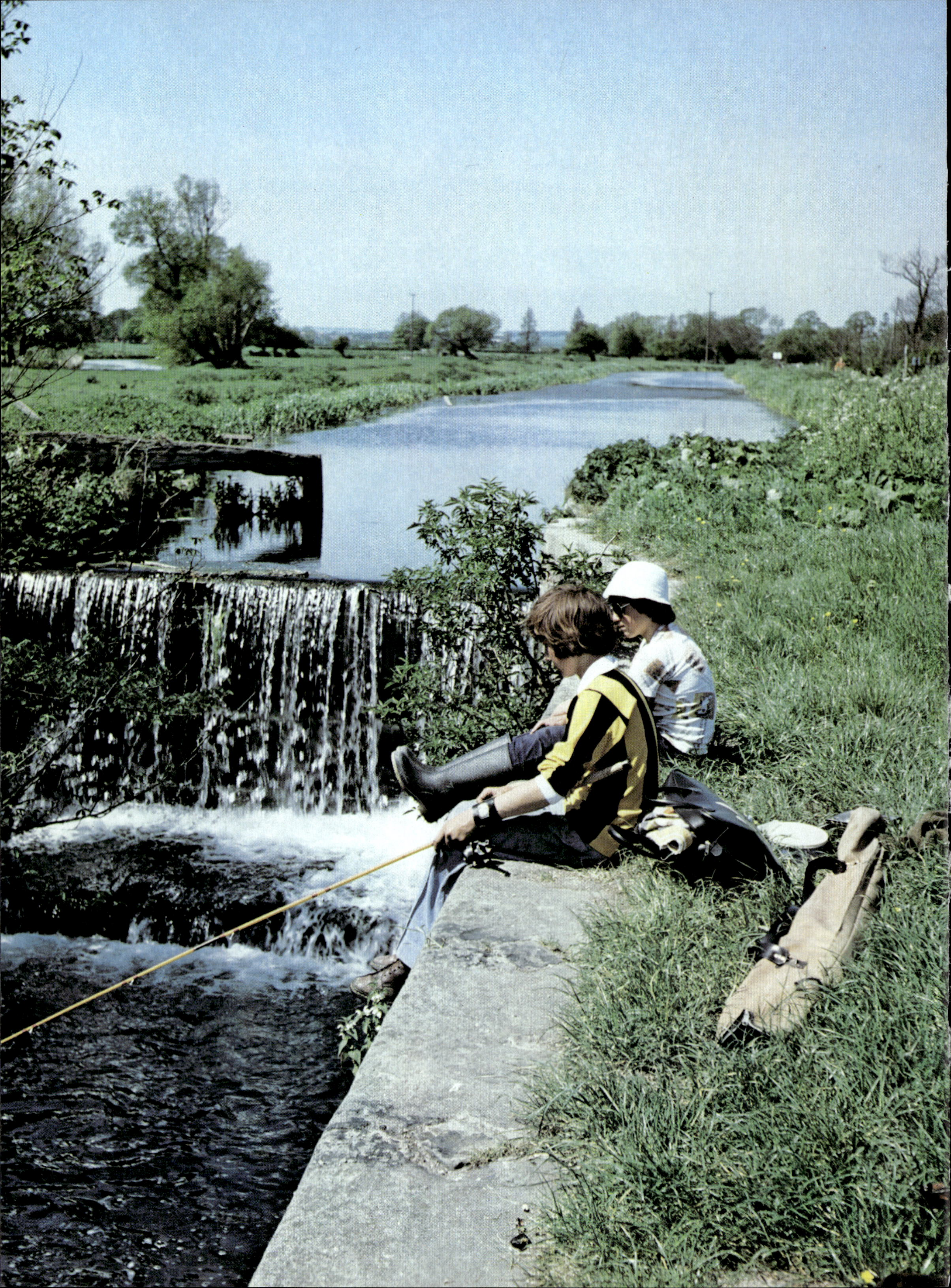

Introduction

A Sunday walk along any river bank or beach will quickly show you that fishing is the country's biggest participant sport. Wherever you look, you will see the modern disciples of Izaak Walton – in fact, at any weekend during the fishing season there are more people out fishing than there are spectators attending all the country's football matches. At the last count there were more than three million anglers in Britain.

If you ask ten anglers why they enjoy the sport, you will receive as many answers, for angling is all things to all men. Some like the fresh air and the peace of the countryside, while others enjoy the challenge of pitting their wits against a truly wild creature. Some enjoy the gregarious atmosphere of a fishing-club coach outing, while others prefer the solitude of a quiet river bank. The really skilled angler may win cups, money and glory.

We should not forget either that, when sea and game fishing, the successful angler can have the extra enjoyment of eating freshly-caught fish.

Fishing is a sport which can be enjoyed by the whole family. Both young and old of either sex can participate, for it does not demand outstanding physical fitness or great stamina – the main qualities needed are enthusiasm and the desire to catch something more interesting than the tiddlers which schoolchildren scoop up in their home-made nets.

The aim of this book is to explain to the beginner enough of the basics of freshwater and saltwater fishing to enable him or her to start fishing safely, without making too many mistakes or buying the wrong tackle.

Throughout the book you will find the terms angling and fishing used. These terms are interchangeable, though it is customary to call the participants of the sport anglers, as the word fishermen has a wider meaning.

Experience is a great teacher. The more you go fishing, the more you will learn – and the greater your knowledge, the more you will enjoy this fascinating sport.

Gerry Hughes

The author, Gerry Hughes, prepares for a day's fishing ▶

◀ The beginner need not have an armoury of tackle and a wealth of knowledge to catch enough fish to make a day's sport interesting and enjoyable

Coarse fishing

Anglers who spend their time catching the so-called coarse fish – the term applied to all freshwater species except salmon and trout – make up the greatest majority of the country's angling population. Many will say that theirs is the most skilled, varied and interesting branch of the sport. They have more than twenty different species to choose from, fish which range from the greedy little gudgeon which rarely weigh more than 56g (2oz), to the mighty carp which can weigh 18kg (40lb) or more. Their quarry can be found in a wide variety of waters from ponds to lakes, dikes, reservoirs, rivers and canals. Their sport can take them to the wide, featureless rivers of the Fens, the lush chalk-stream country in the south or the concrete-sided drinking-water reservoirs found in the heart of most cities.

A really good coarse angler will have a variety of skills at his fingertips, from the technique of catching small fish at high speed, so often needed in matches, to the knowledge and patience needed to outwit big, cunning fish. He will also have a wide selection of tackle to cope with the many different situations in which he may find himself.

However, the beginner need not worry about gathering an armoury of tackle and a wealth of knowledge when he or she first takes up the sport. Catching enough fish to make the day interesting and enjoyable is not difficult and good tackle will not cost a fortune. Modern technology and new materials have done much to improve design and keep down prices. Twenty years ago a fair quality rod cost nearly a week's wages and you would have paid the same amount for a reel. Now you can buy a virtually unbreakable glass fibre rod for little more than a day's wages and a reel costs even less.

For the beginner, it is important to know that he cannot fish when and where he likes. A licence is needed for all parts of the country except Scotland, and the proper season must be observed. In England and Wales you may fish for the coarse species from June 16 to March 15. The only exceptions are Yorkshire, where the season opens and closes a fortnight earlier than the rest of the country, and Cornwall, which has no close season. Scotland, too, has no close season for coarse fish. Rod licences (obtainable at most fishing tackle shops) are issued by the ten regional Water Authorities which cover England and Wales (see page 121) and their by-laws regarding the removal of fish, permitted sizes of keepnets (the nets in which anglers retain their catches) and methods of fishing must also be observed. The Water Authorities are responsible for land drainage, water supply, flood control and the administration of fisheries. However, the possession of a rod licence alone does not give the angler permission to fish private waters. It puts him in the same position as the shooting man who must have a Shot Gun Certificate but must also obtain a landowner's permission to use it on his land.

Having bought a rod licence for the area in which you intend to fish – and it can cover periods varying from one day to a complete season – you then have to find somewhere to fish. This is fairly easy, as there is almost certain to be some sort of free fishing in your area, and many river stretches or lakes controlled by angling clubs have day-ticket facilities allowing non-members to use the water for a nominal fee. In most cases the bailiff sells the tickets as he does his rounds.

The best advice for any beginner is to make a few enquiries in his home area and find out where the local fishing clubs have their headquarters. Joining a club is always a wise move. The more experienced members will gladly offer practical help when needed, and you will have access to its members-only waters. Many of the bigger clubs have a family membership scheme, and most run outings to fisheries outside the area. Smaller clubs are often affiliated to bigger associations, thus increasing the range of fisheries available.

A day's fishing can be enjoyed by the whole family, for every member can participate in the sport regardless of age, experience and physical fitness

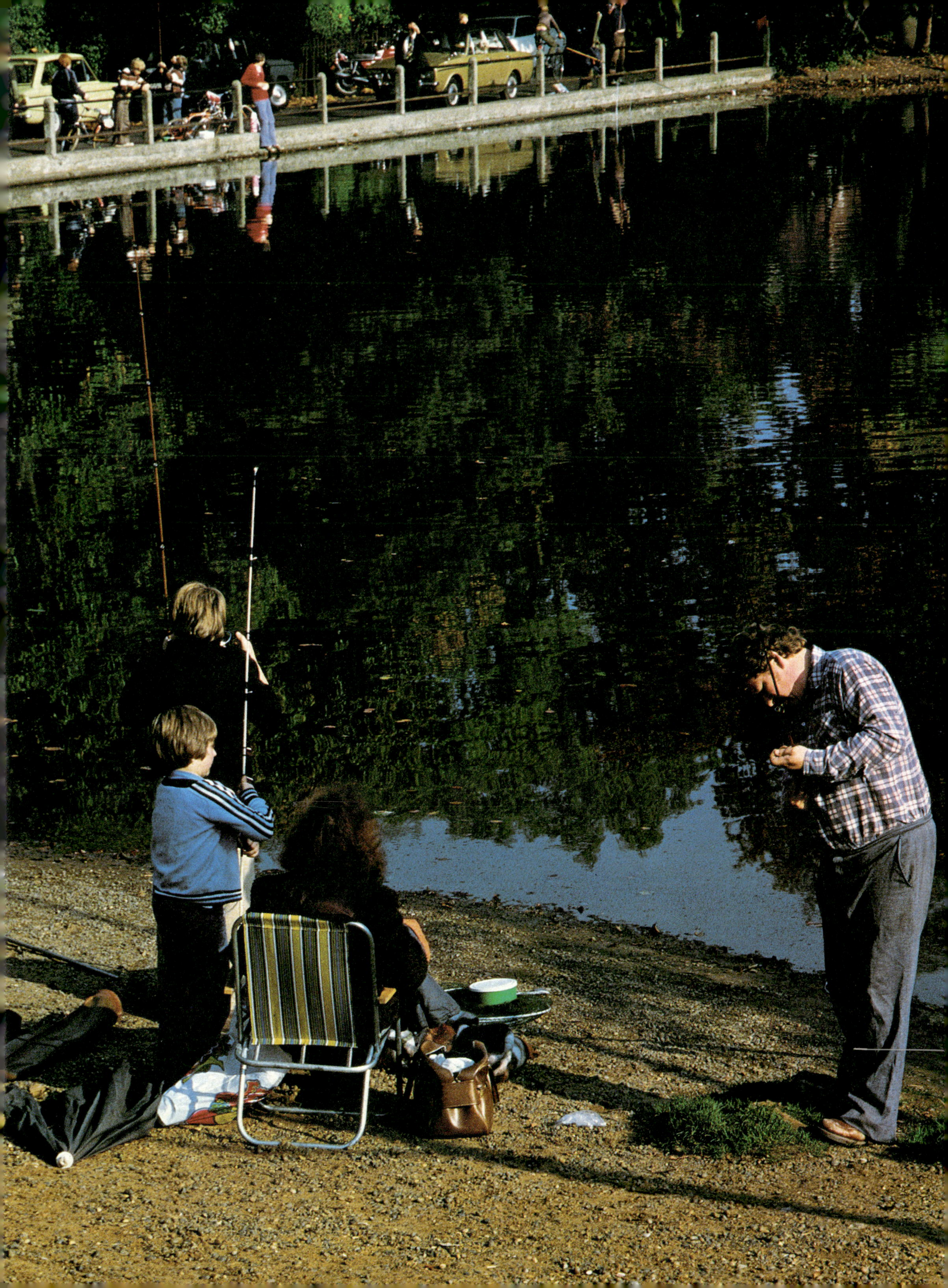

Coarse fishing
Tackle

The first visit to a good tackle shop is rather like entering Aladdin's Cave. The walls are hung with scores of rods, each designed for a particular purpose. The showcase houses a collection of reels, there is a rack of special clothing and a pile of nets. Floats of every shape, colour and size are hung on cards. There is a bewildering range of hooks, lead shot, baskets, stools and haversacks, plus a thousand specialized gadgets whose uses you can only guess at! Do not be put off, however. Although everything in the shop has its use at certain times and under certain conditions, to begin with you need bother only about the basics.

The most obvious requirements are a rod, reel, line, floats, hooks and lead weights, but you will also need a haversack or shoulder bag in which to carry the smaller tackle items, a stool to sit on and a keepnet to hold the catch.

As a beginner you will not be specializing in any particular aspect of angling, so you should choose just one rod that will do several jobs. Luckily, today's glass fibre rods, light and almost unbreakable, are versatile tools and you will have no trouble finding a general-purpose rod of

▲ Choose a rod of the right length and with the correct action. A general-purpose rod of about 4m (12ft) is ideal

▼ Aladdin's Cave! There are thousands of different items inside this large London tackle shop but you will need only a few to begin with

about 4m (12ft) in length. Do not be tempted to buy a much shorter rod because you think it will be easier to manage – it will not. Short rods are a disadvantage when fishing a river bank with a soggy or reed-fringed margin, as they will not allow you to reach over the margin and into the water. They are also a handicap when float fishing a deep stretch (see pages 18 and 19), where the depth of water is greater than the length of the rod, as they make casting difficult.

The general-purpose rod will cope with most sorts of fish and situations, except the specialist styles needed for big carp and pike.

There are three types of reel to choose from: the centrepin, which is now rarely used except by a few traditionalists and some matchmen, the fixed-spool (see photograph above right) and the closed face, which is a variation of the fixed-spool. The most widely used of the three is the fixed-spool, a reel which takes a lot of headaches out of casting. It has a slipping clutch which helps avoid sudden line breakage, can be bought in either left- or right-hand wind and has the added advantage that spools can be changed in minutes. This means that you can carry three or four different spools, each loaded with a line of a different breaking strain, and switch them around according to the species you are after or varying water conditions.

Modern lines are made from nylon monofilament, which is cheap, rotproof and has a degree of elasticity which acts as an additional safety factor in the hands of the beginner. If you are buying a number of extra spools, choose a range of different breaking strains, 1kg, 2kg, 3·50kg and 4·50kg (2lb, 4lb, 8lb and 10lb), so that you can cope with the varying situations you may meet. If you are not likely to be catching big fish and you do not want to buy too many reel spools, stick to 1kg and 2·75kg (2lb and 6lb). Read through the instructions which come with every reel to find out the line loading of each spool. A shallow spool may take 91m (100yd) of 1kg (2lb) line, while a deeper one may accommodate a longer length of thicker line. Make sure you stick to the correct loading, for the amount of line on the spool can affect the casting. Too little will cut down the distance you can cast, too much will have line spilling over the edge and can cause tangles.

▲ The fixed-spool reel is sturdy and trouble-free, needing very little maintenance, but keep it in a bag or pouch to prevent dirt and mud getting into the works

▲ You will need a selection of lines of different breaking strains to cope with various species and water conditions

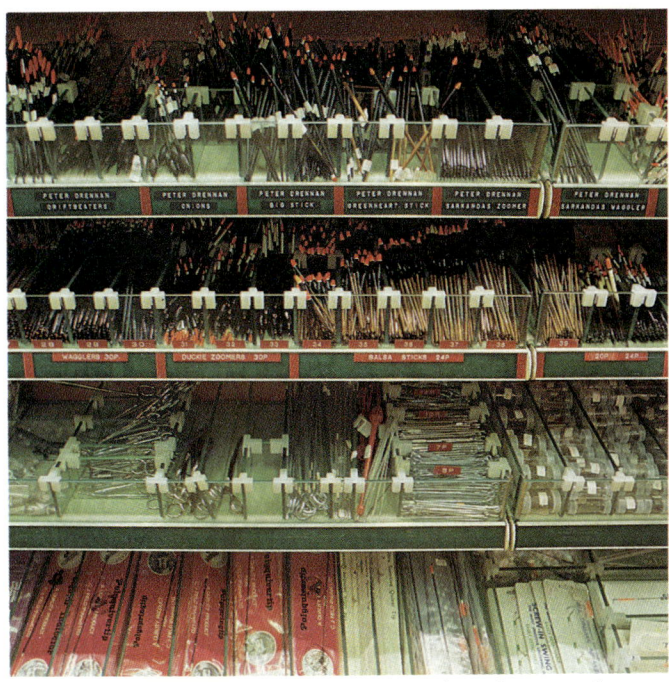

▲ From this collection of floats you need to choose only a couple of basic types for river and lake fishing

13

Coarse fishing

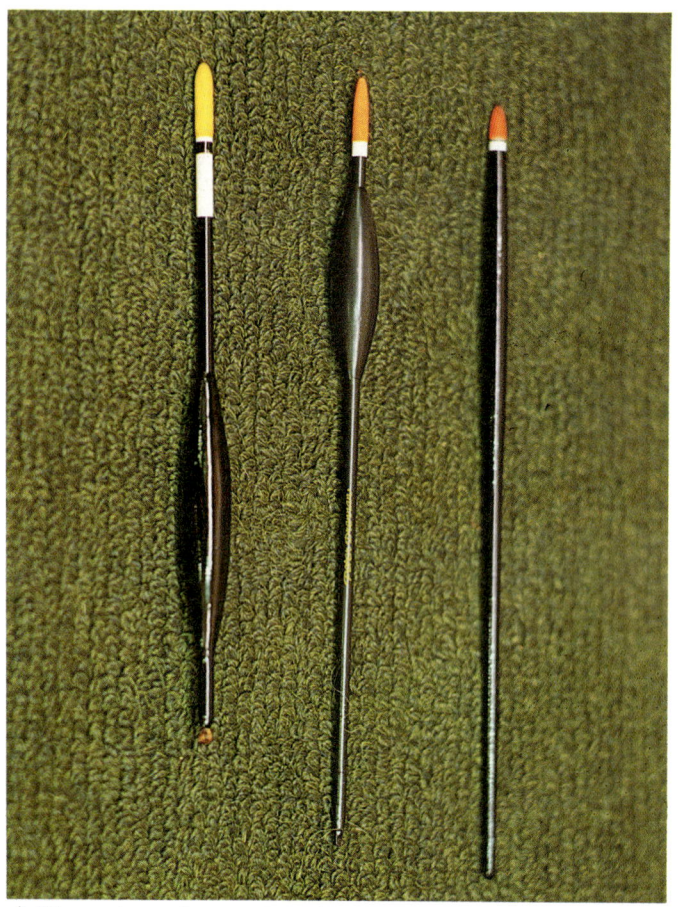

▲ These three floats – from left to right, Antenna, Avon and Stick – are a basic selection for use in still and running water, but you need several sizes of each. On pages 20 and 21 you will see how to use and weight them

▲ You will need an assortment of split shot to balance the float, and the most convenient way of buying it is in a container holding a range of sizes

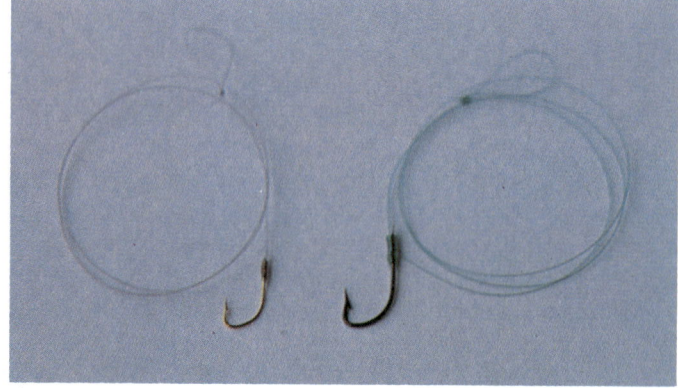

▲ Hooks that are ready tied to lengths of nylon are a good choice for the beginner. Make sure you have plenty and buy a number of different sizes

Next we come to floats – and a headache if you let yourself be dazzled by the display in the tackle shop. Look at the whole range and you will see such odd-sounding names as Duckers, Trotters, Sticks, Zoomers, Avons, Antennas, Missiles, Carrots, Arrows, Swingers, Onions, Wagglers, Darts and a dozen or so more. The purpose of the float is to put the hookbait in a given area or depth of water and to tell the angler when he has a bite. The floats can be made of wood, cork, pith, plastic, quill, reed or polystyrene. However, you will need only a couple of basic types for lake and river fishing. For stillwater (lake) use you will need a float with its buoyancy at the bottom end – an Antenna is a good example. For river fishing you will need an Avon, Stick or similar float, and a good old-fashioned standby for many situations is a length of peacock quill.

Buy an assortment of split shot – lead balls with a slot cut halfway through, used to balance the float – in various sizes, and some Arlesey bombs. The latter are pear-shaped leads with a brass swivel set in the narrow end, and are used for ledgering (see page 22), which is fishing with the bait on or near the bed of the lake or river. You should also buy a maggot dropper, a very handy gadget which puts the maggots exactly where you want them on the river bed, and some swimfeeders (see page 23), which serve the same purpose with groundbait (see page 43).

The tackle shop will sell three types of hook: spade-end and eyed (which are bought loose and have to be tied to the end of the line), and thirdly, hooks ready whipped to lengths of nylon. The latter are slightly more expensive but they are easier for the beginner as they do not involve any knot-tying. You simply tie a loop at the end of the main line and slip it through the loop at the end of the hook link (see diagram on page 18).

Get a swing- or quiver-tip which screws into the top rod ring (see page 25). Both are designed as bite indicators when ledgering,

▲ Arlesey bombs and drilled bullets are leads used for ledgering, when you need to keep the bait on or close to the bed of the lake or river

▲ These are two types of plummet, an invaluable aid in finding the depth of the water you are fishing. It helps you set the float at the proper level

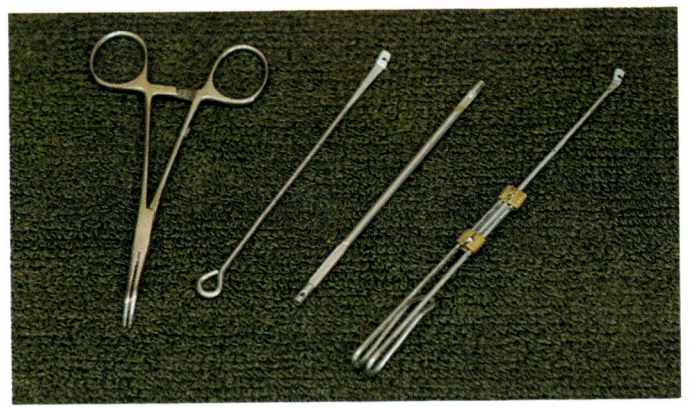

▲ Disgorgers are used for removing the hook from a fish's mouth and there are several types available. They can be lost quite easily, so keep a spare in your pocket. Artery forceps do the job better but are more expensive

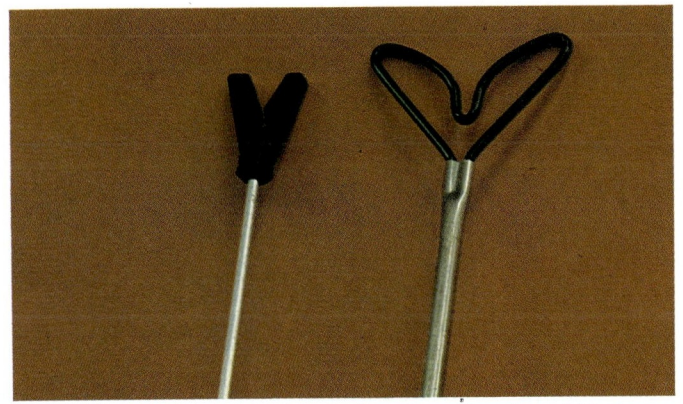

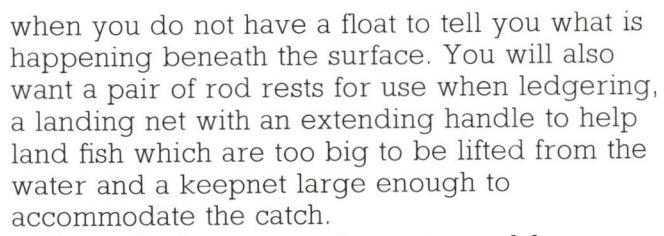

▲ Rod rests are useful when ledgering. The deep V helps to prevent the line being trapped between rod and rest

when you do not have a float to tell you what is happening beneath the surface. You will also want a pair of rod rests for use when ledgering, a landing net with an extending handle to help land fish which are too big to be lifted from the water and a keepnet large enough to accommodate the catch.

You will also want a plummet, used for checking the exact depth of water when float fishing, a disgorger for removing the hook from a fish's mouth, and a pocket knife, handy for all sorts of jobs.

Finally, you need something in which to carry all the odds and ends, plus the day's food and drink, and something to sit on. The old-fashioned cane basket or its modern glass fibre equivalent will do both jobs, but it has the disadvantage of having no back rest. The alternative is to buy a haversack or shoulder bag in which to carry the bits and pieces and a separate stool, with a back. This is a matter of personal preference, so see what the shop has to offer and make your choice.

▲ Some of the equipment that the beginner may consider buying includes a keepnet, a landing net, stool, bait box, haversack, umbrella, boots and rod case

Coarse fishing
Tackling up

✓ A correctly filled spool will offer the minimum of friction during the cast

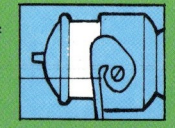

With the reel positioned near the top, the rest of the handle can be tucked under the forearm, which helps control

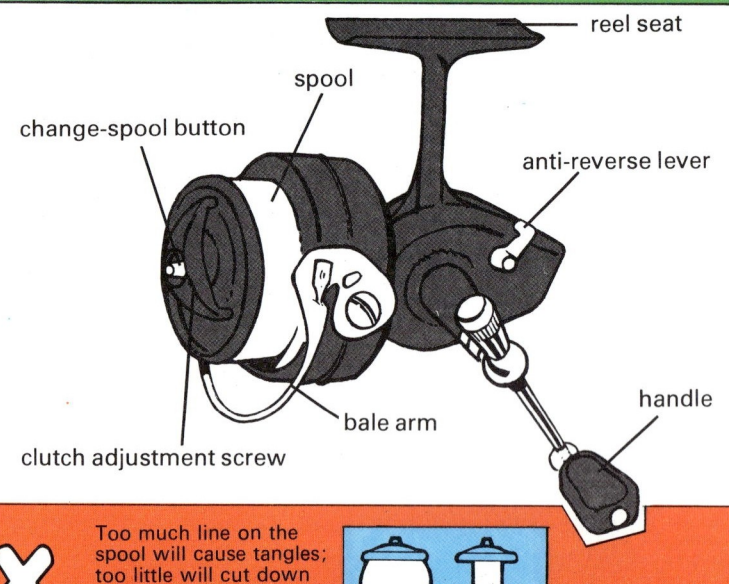

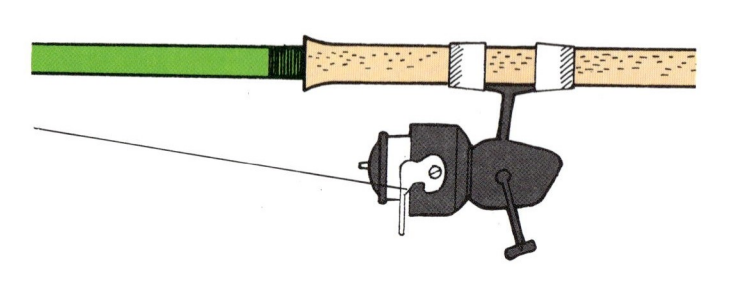

Labels on reel diagram: change-spool button, spool, reel seat, anti-reverse lever, bale arm, handle, clutch adjustment screw

✗ Too much line on the spool will cause tangles; too little will cut down casting distance

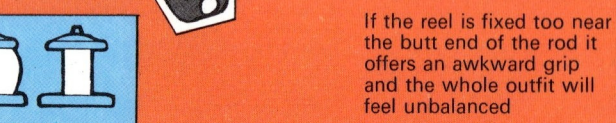

If the reel is fixed too near the butt end of the rod it offers an awkward grip and the whole outfit will feel unbalanced

▲ The fixed-spool reel has a built-in slipping clutch on the front of the spool which helps to avoid breaking the line by a sudden jerk. You set the clutch by turning the knob and test it by pulling the line. The clutch should yield just a little line. Make sure that the spool is correctly loaded with line or the casting will be affected

▲ The reel should then be positioned underneath the rod handle by means of the special fittings, which should be pushed tight so that the reel does not move. Place the reel near the top end of the cork handle so that the rest of the handle fits comfortably underneath the forearm

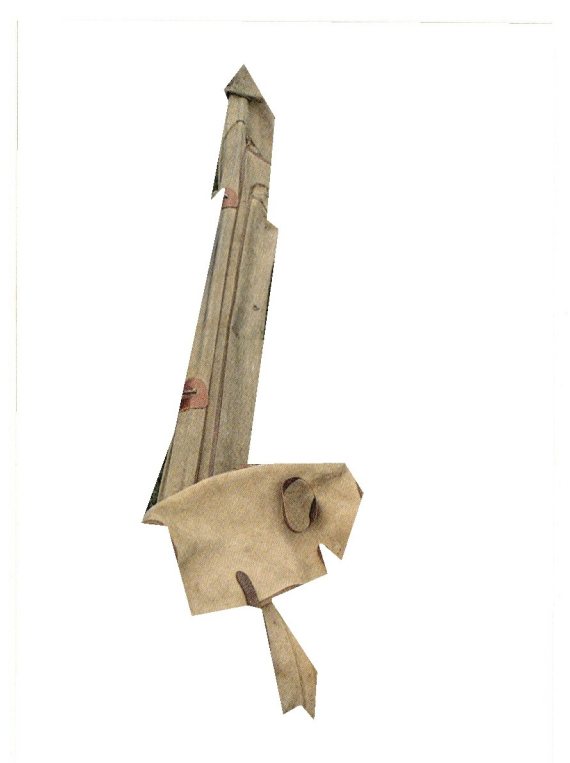

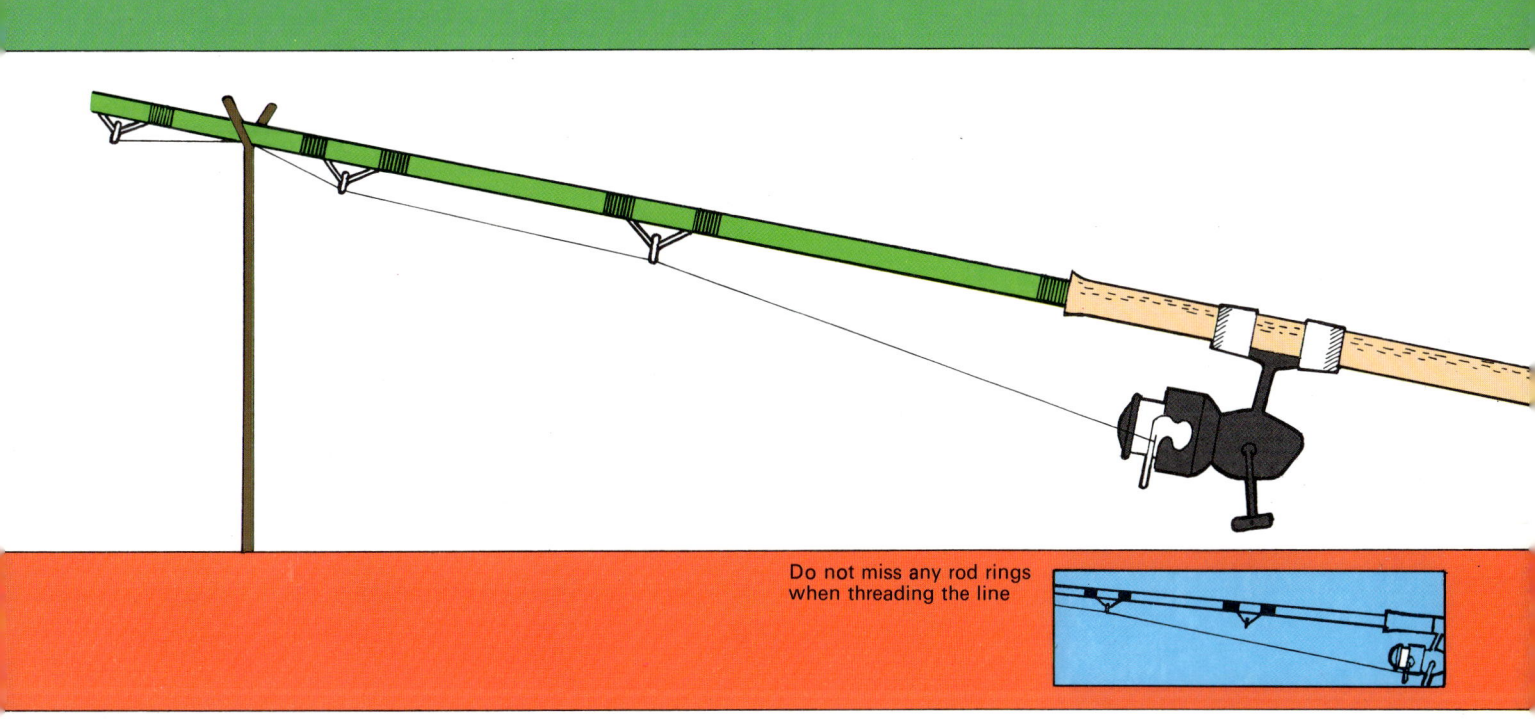

Do not miss any rod rings when threading the line

▲ It is easier and safer to prop the rod against a rod rest when threading the line through the rings. Push open the spring-loaded pickup, or bale arm, at the front of the reel to allow the line to be pulled off; then thread it through the rings to the top of the rod, leaving an extra couple of metres on which to fix the terminal tackle. Check that you have not missed any of the rings

Fitting all the tackle together is not difficult, but you must do the job in the right order. First, fit the rod joints together, making sure that all the rings are in a straight line. Most modern glass fibre rods have spigot ferrules, the male half fitting inside the female. These ferrules are designed with a taper to allow for wear, which means that when a rod is brand new there will be a slight gap showing even when the joint is fitting snugly. Do not try to force the ferrules any tighter than this, as you will only damage the rod.

The reel fits on the rod handle next and the positioning is important. If the reel is placed too low down, the balance of the rod will feel wrong and you will fish badly. Place the reel near the top, so that when you hold the rod parallel to the ground the rest of the handle fits comfortably under the forearm. The rod should feel almost like an extension of the arm, making casting and playing a fish much easier.

You then have to thread the line through the rod rings, and the best way to do this is to stick a rod rest in the ground first and lean the rod against it. A rod lying on the bank is in a dangerous position as it can get trodden on and damaged all too easily, either by the owner or a passer-by. Open the reel pickup, or bale arm, and thread the line through the rings, checking once you reach the top ring that you have not missed any. Then pull a couple of metres of extra line through to make the job of tying on the terminal tackle easier.

◀ Try to keep your tackle neat and tidy on the bank. It makes the job of finding bits and pieces easier, as well as preventing accidental damage by passers-by

◀ Do not be in too much of a hurry when putting the rod joints together. Always check that the rings on each joint line up with each other

Coarse fishing
Terminal float tackle

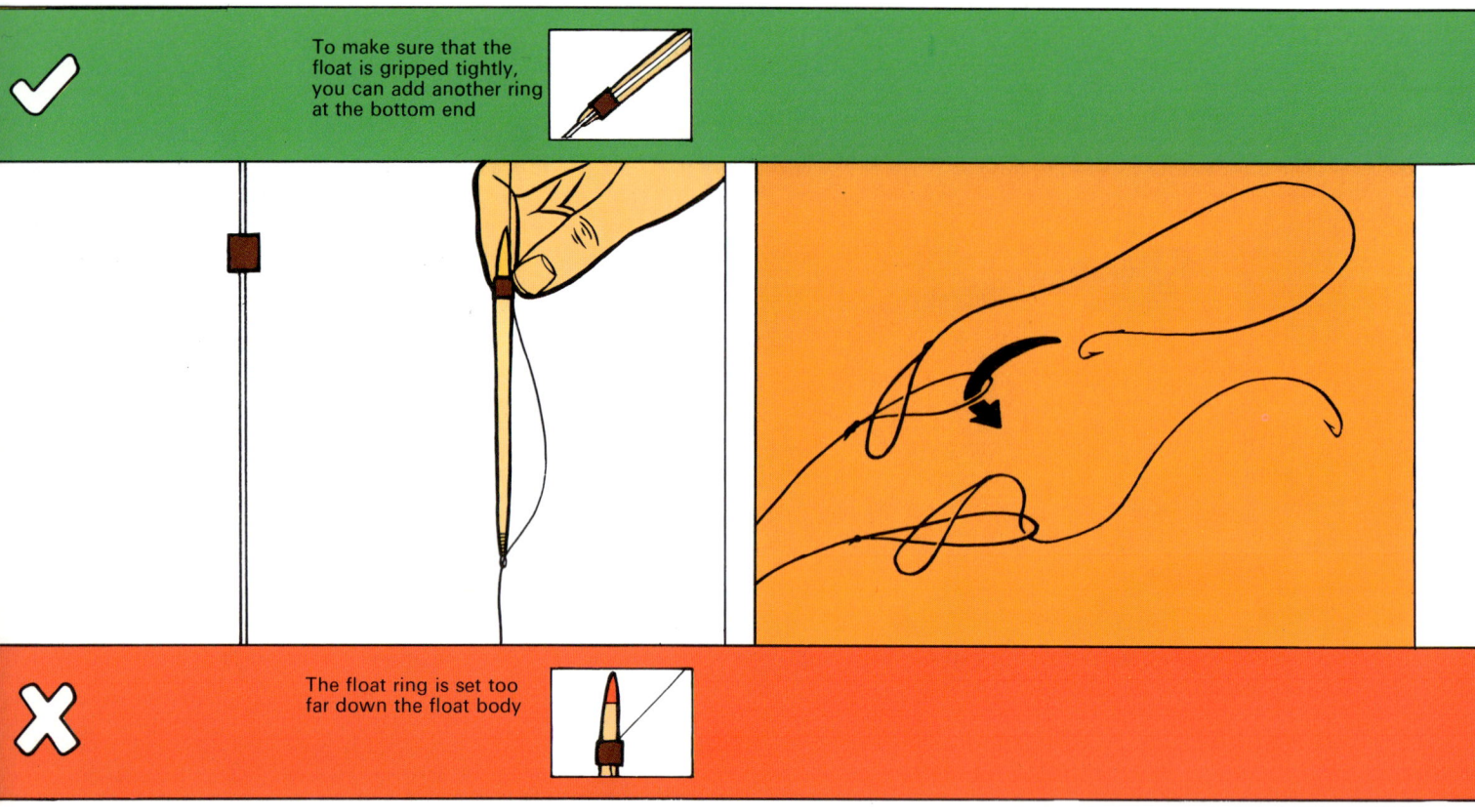

To make sure that the float is gripped tightly, you can add another ring at the bottom end

The float ring is set too far down the float body

▲ To attach the float, thread the ring on to the line, then slip the line through the ring at the other end of the float. Push the ring back on to the float body, but wet the body first to make the job easier. The ring should be a snug fit so that the float will not slip in use and thus alter the depth at which the bait is being fished

▲ Hooks already tied to a length of nylon are the easiest for the beginner to use, and the diagram above shows how such a hook is attached to the main line. Tie a loop at the end of the main line, and slip it through the loop at the end of the hook link. Pass the hook through the loop at the end of the main line, then pull gently to tighten it up

Once the rod, reel and line have been put together, you come to what is known as the terminal tackle, that is, the float (or ledger weight), shot and hook.

If the float has a rubber ring at each end, take them off and slip them on the line, then replace them on the float. They will slide more easily if you wet the body of the float first. Make sure that the rings are a firm fit, otherwise the float will move on the line. You balance the float by attaching split shot to the line beneath it, and with modern floats the amount of shot needed will be marked on the side. Shot sizes range from swan (the heaviest) down to dust (the lightest) and they are simply lead balls with a slot cut halfway through. Put the line in the slot and press the two sides together with your fingers or your teeth.

◀ Although these anglers are fishing close to the water's edge, the bushes on the sloping bank behind will help disguise their silhouette against the skyline

Put the hook through the eye of the plummet and then stick it into the cork strip on the bottom

If the shot is bunched up beneath the float, the bait will stay near the surface

▲ Shotting patterns vary according to the type of float being used, but the one shown above will give a natural bait presentation in most situations. Graduate the shot in size, starting with the heaviest nearest the float and working down, so that the lightest is near the hook. Do not squeeze them on with pliers or you may weaken the line

▲ Use a plummet to check the depth before you begin fishing. If the float is not set deep enough it will sink when you cast in. If it is too deep the float will lie flat on the surface or not cock properly. You have judged the depth accurately when the float just shows, but remember that the depth can vary in any given area

Do not pinch them too tightly or you may nick the line. Fix the heaviest shot nearest the float, graduating them so that the lightest ones are near the hook.

To attach a ready-tied hook, tie a small loop in the end of the reel line and slip it through the loop at the end of the hook link. Then push the hook through the loop at the end of the main line and pull it tight.

Before you start fishing you must check the depth of water in front of you, and this is where the plummet is used. With the plummet attached to the hook, cast in and watch the float. If it sinks, the float is set too shallow and the hook will be off the bottom when you start fishing. If it lies flat it is set too deep. You have the correct depth when just the tip of the float is showing.

This young lad has just hooked an eel in his local canal. ▶
He is not suitably dressed for fishing, however, as his bright clothes could frighten away wary fish

Coarse fishing
Floats and shotting

Shy bites are easier to spot if only the tip of the float is showing

The line should pass through the ring on the bottom part of the float

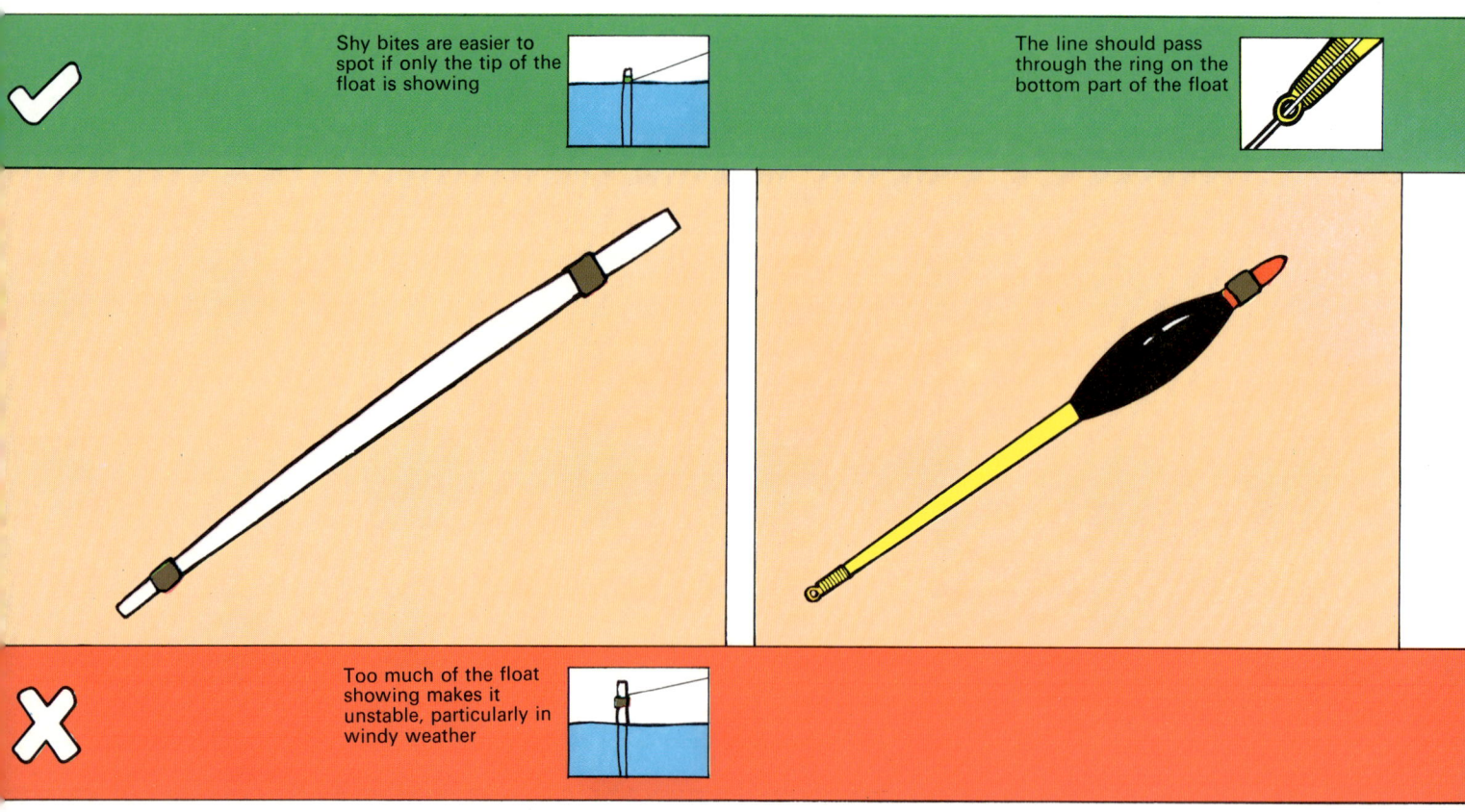

Too much of the float showing makes it unstable, particularly in windy weather

A piece of simple white peacock quill makes a very versatile float. It can be cut to length to suit the conditions and may be used on still or moving waters. You can use it just as it comes from the shop, or paint the tip in various colours to cope with different light conditions. The shotting pattern shown below would be used in a situation when the bait needs to get to the bottom quickly

The Avon float, made with a cane stem and balsa wood body, is ideal for use on fast-running rivers. The float is held in position by the float ring at the top end of the stem. It should always carry sufficient shot to sink the body, leaving only the top of the stem showing above the surface

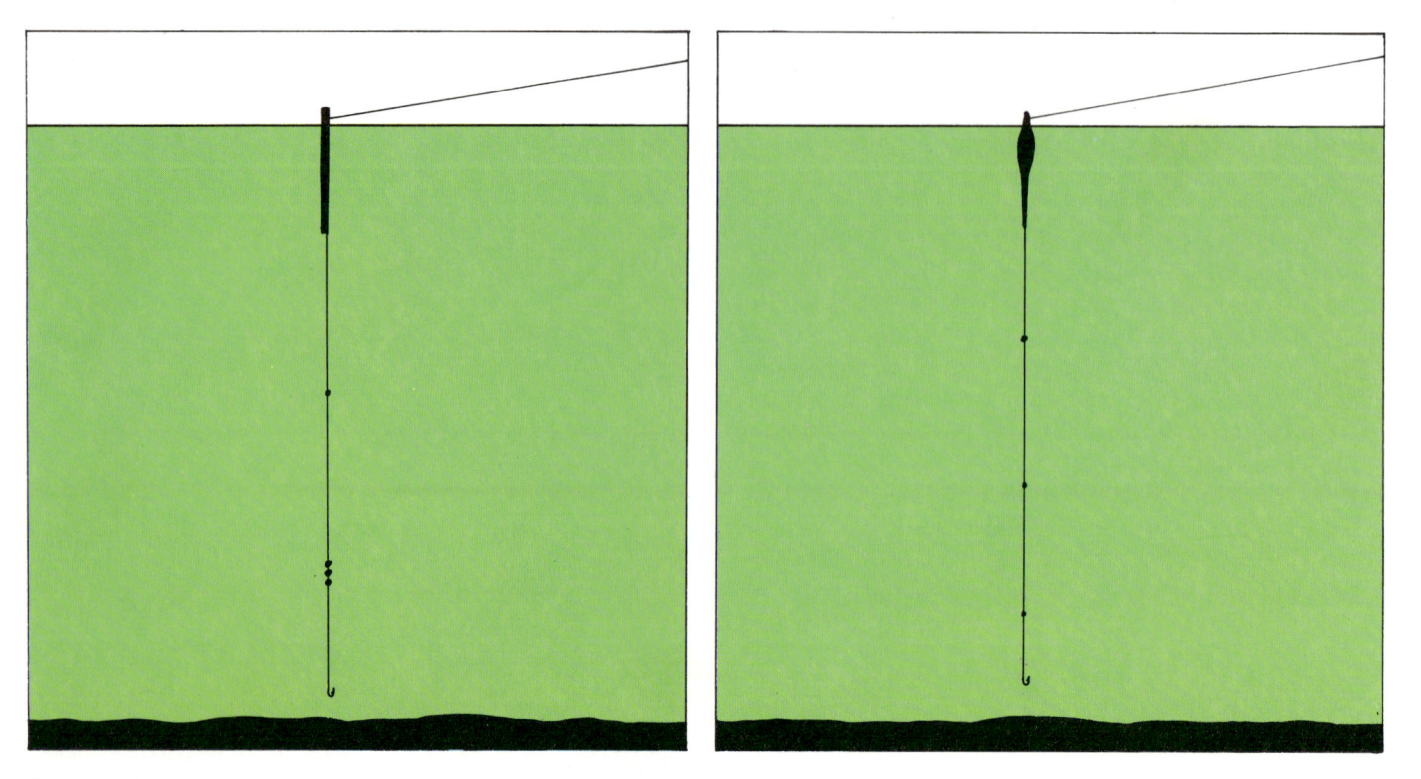

The line should go through the float rings

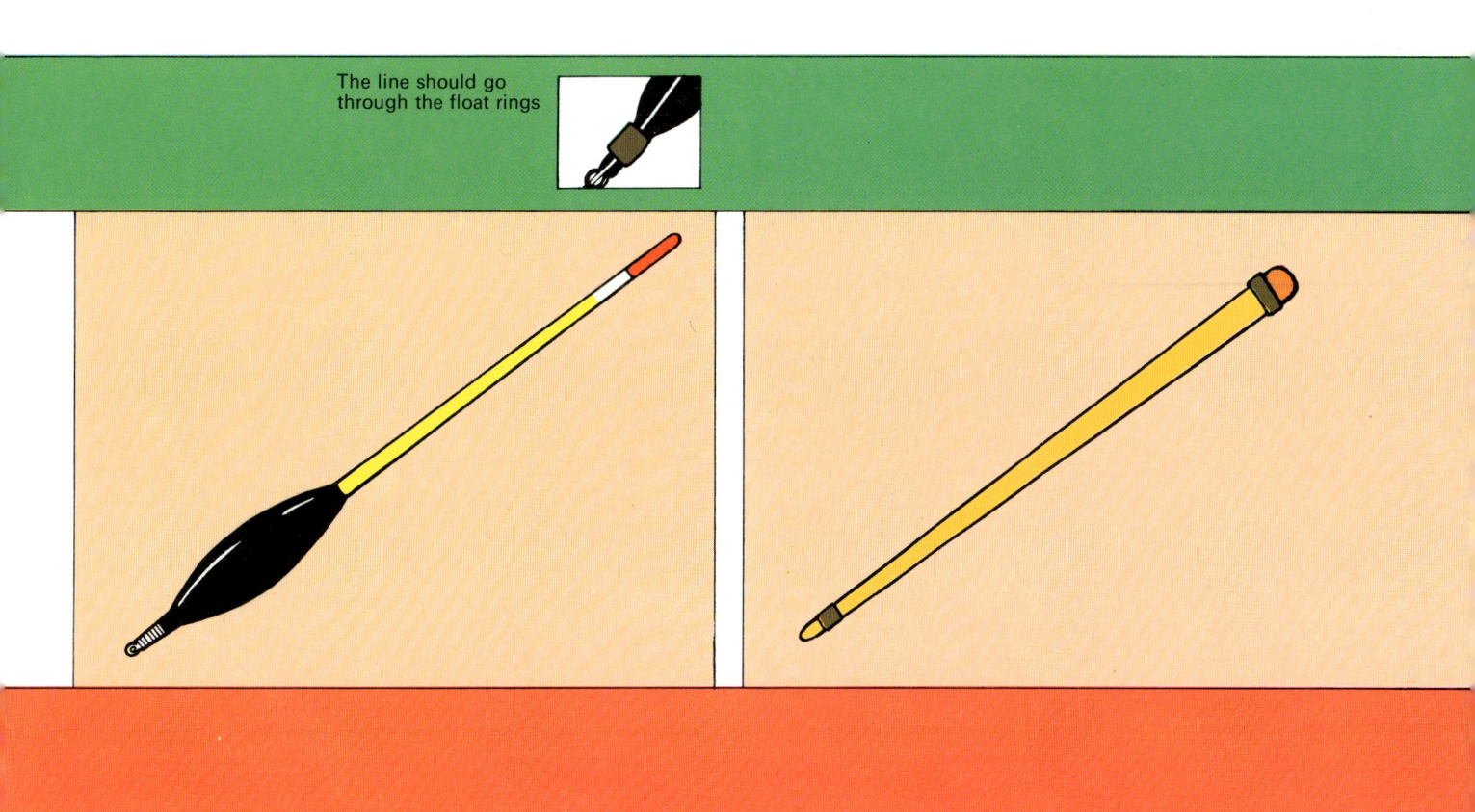

The Antenna is one of the family of floats designed for use in still or slow-running waters where waves on the surface make float control difficult. The Antenna is meant to be fished with the body, its most buoyant part, sunk deep enough under the surface not to be affected – otherwise the line on the surface would be blown about and drag the float out of position. It is attached via the wire ring and a float ring at the bottom, so the last part of the line is sunk

The tapered Stick float, made of balsa wood with a cane stem, is best used on those rivers which have a steady flow and is useful for fairly close work – you cannot fish it at the same distance as you can an Avon. It is meant to be used with light bait such as maggots, and is always fished with the shot evenly strung out between float and hook

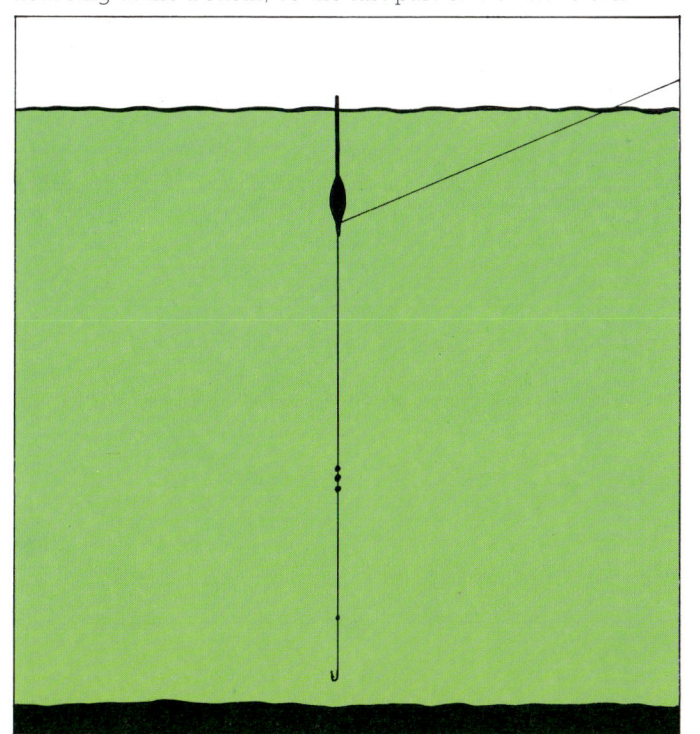

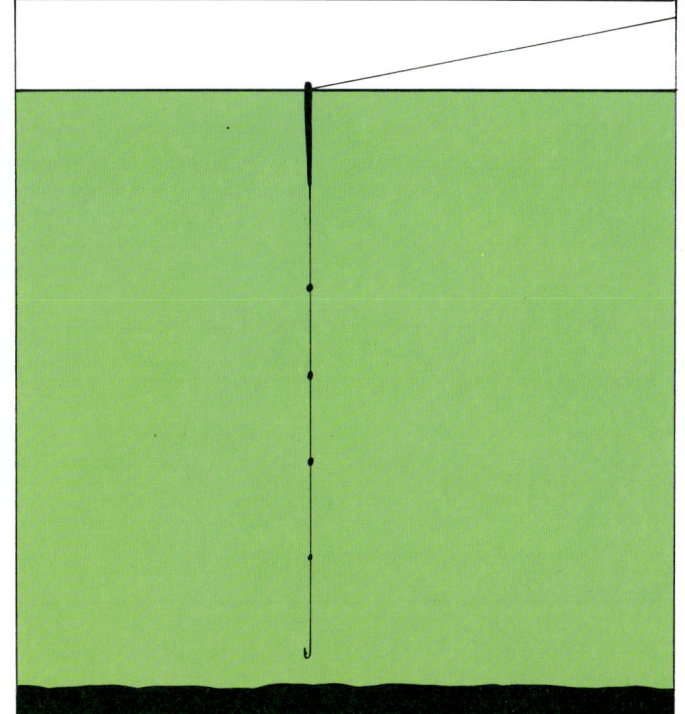

21

Coarse fishing
Ledgering

One of the differences between ledgering and float fishing is that bites are indicated in different ways. Float fishing allows the angler to present his bait at varying depths, from the bottom to the surface of the water, with the float itself showing when a bite is developing. The idea of ledgering is to get the bait right down to the bed of the lake or river and keep it there. By holding the rod and keeping a light grasp of the line just above the reel you can tell when a fish has taken the bait, but the more usual method is to lay the rod on two rests and rely on one of the special bite indicators which will do it for you.

Quiver- and swing-tips are tailor-made for the job, as are the various visual and audible indicators. There are also a number of old-fashioned, but still effective, ways of spotting the bites. The dough bobbin is simply a piece of bread paste moulded round the line between the reel and the first rod ring. The weight of the bobbin will keep a V shape in the line and the bobbin will rise as a fish takes the bait and straightens the line. On a calm day silver paper rolled round the line or folded into a V and looped over it will serve the same purpose.

The quiver-tip is a length of fine glass fibre which is screwed into the special top ring of the rod by means of a small threaded attachment, and it can be taken off when the rod is used for float fishing. Because of its sensitivity, the quiver-tip reacts to any movement of the line.

The swing-tip is attached to the rod in the same manner as the quiver-tip, but differs from the former in that it dangles at an angle from the rod tip. A fish lifting the bait will move the swing-tip.

At the terminal end of the tackle, the type of lead most commonly used nowadays is the Arlesey bomb, a pear-shaped lead with a brass swivel set in the narrow end. The round drilled bullet is also a popular lead. The shot ledger – a piece of spare line weighted with split shot – is a versatile rig, while the swimfeeder allows the angler to ledger and distribute samples of hookbait and groundbait at the same time. A split shot is always put on the line to stop the lead sliding down to the hook.

The swimfeeder is a particularly useful terminal rig in running waters. There are three types: the blockend, which has each end sealed with a cap, the open-ended and the conical, and they serve a dual purpose. Their most important function is to distribute free samples of hookbait in the area to be fished and also, being self-weighted, they need no extra lead on the line. With the conical feeder, the line passes through the centre, the wide end of the feeder being nearest the hook. The other types are attached to the reel line by a brass swivel.

▼ Ledgering is often a way of catching bigger fish, such as this barbel, which fell to an Arlesey bomb set-up

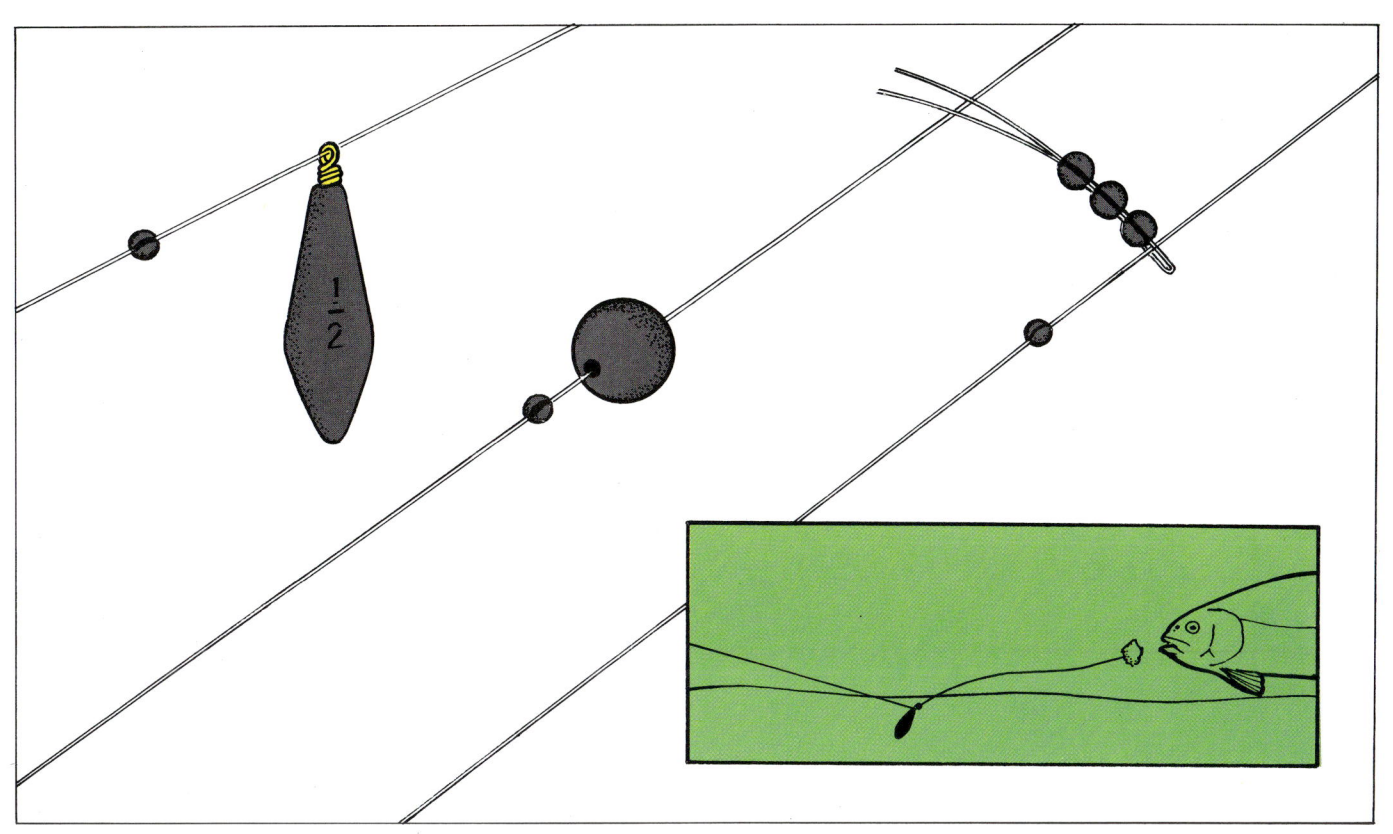

▲ Three types of ledgering rig. The Arlesey bomb (at top) can be made to hold the bottom or to roll with the current. The drilled bullet (centre) is another good rig for searching out swims (areas holding fish) on rivers. The shot ledger is a very versatile rig: weights can be put on or removed without breaking down the tackle. A split shot is put on the line to stop the lead sliding down to the hook

▼ Three different types of swimfeeder. The blockend (left), which is sealed with a cap at each end, trickles maggots into a swim at a slower rate than that of the open-ended feeder (centre) which can be used for maggots providing each end is plugged with groundbait, and is also useful for bigger bait particles. The conical feeder is another version of the blockend, but is attached to the line in a different way

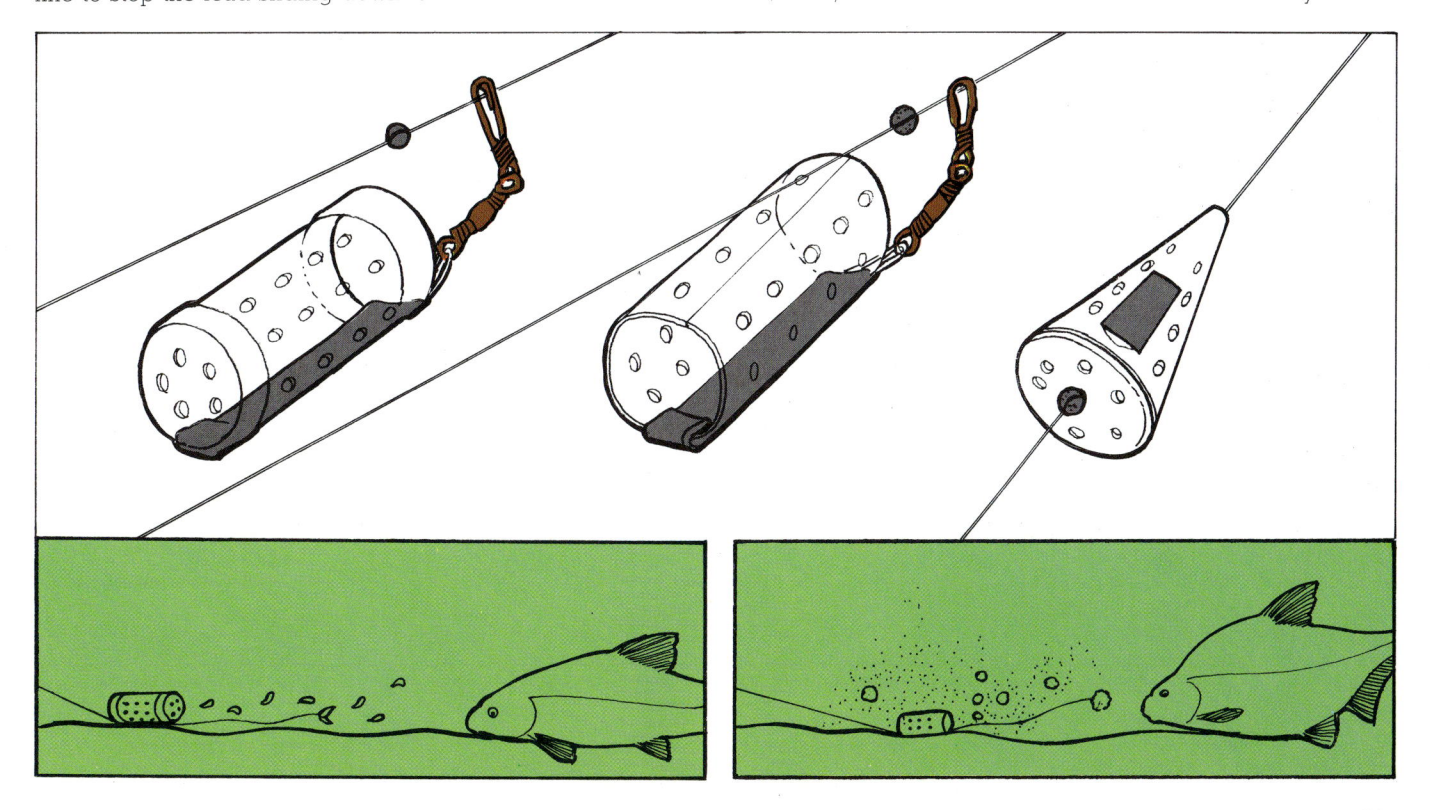

Coarse fishing
Bite indicators

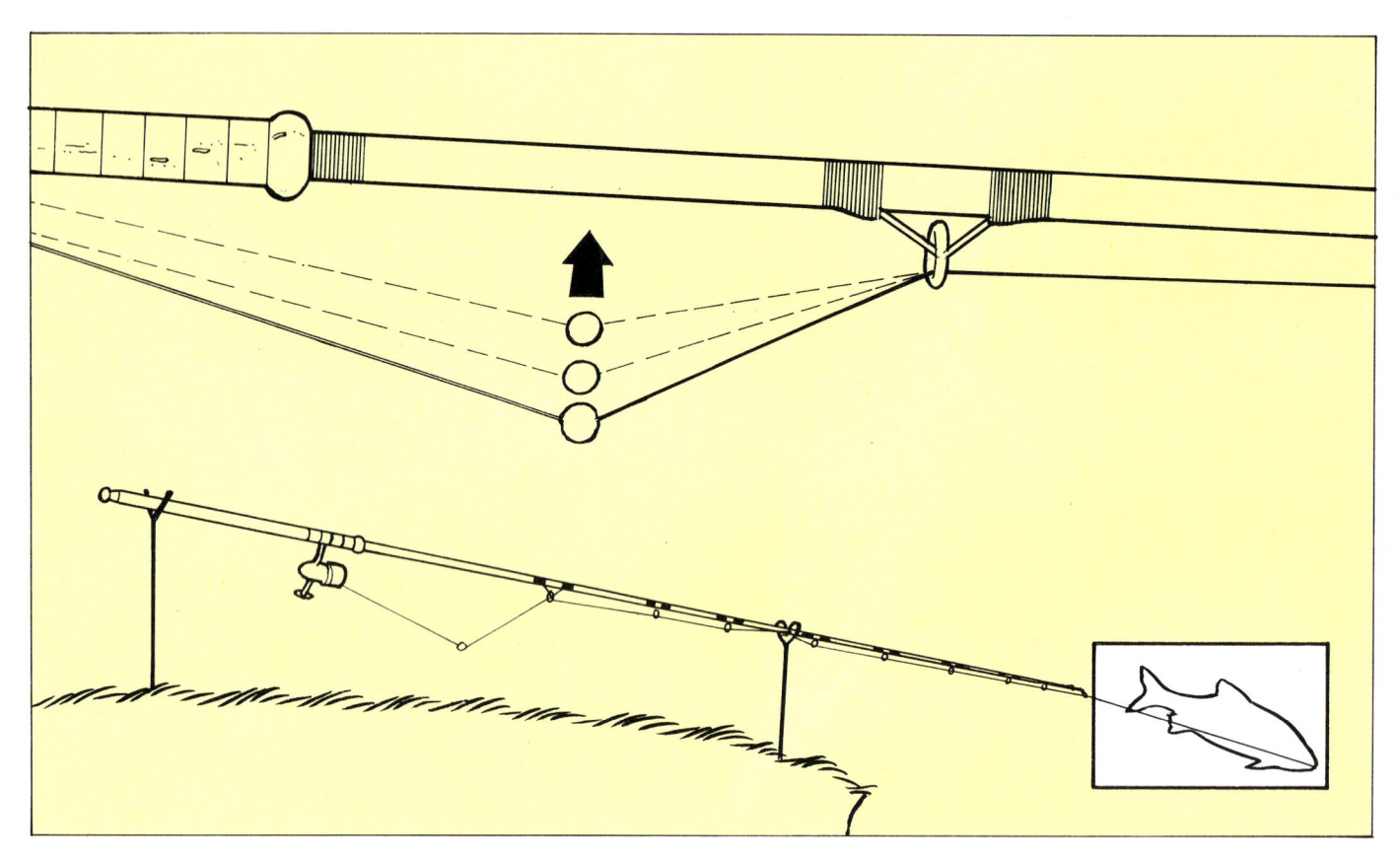

A simple visual bite indicator when ledgering can be made from a piece of bread paste. This is known as a dough bobbin. The rod is placed on two rests and the bobbin squeezed on to the line below the bottom rod ring (see above). When a fish moves off with the bait, the bobbin will move up. Alternatively, you can roll a tube of silver paper round the line in the same position (see below). If it blows about too much, fold it over, lay it on the ground and weight it with a couple of small stones. Tackle shops also sell purpose-made indicators which are attached to the end of the rod (see the diagrams on the opposite page), or you can buy the sensitive but rather expensive electronic or battery-operated indicators that give visual and audible warnings

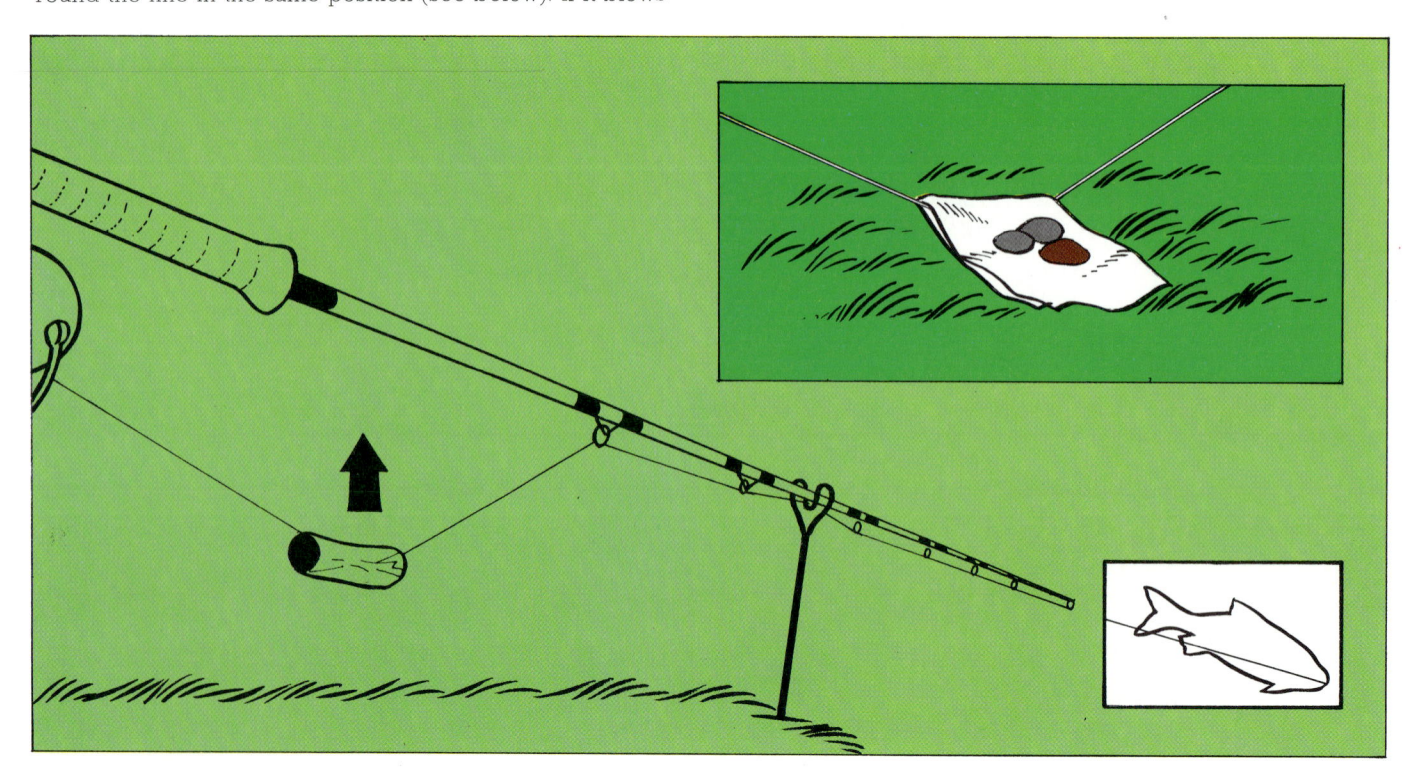

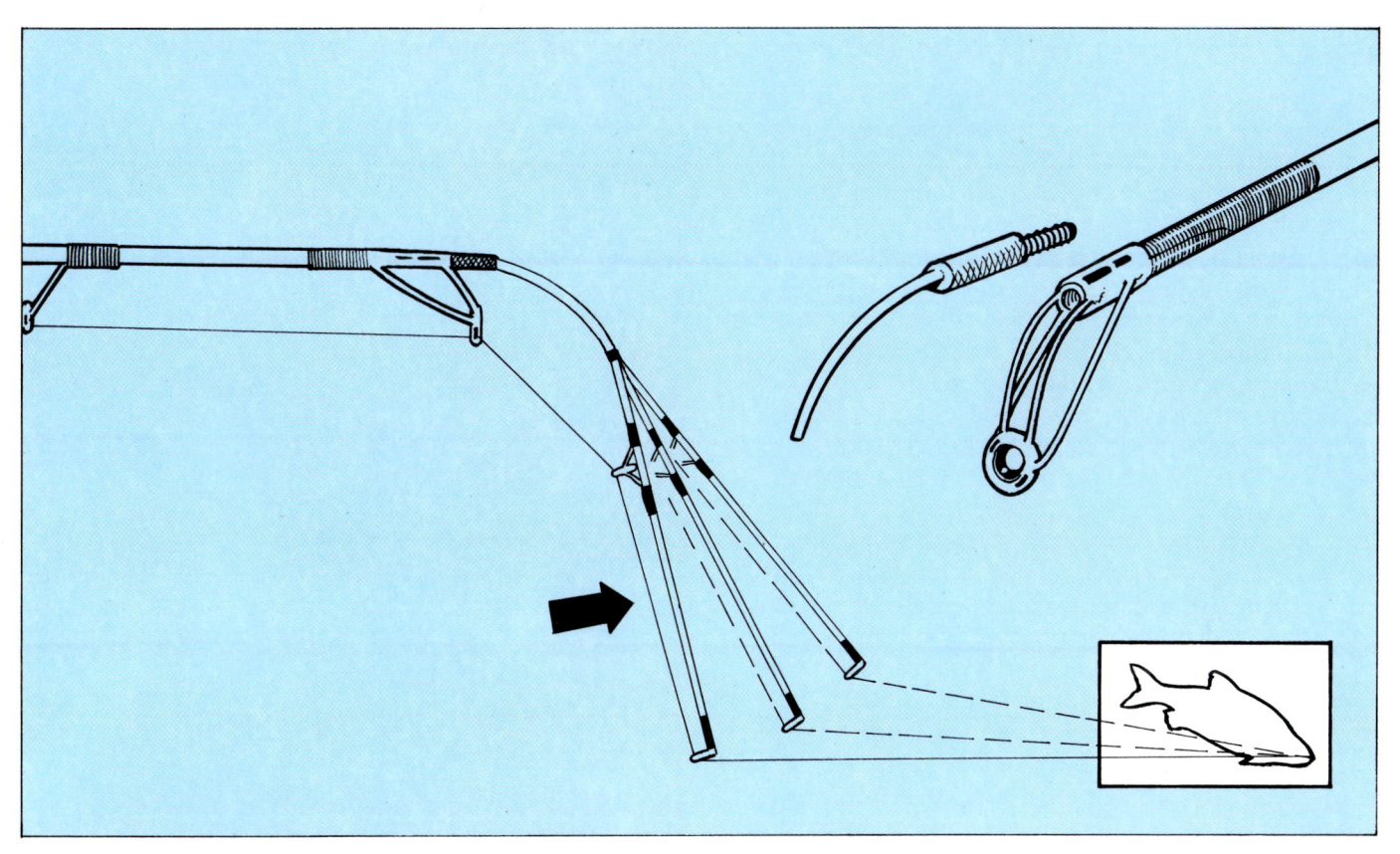

Swing-tips and quiver-tips are commercially made, sensitive bite detectors which are fitted to the rod itself, instead of being attached to the line near the butt as with the dough bobbin or silver paper. Both are screwed into the top rod ring by means of a special threaded attachment. In use, the swing-tip (see above) hangs down at an angle from the rod tip and will move up or straighten out when a fish takes the bait. The quiver-tip (see below) is a slim, straight length of glass fibre that will flick or quiver when the angler gets a bite

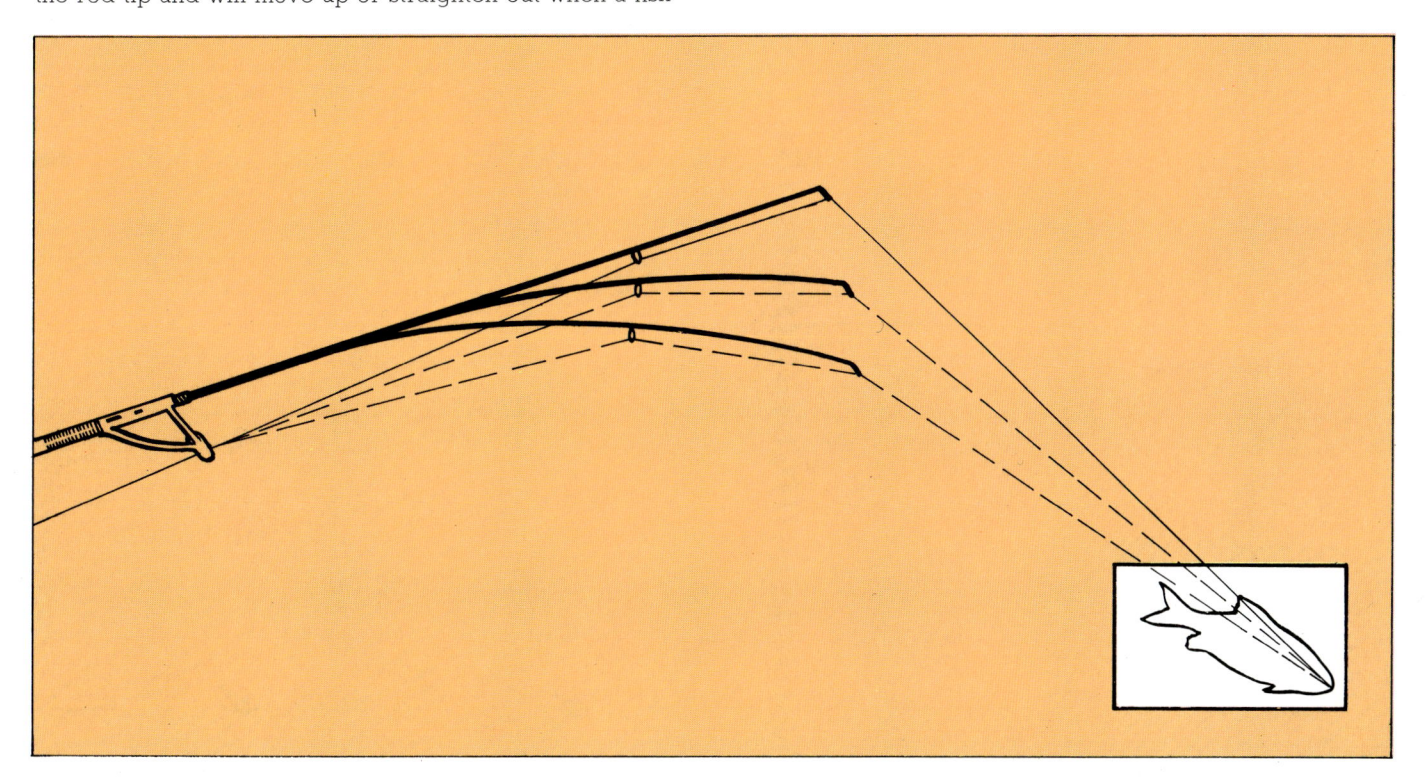

Coarse fishing
Spinning

Spinning differs from all other forms of coarse fishing in that an artificial, moving bait is used while the angler roves the banks and seeks fish rather than trying to attract the fish to one area. It is a method designed to catch predators, such as pike and perch. The bait – which can be made of wood, metal or plastic – is designed to imitate the actions of a small fish, and it is the action which is most important.

The term spinning is rather misleading, for not all lures (the general term used for artificial bait) actually spin in the true sense of the word. The metal ones called spoons are among the lures that are designed to wobble, dip, dive or wriggle. You can buy wooden plugs which float on the surface when stationary but dive when the line is reeled in. Other lures make popping sounds on the surface, just as small fish do. Most do not resemble actual fish in appearance. Their purpose is to make vibrations (when reeled in properly) which the predatory species will pick up. The fish home in on the cause of the commotion and hit the lure with a solid thump.

Different lures will succeed on different days, depending on their colour, action and the weather conditions. The usual method is for the angler to carry a selection with him, so that he can ring the changes when necessary. To combat the pike's sharp teeth, a short wire trace is used to join lure and line. The normal general-purpose rod used for bottom fishing is not suitable for spinning. A more specialized rod is called for, something which can flick a lure to a precise spot and cope with a heavy fish when the need arises.

▲ The mullet is a saltwater fish but is often found in the brackish waters of river estuaries. This one was caught on a small spinner

▶ Spinning keeps you on the move on those cold winter days when the banks are less crowded and there is plenty of room for everyone

▼ Plugs, generally made of wood, can be fished on the surface, at midwater or down near the bottom

▼ Spoons and spinners made of metal have different actions, depending on the speed and style of the retrieve

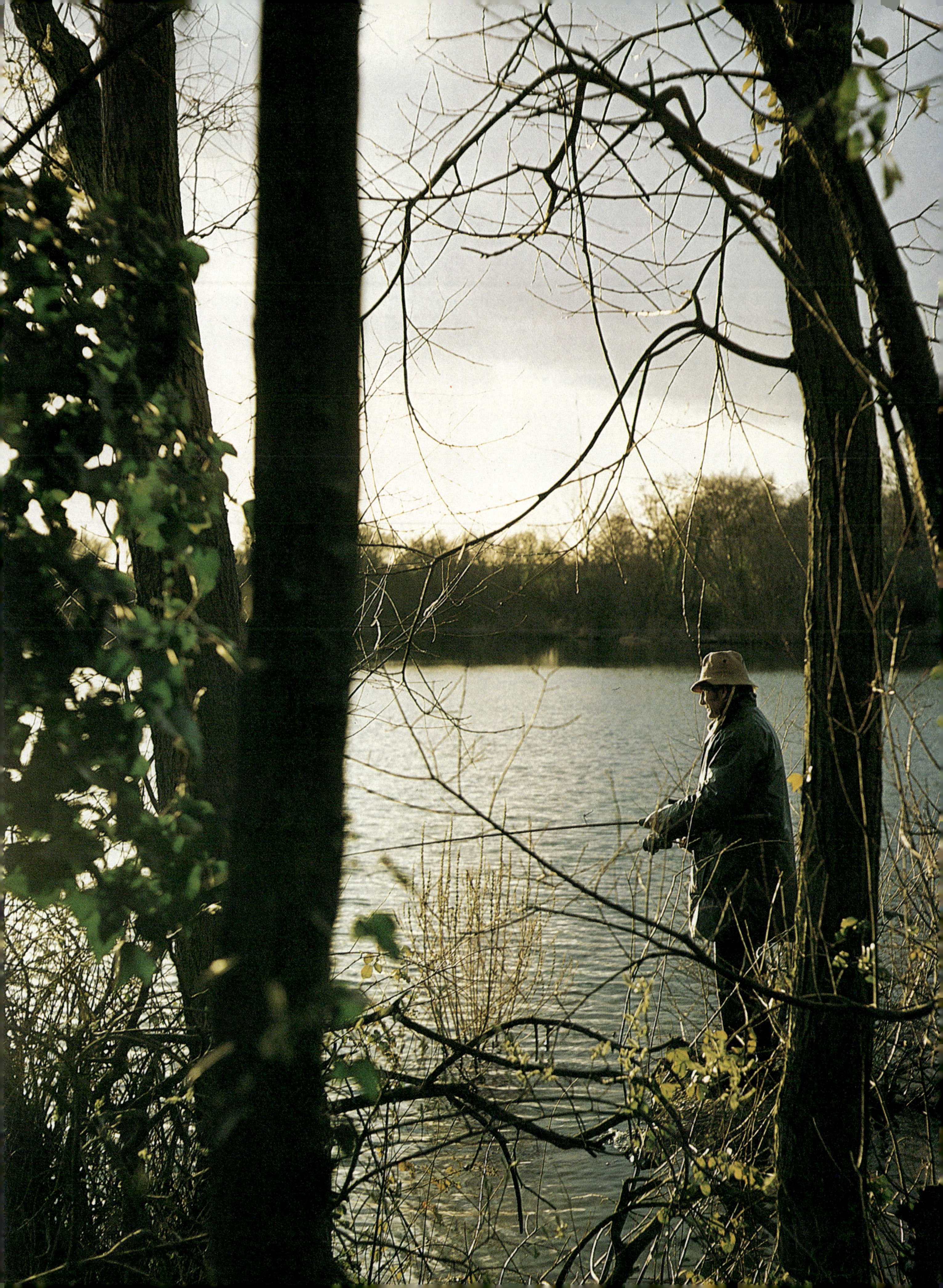

Coarse fishing
Locating a swim

You have bought the tackle and bait, the sandwiches are packed and you are ready to go – but do you know exactly how to start fishing? There are two important things to bear in mind before you get on the bank. The first is that fish are wild creatures which, like any other, are easily scared. So do not rush down to the water's edge because you will frighten them, particularly on small waters. Approach softly so that the fish's sensitive lateral line does not pick up your vibrations. Wear drab clothing, keep your shadow off the water, and take advantage of any trees or bushes that break up your silhouette and help you to merge with the background.

The second point is that fish will not be spread evenly along a river or lake like currants in a cake. Certain areas will be almost devoid of fish because they offer no cover or contain little food. You will have to learn to 'read' a water to enable you to find a promising place – which anglers call 'finding a good swim'. On a river you will be looking for different things, depending on the species of fish you seek, such as an even run of current alongside a weedbed, an area of slack water where food collects, an underwater boulder or fallen tree, or a bend where the current swings away from the bank. A depression or gully at the end of a stretch of fast water is a likely spot, as is the area round the raft of rubbish which collects against the trailing roots or branches of a bankside tree. 'Reading' a water is something you learn from experience, of course, but you can pick up useful pointers by watching more experienced anglers, noting the spots they are fishing and the type of fish they are catching.

Stillwaters – particularly the larger ones – can be more difficult to assess because there are no currents, bends or other visible signs to help you. There are still certain points to watch for, however. Big, open waters exposed to the wind are rarely still, for the wind itself will push the water against one particular bank, and that area is always worth a try, even if you are not keen on fishing with the wind in your face. It will be attractive to fish because the wave action will oxygenate the water and, more important, food items will be washed into that bank. Any promontory enabling you to reach deeper water is well worth a try, as are the small, open areas between weedbeds. Never be put off by weedbeds, for in every sort of water they offer the fish both shelter and food.

Never choose a particular fishing spot because it is a comfortable place to put your stool, because the ground is even or because it is tucked away out of the wind. A good swim is good only in the terms of the fish it may hold, not of the convenience it offers an angler.

▶ This fortunate angler plays a lively carp from a spot where he has bushes on each side to help give him a little cover. The felling of the trees in the foreground allows more light to reach the water. Light encourages weed growth that will give both food and shelter to the fish

▼ These lads have found a likely-looking spot just downstream of a bridge. Wading could frighten away any fish in the vicinity, however, so don't go in the water unless it is absolutely necessary

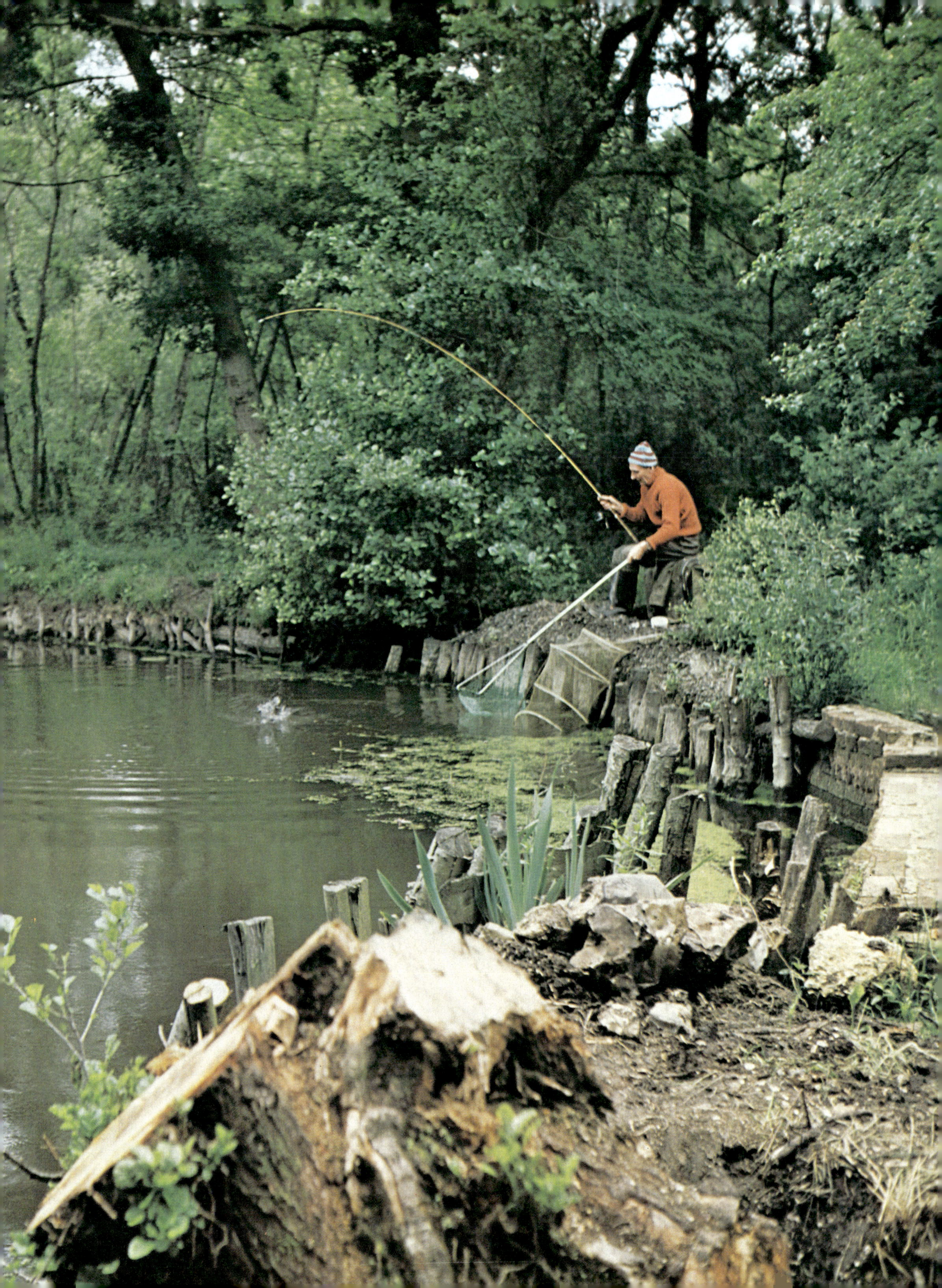

Coarse fishing
Finding the fish

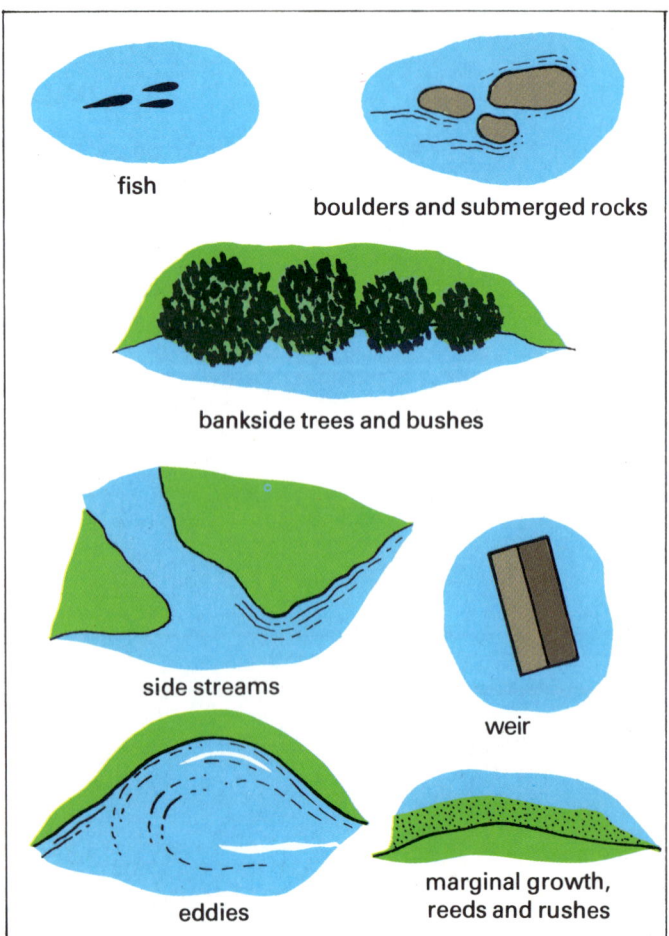

No two rivers are the same. They vary in depth, flow and clarity as well as the nature of the bottom, but the fish-holding areas are common to all. Learning to read a water is an essential part of the angler's expertise and a skill that stands him in good stead when visiting an unfamiliar water for the first time. The illustration above shows some of the places that various fish favour, because they offer either shelter or food or, in the case of predatory fish, a likely ambush point.

Bankside trees are often a good holding point for chub, which seek the shade they offer in summer. The trailing branches will often gather rafts of floating rubbish in times of high water and these are also good chub areas. A rolling ledger cast into the faster water and then allowed to roll into the bank will put the bait in the right place. A bed of reeds growing along the margin not only provides food in the form of the insect life it holds, but also sanctuary from predators. If the water close to the reeds is deep, without too much current, it is a likely place to find roach. Rocks or similar obstructions, such as a fallen tree which has become wedged on the bottom, are holding points for many species, particularly barbel and chub.

Eddies are worth trying for any species which do not like too much of a hard current. Bream and perch have a particular liking for them, and in times of flood when the main river is full and turbulent, they offer a resting place to fish of every kind. In such conditions they will also be full of rubbish, such as leaves, branches and other waterborne debris, so be prepared for false bites. The mouth of a side stream is always worth a try, either at the point where it enters the main river or just a few metres downstream on the main river itself. Roach and chub are the most likely species to find there, but at the end of the season they can be excellent for pike, which gather in such places prior to spawning.

The fast water at the tail of a weir is a magnet for fish of all sorts at the start of the season, when they gather to take advantage of the highly oxygenated water after spawning. Barbel will stay there nearly all season, as will chub and dace, while pike will never be far from such a well-stocked larder. Weirpool fishing can be expensive in lost tackle because of the snags which often litter the bottom, but those same snags offer shelter to the fish, so it is worth the risk. The fast glides above a weirpool are nearly always deep and will have a strong pull. Put a float-fished bait close to the bottom and you will pick up the bigger dace as well as roach.

▼ The island of sedges in front of these young anglers shows that the centre of the lake is shallow, but the water plants surrounding it will harbour various forms of aquatic life on which fish feed

Coarse fishing
Recognize the species

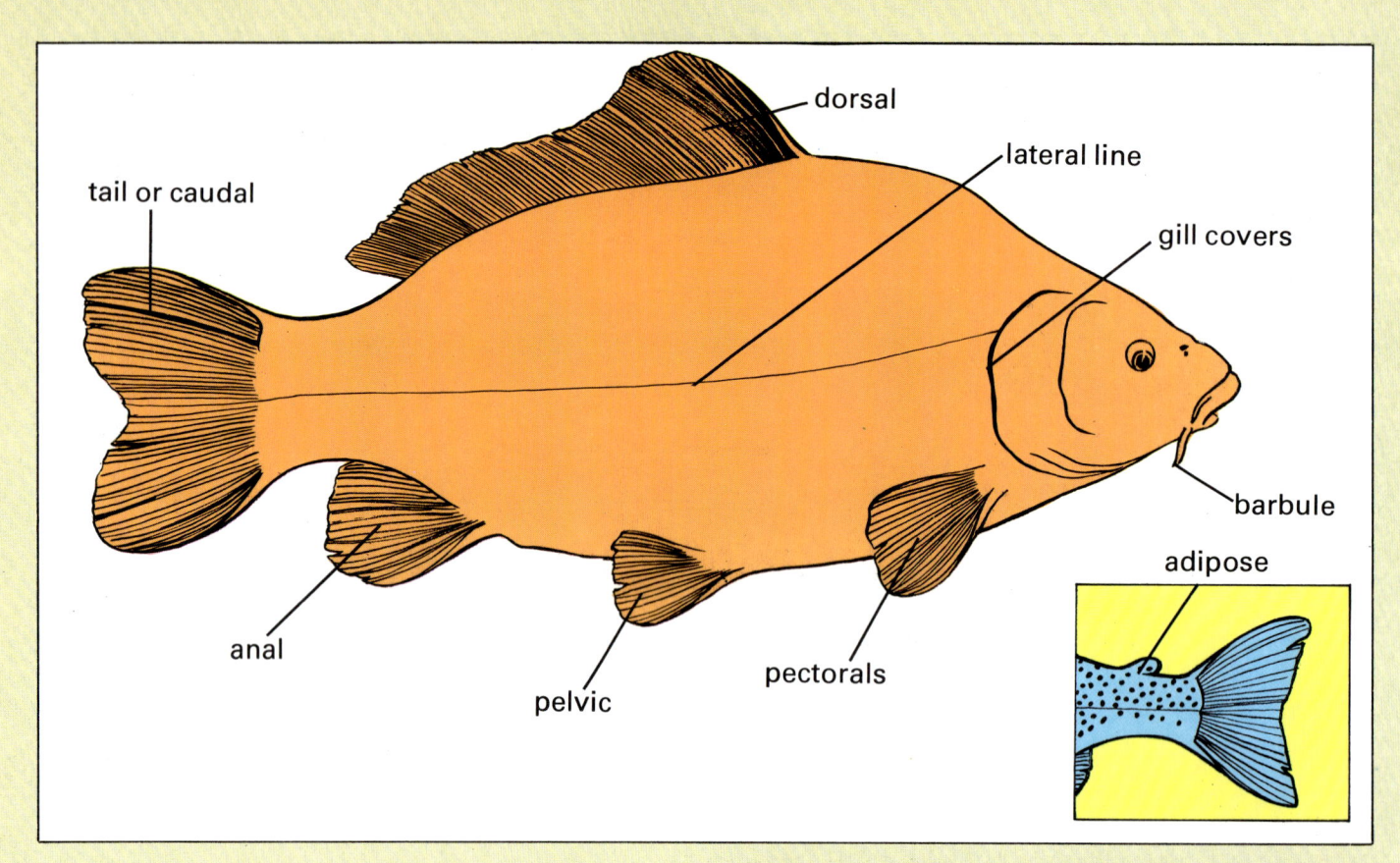

Labeled fish diagram: tail or caudal, dorsal, lateral line, gill covers, barbule, adipose, pectorals, pelvic, anal.

To be able to identify any fish correctly the beginner really needs to know its obvious external features, for colouring alone is never a sure guide. A fish's colour can vary according to its surroundings and it can also change with age, but the positioning of the fins in relation to other parts of the body, the number of rays they contain and the scales along the lateral line can be a great help in identification. The fish illustrated above is a composite one, but it shows the main points. The fleshy appendage found under the chin in some species is known as the barbule and the fin on the top of the body is the dorsal. The fins on the lower part of the body just behind the gills are the pectorals, and the pelvic – also known as ventral – fins are the pair on the forward part of the belly. The anal fin is the one behind the vent, and the tail is also known as the caudal fin. Game fish differ from all others in having a small, fleshy fin, called the adipose fin (inset), just in front of the tail.

Coarse fish should never be killed deliberately. There is no reason to do so, as nearly all of them are inedible by British standards. They should be retained in a keepnet until the end of the day's fishing, and then gently returned to the water. If they show distress in the keepnet, they should be returned to the water immediately.

BLEAK (Record weight 111·6g/3oz 15dr)
Small and silvery, the bleak is a favourite with competition anglers, who can often build up a winning weight with a netful of these eager feeders. They are found in rivers where the surface is often dimpled with shoals of them. To find out if there is a shoal near you, throw some maggots or casters (the pupae of the maggot) in the water and watch – if the water 'boils' with rising fish, the odds are that they are bleak.

Tackle is simple: the lightest of rods and line, the smallest of floats and a size 16 hook baited with a single maggot. The bleak will grab the maggot almost as soon as it is cast in so long as there is no more than 30cm (12in) between hook and float. A handful of maggots thrown in now and again will keep the shoal in your vicinity.

BREAM (Record weight 6·12kg/13lb 8oz)
For every angler who complains that the bream is a slimy nuisance there are twenty more who will not hear a word said against it, for it has many points in its favour. Bream live in shoals, so if you catch one you are almost certain to catch more. They run to a good average size, so you finish with a good weight of fish at the end of the day. They can be found in most parts of the country, will take most bait and are usually fairly easy to catch.

Bream are deep, slab-sided fish with a silvery appearance when small, changing to brown, sometimes almost black, as they grow bigger, depending on the local environment. They love still or slow-moving waters – the Fenland waterway system is a famous bream area – but can also be found in medium-paced rivers such as the Thames, Severn and Great Ouse. Like tench, bream spend most of their time feeding on the bottom, although on bright sunny days you will sometimes see them swimming near the surface, especially on stillwaters.

Whatever type of water they live in, bream shoals have regular patrol routes. On a river they may cruise upstream near one bank, then turn round and go down the centre. In a lake they may have routes which take in certain banks and then cross the centre. The trick is to be fishing a patrol route as the bream come along. Feed in plenty of groundbait so that they stop to investigate.

Plenty of groundbait means just that when talking of bream. A shoal of bream is like a fleet of vacuum cleaners which can gobble up any amount of groundbait before moving on. Put in half a bucketful before you start fishing and keep on putting in smaller amounts once you have caught a couple of fish. Maggots (in bunches), worms, casters and bread are all good bream bait. The groundbait needs to be stodgy so that it sinks straight to the bottom and has enough nourishment for the bream's healthy appetite.

Although there are odd times when you will catch bream in midwater, most are taken when they are grubbing along the bottom eating up groundbait, so that is where your baited hook should be. You can use either float or ledger tackle, the choice is yours. When float fishing a medium-paced river, have the hook just touching the bottom, and hold the float back slightly so that it is travelling more slowly than the current. Ordinary shoal fish – bream to around 2kg (4lb) – are not renowned as great fighters so you do not need a heavy tackle. Line of 2·30kg (5lb) breaking strain will be heavy enough, with hooks varying from a 16 to a 12. A roach rod will easily cope with fish of this size.

Less common than the bronze bream is another variety known as the silver bream which rarely grows to more than 450g (1lb) in weight. Immature specimens of the bronze are often confused with this smaller bream, which is found mostly in East Anglia.

CATFISH (Record weight 19·59kg/43lb 3oz)
The catfish is a European species, originally stocked in the Woburn Abbey waters in Buckinghamshire around the turn of the century, and is limited in its distribution to a few lakes in that immediate area, thus putting it out of the reach of most anglers. Big and strong, it has a broad, flat head with two very long barbules on the upper jaw and four shorter ones on the lower. It lives and feeds on the bottom and is usually caught on small dead fish or worms.

Coarse fishing

BARBEL (Record weight 6·24kg/13lb 12oz) Possibly the hardest-fighting fish in English waters, the barbel has been described as a torpedo with fins and it lives in fast, strong-running rivers. The distribution of the species prevents barbel being more popular than it already is. Many parts of the country have no barbel at all. The best areas are the River Thames and its tributaries, the River Severn, the Hampshire Avon and Dorset Stour and some of the Yorkshire rivers. Other rivers – the Great Ouse and sections of Hertfordshire's old River Lea are typical examples – hold barbel, but they show up less often than in those first mentioned.

One look at the barbel's underslung mouth tells us that it is a bottom feeder, and for much of the time its golden and olive-green body, with large coral-pink fins, is down near or on the bed of the river. Like tench and carp, barbel are very much summer and autumn fish, and once the water temperature drops it is best to turn your attention to another species. In the early part of the season barbel will shoal in any area where the water is fast, streamy and well oxygenated – weirpools, for example – and they have a particular liking for a gravel bottom. Find a stretch of river with gravel bars on the bottom, a weedbed or two and a fast current and you should be successful.

Big barbel – fish of 4·50kg (10lb) or more – are difficult to catch, but the smaller ones offer no particular problems, especially on those stretches of river which have a lot of anglers on the banks. (The more anglers there are on the bank the more bait there will be in the water, which will wean the fish off their natural food.) The match stretches of the River Severn are a good example. Competitions are held every week and the barbel are caught as regularly as dace or roach on other rivers.

These are the areas the beginner should head for, and a good way to start is to use float tackle and maggot bait. It is essential to keep the bait tripping along the bottom, so make sure that you have plumbed the depth correctly. Another essential in this situation is the maggot dropper, which gets the loose maggots used as groundbait straight down to the bottom where the barbel are. If you simply throw the maggots in, the fast current will immediately carry them downstream and it will defeat the object of the exercise, which is to get the fish feeding close to you.

Another very effective barbel method – and one used to catch big bags of Severn barbel – is the swimfeeder ledger rig. The feeder is packed with maggots, plugged with a little groundbait at each end and cast into the swim. This method puts the hook samples exactly where you want them. When the barbel swim up to find the source of the free samples, they also find the baited hook.

A rolling ledger rig incorporating an Arlesey bomb (see diagram on page 23) is another recognized and successful method, and you can use a variety of bait. Sausage or luncheon meat, cheese paste, bread, worms and wasp grub are old-established barbel bait. More recently sweetcorn and tares (a form of dried pea) have been used with great success.

Whichever bait or method you use, remember that barbel are powerful fish and even the small ones fight like tigers, so make sure the tackle is strong enough for the job. Line should be around 2·75kg (6lb) breaking strain and hooks, anything from size 12 to 8 depending on the size of the bait being used, should be the strong, thick-wire type. The rod should be based on the famous Mark IV Avon.

Barbel will often fight to the point of exhaustion when hooked, so treat the fish carefully when you have landed it. If you should use a keepnet – though it is best to return the fish at once to the water – make sure that it is pegged in a streamy run, where the caught fish will get the full benefit of the oxygenated water. If a fish shows any signs of distress, return it immediately, holding it with its head pointing upstream until it has fully recovered.

CRUCIAN CARP (Record weight 2·57kg/ 5lb 10½oz)

The crucian carp should not be confused with other members of the carp family, the leather, common and mirror, all of which are much bigger and more difficult to catch. Identification is fairly straightforward, the crucian having no barbules on its chin, and having a deeper, more compressed, bream-like shape.

Seasoned anglers do not take the crucian very seriously for the reason that beginners like it, because it is easy to catch! You will find crucians in stillwaters and more usually in small ponds, where there might be a great number of them, even though they will be small. Like the other carp, it is a summer and autumn fish. Its great value to the beginner is that it is always willing to feed. A handful of light groundbait laced with maggots will soon bring a shoal foraging around, and it will not be long before your float registers a typical crucian bite. It will lift, move sideways, dip, bob and do all manner of things except a straightforward slide beneath the surface. The best bait is either maggots or bread, and to get the most enjoyment you should use light tackle. The roach rod, 1kg (2lb) breaking strain line, a light float and a size 14 hook are needed.

DACE (Record weight 574g/1lb 4oz 4dr)

The dace (illustrated above right) is a handsome, lively little fish, found in fast rivers all over the country. It can be confused with a small chub, the main differences being that whereas the anal fin (the one on the lower part of the body and nearest the tail) of the dace has a concave edge, that of the chub is convex. The dace has a small, neat mouth compared to that of the chub, and a slimmer and more streamlined body. Place the two side by side and you will spot the differences immediately.

Dace will feed at any depth, and the usual way of catching them is with light float tackle. They are confident feeders and will normally give a decisive bob of the float as they take the bait, which should be casters or maggots, although small redworms and hempseed will also catch them. Find a fast, shallow section running over a gravel bottom and throw in a few handfuls of hook samples mixed with light groundbait at the head of the spot. Then let the float go downstream. In recent years the blockend feeder loaded with maggots has accounted for plenty of dace, particularly from the River Thames.

You do not need heavy tackle if you want to get the most enjoyment from dace fishing A roach-style rod, 1kg (2lb) line and a size 16 hook are suitable.

EEL (Record weight 3·91kg/8lb 10oz)

The eel is so well known that it needs no description. You will find it almost everywhere, from the smallest of farm ponds to the widest of rivers, and though many anglers regard it as a pest, it is a fish that the beginner is bound to catch at the start of his angling career. Small eels, known as 'bootlaces', will take any worm or maggot being fished on the bottom, and make a tangle of the terminal tackle as well! They invariably swallow the hook and often manage to tie knots in the line and transfer sticky slime to everything they touch.

For those who set out to catch them deliberately, bigger eels – those weighing over 450g (1lb) – are a different proposition. Small dead fish, worms or strips of liver make good bait, and they are used in conjunction with ledger tackle, for the eel is very much a bottom feeder. Serious eel fishing is nearly always carried out at night, when eels are most active. You will need tough tackle; the eel is a strong fighter and a carp rod and 4·50kg (10lb) breaking strain line are necessary. When you land an eel, do not try to unhook it. Simply cut the line below the lead, drop the eel in the keepnet and tie on a fresh hook.

Coarse fishing

will give a good account of itself. Tackle need not be heavy – an all-purpose match rod coupled with 2·30kg (5lb) line will cope with most situations. Do not use too small a hook, as perch have large, soft mouths and a tiny hook is unlikely to gain a secure hold. A size 8 or 10 hook is needed.

If you prefer a more active form of perch fishing – and one that will cover a lot more ground – try spinning. There is a wide range of suitably small spinners that will take perch, and it is worth taking a selection with you so that you can ring the changes. A wire trace is not needed.

PERCH (Record weight 2·15kg/4lb 12oz)
Handsome is the word that springs to mind when you catch sight of your very first perch, one of the most distinctive of all Britain's freshwater fish. A hump-shouldered predator, it has a big, spiky dorsal fin and tiger-like stripes running vertically down its body, stripes which are very noticeable in small fish but which fade gradually as the perch grows bigger.

It can be found in all types of water, but the species suffered a setback in the mid-sixties when populations in some parts of Britain were all but destroyed by disease. Happily, they are now making a comeback but their distribution is patchy – some waters swarm with small perch, while others seem to have very few. Like the pike, the perch is a hunter of small fish, and prefers cover for its ambush. Perch will often betray their presence by chasing small fish to the surface. If you see a shoal of small fry suddenly explode on the surface, or a lone small fish frantically skipping its way along the top, you can be almost certain that a perch is responsible. Any places where shoals of fry gather are worth trying for perch. In rivers these could be patches of slack water, eddies, undercut banks or bridge buttresses. In stillwaters perch are more likely to be in the vicinity of weedbeds.

Float or ledger tackle can be used for perch fishing, the important point being that the bait must be kept on the move. An Arlesey bomb ledger, with lobworm as bait, will work better if the bait is twitched back across the bottom at intervals. A live minnow hooked below float tackle is effective, as are other small fish, such as bleak or gudgeon.

The perch's good looks are matched only by its fighting ability, and any reasonably sized fish

GRAYLING (No current record)
Although the grayling carries the small adipose fin which marks fish of the game family, it is generally regarded as a coarse fish, for it spawns in spring, at the same time as the rest of the coarse species. A slim, beautiful fish with silvery grey sides overlaid with an iridescent greenish gold tinge, it has a huge dorsal fin.

It is a fish of fast, clean rivers and is found all over Scotland, but its distribution in England is patchy. Yorkshire is good grayling country, as are the southern chalk rivers such as the Test, Itchen, Hampshire Avon, Wylye and Nadder. Generally speaking, you will find grayling in the same shallow swims that hold dace, and the fishing methods are similar. Use float tackle with maggot or small redworms on a size 16 hook and line of around 1kg (2lb). The grayling gives a peculiar fight, a wriggling plunge similar to that of a big eel. It does not take kindly to being retained in a keepnet and will quickly turn belly up, so any grayling that you catch should be returned to the water immediately.

CARP (Record weight 19·96kg/44lb)
The carp is probably the most exciting of all British freshwater fish. Big and wary, it is a fish of stillwaters although, like the tench, it can also be found in some of the slower rivers. The average angler is likely to catch carp only during the summer months when the fish are active. Trying to catch carp in winter is a job for the specialist with time, knowledge and patience to spare, for they move and feed very little once the cold weather sets in.

The original English carp, known as the wild carp, is comparatively rare nowadays. However, lakes, ponds and reservoirs all over the country have been stocked with mirror, common or leather carp, all strains of the same fish which originally came from Europe. The mirror (illustrated above right) can be recognized by the large, irregular scales dotted along its flanks; the leather has scales so small they can hardly be seen and the common has normal scales in an even pattern.

Carp are bottom feeders, sifting through the mud on the lake bottom for bloodworms and other small forms of insect life. When they get their heads down and root through the mud, they will often betray their presence by sending up clouds of bubbles. Carp are easily spotted on warm summer days, when they bask just below the water surface. If the lake has weedbeds and lilypads, keep an eye on them, as carp browsing through the stems will often move the leaves on the surface. On bigger waters with no visible signs of the fish, it pays to look for special features such as fallen trees, a gravel bar rising near the surface, an island or an area of shallower water interspersed with deeper channels, as carp often frequent these areas.

Carp fishing demands a stealthy approach. They are wary fish, and bankside disturbance will send them to the middle of the lake and out of casting range. Most of their feeding is done during the hours of darkness so, for the best results, that is the time to fish. Early mornings and late evenings are good times if you cannot manage a night trip. If you fish during the day, try to keep as far away from other anglers as you can, and find a quiet corner.

The most common method of fishing for carp is with a light ledger or, better still, no weight at all but simply a baited hook. Using bread crust on an unweighted line is an effective way of fishing for those carp seen basking near the surface, as the bread crust will float. Dunk the crust in water to give it a bit of extra weight which will help in casting, and flick it out to the cruising carp, throwing out a few loose crusts as free offerings. It is an exciting way of fishing, as you actually see the fish take the bait. Bait of all kinds may be used for conventional ledgering – maggots, worms, cheese, luncheon meat, a paste mixture of tinned cat food and sausage rusk, peas, beans, sweetcorn – the list is endless. One of the secrets of successful carp fishing is to try to find a bait that has not been used on the water you are fishing. Carp are quick to profit from their mistakes – once they have been caught on a particular bait, they soon learn to leave it alone. The trick is therefore to find something they have not learned to be frightened of. Some loose samples scattered in one or two places will give them the taste and make them less suspicious.

The carp is one of the strongest freshwater fish, and tackle has to be chosen to suit it. The rod should be one of the many sold specially for the purpose, and it is unwise to use line lighter than 4·50kg (10lb), even in clear, open water with no weedbeds or fallen trees. Hooks should range between a size 2 and 6 and should be tied direct to the main line. Ready-tied hooks should not be used, as they have a weaker link. When ledgering, it is essential to keep the bale arm of the reel open, as carp often pick up the bait and swim for cover. With the pickup closed, the carp will either break the line or pull the rod clean from its rest and into the water. Alternatively, if it feels the resistance caused by a closed spool, it is likely to drop the bait before a run develops.

The size of the carp you catch depends very much on the water you fish. There are places which teem with small fish around the 450-900g (1-2lb) mark, and ordinary tench tackle (see page 40) will be sufficient in this situation. Club lakes often hold fish to 9kg (20lb), with the average size running to 4·50kg (10lb). Waters holding the much bigger carp tend to be in the hands of private syndicates and smaller clubs.

Coarse fishing

CHUB (Record weight 3·35kg/7lb 6oz)
The chub is one of Britain's most obliging fish. Looking like a bigger version of the roach, it has large, leathery lips and a cavernous mouth with an appetite to match. Described by Izaak Walton as 'the fearfullest of fishes', the chub is a fish of the rivers, wide, narrow, slow or fast, and there is not a bait it will not take – maggots, worms, cheese paste, slugs, spinners and even small livebait.

A cautious approach is needed if you want to catch a chub from a small stream, but on the bigger rivers it is not so easily scared away. Chub like cover such as that offered by overhanging tree branches, rafts of debris caught up on an underwater obstruction and the waving ends of weedbeds.

Early in the season the chub can be disappointing once hooked, for it does not take long to beat. In winter, however, when the fish is in the pink of condition, it is a different story and it will give a good account of itself. On a small river you can often spot chub quite easily and cast the bait almost directly to them, providing it is done with little disturbance. On a big river, try any area of slack water, but if you cannot find one, do not worry – chub can turn up almost anywhere!

They can be caught on float or ledger tackle and the latter often pays off best, for chub like a static bait.

One of the best ways to test a likely-looking chub area is to use the rolling ledger, baiting with either lobworm or a lump of cheese paste. Use an Arlesey bomb, just light enough to hold the bottom, and cast into the top end of the swim. Hold the rod and, if no bite develops, just lift the rod and let out a little more line. The bait will roll across the current and will often be taken by the chub as it swings past. You can do the same thing with a swimfeeder rig, the feeder loaded with maggots or casters. A chub bite is usually a confident, healthy thump felt at the rod tip, but there are times in winter when the only indication is a momentary pluck on the line.

If you are fishing in traditional chub-holding areas, such as weedbeds or sunken snags, make sure that the tackle is strong enough for the job. Line should be no lighter than 2·30kg (5lb) and tie your size 6 hook direct to the reel line.

RUDD (Record weight 2·04kg/4lb 8oz)
The rudd is a species which is active in summer and autumn but offers the angler much fewer chances during the winter months. It is a fish of still or very slow-moving water, and is similar in appearance to the roach but has a more golden sheen overall.

Rudd are active surface feeders, and light groundbait or pieces of bread scattered on the surface will show you where the fish are feeding. Light float tackle, with most of the shot just below the float so that the bait sinks slowly, is effective, using either maggots or bread as bait on a size 14 hook. Line of 1kg (2lb) breaking strain is suitable.

However, rudd are not always found near the surface. Many of the bigger fish are caught in midwater or on the bottom, and in the latter situation it is worth trying ledger tackle. Distribution of the rudd is patchy. The Fens and many Norfolk waters hold plenty of them, but in other parts of the country they are hard to find.

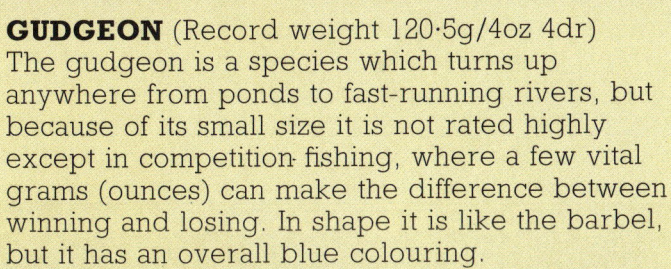

GUDGEON (Record weight 120·5g/4oz 4dr)
The gudgeon is a species which turns up anywhere from ponds to fast-running rivers, but because of its small size it is not rated highly except in competition fishing, where a few vital grams (ounces) can make the difference between winning and losing. In shape it is like the barbel, but it has an overall blue colouring.

Despite its small size, the gudgeon is a bold biter and pulls the float down in a decisive manner. It is an ideal beginner's fish, for gudgeon travel in shoals, and where you catch one you will be almost certain to catch more. A bottom feeder, it can be caught on either float or ledger tackle, but the most enjoyment comes with the former. A little groundbait will keep the shoal interested. A light rod, 1kg (2lb) breaking strain line and a size 16 hook below the smallest of floats is sufficient in the way of tackle. The best bait to use are maggots, small redworms or the tails of bigger worms.

ROACH (Record weight 1·84kg/4lb 1oz)
Every angler loves the roach (illustrated above right) – and with good reason. Often described as Britain's most popular fish, it is to be found in every conceivable type of water, from the smallest of farm ponds through to the swiftest of rivers. You can catch it at any time of the season, using a variety of methods, and it will take most bait – but that does not mean that it is an easy fish to catch.

Some ten years ago a mystery disease hit the country's roach population and their numbers dwindled, but now they are making a recovery and can be found in most of their old haunts. The colouring of the roach depends on the environment in which it lives, but generally it has silver sides, a dark back and red fins. Because of their general similarity, roach and rudd are often mistaken for each other. The roach will also interbreed with bream, which leads to identification problems that can only be sorted out by experts. In a straight roach or rudd identification test, remember that the roach's top lip protrudes over the lower, while the reverse is the case with the rudd.

How you set about catching roach depends on the water you are fishing, but wherever you are it pays to use light tackle, for they can be shy fish, easily frightened by a clumsily presented bait. Although bigger roach are often caught on ledger tackle, there is no doubt that most fall to float-fishing tactics, using anything from a single maggot below a tiny float on a canal to a piece of bread beneath a heavy float on the fast, pushing water of a river like the Hampshire Avon.

Except when using a swimfeeder while ledgering, you will rarely need to have your reel loaded with line of more than 1kg (2lb) breaking strain, with hooks between size 16 and 10. Bite indication will not necessarily be a straightforward dip of the float. Sometimes it will move sideways a little, it might give a sharp bob or it could lift fractionally – any of these indications mean that a roach is interested in your bait.

Another thing to remember when roach fishing is that groundbaiting pays off – but do not overdo it. A few loose samples of hookbait mixed with groundbait and fed into the swim at regular intervals will keep the shoal interested.

Roach shoals will nearly always consist of fish of the same size, and a general rule of thumb is the smaller the shoal the bigger the size of the individual fish. On a river where the food supply is limited you might get roach of about 230g (8oz), but on the famous roach rivers, such as the Hampshire Avon and Dorset Stour, they will be nearer the 1kg (2lb) mark. Tring Reservoirs in Hertfordshire – open to day-ticket visitors – contain plenty of roach around the 1kg (2lb) weight.

Coarse fishing

TENCH (Record weight 4·57kg/10lb 1oz 2dr)
With its small, red eyes and an overall colour which can vary from black to a dark olive-green, the tench is an easy fish to identify. It is a stillwater species, though it can also be found in the slower-moving rivers, and it is traditionally a summer fish and becomes much harder to catch during the winter months. A nocturnal feeder, it is active during the dawn as well. Bright sunlight will usually kill sport, though you will catch tench on dull, cloudy days.

The tench is a bottom feeder, whose natural food is found in the mud on the bed of a lake or pond. One sure sign of a shoal of feeding tench is the patches of tiny bubbles which burst on the surface as the fish grub around on the bottom. Tench like weedbeds, and one of the time-honoured methods of catching them is to find a dense weedbed, drag a clear patch through it with the aid of a piece of heavy metal on the end of a rope, and then fish the newly cleared patch. The tench will come foraging through the disturbed weed, into which you will have thrown groundbait, and will find the hookbait.

There are times when tench will take bait presented at different levels in the water, but generally the angler has his bait lying on the bottom, using float tackle at close range or a ledger when fishing further out. The average run of tench weigh 700g-2kg (1½-4lb), depending on the richness of the water, and they are strong fighters no matter what their size. Because of this and the fact that you are likely to be fishing near weedbeds in which the tench will try to take refuge when hooked, it is unwise to fish with line lighter than 2·30kg (5lb).

Where the fish run fairly small, you can use a normal general-purpose rod, but if you fish regularly for tench over the 2kg (4lb) mark you will need something with a little more backbone. Hook sizes can vary from a size 16 to a size 8, depending on the size of the bait being used. Tench can be caught on all sorts of bait, the favourites being maggots, worms and bread. In recent years sweetcorn has proved a good tench bait, and a favourite for big tench is the freshwater mussel, the flesh of which is cut from the shell and used on the hook. Tench respond well to groundbaiting tactics, and it pays to bait a swim with samples of the hookbait before and during the fishing session.

ZANDER (Record weight 7·82kg/17lb 4oz)
The zander, also known as the pike-perch, was introduced into Britain in 1880, when a few fish were put into the waters of Woburn Abbey, Buckinghamshire. In the mid-1960s, another batch was put into Norfolk's Relief Channel, and they have now spread through many of the rivers and drains that make up the Fenland system of waterways. Unfortunately, they are still confined to that region, so anglers living in other parts of the country have no chance of catching them in their home waters.

A separate species in its own right, the zander looks very much like a cross between a pike and a perch. It has the former's body shape and long, toothy jaw but the perch's spiky dorsal fin and colouring. Like both the other species, the zander is a predator which feeds on smaller fish. The technique and bait used for pike (see opposite page) will also catch zander.

PIKE (Record weight 18·14kg/40lb)
There are more tall tales told about the pike than any other fish in British waters. The ill-informed call it the freshwater shark and a vicious killer. There are tales of savage pike which attack swimmers, fish so greedy that they have eaten every other inhabitant of the pond or lake in which they live. Listening to these tales you might get the impression that it is dangerous to wade in well-known pike waters for fear of having your feet bitten off!

Exciting though the stories may sound, the pike is none of these things. It is a simple predator which feeds on smaller fish, dead or alive. Sometimes it is hungry, at other times it is not, and there are times when it is easy to catch and others when it is difficult.

The pike is easy to recognize, with its long streamlined body, marked in green and yellow, long jaw and big mouth full of sharp teeth. You will find it everywhere in the country, in still and running waters of every description. In some waters there will be plenty of small pike, fish up to the 2·30kg (5lb) mark, and in others there will be fewer but bigger specimens, real giants growing to 9kg (20lb) or more which is the magic target at which pike specialists aim.

The pike is a hunter, but it does not spend its time and energy chasing fish all over the river or lake. Most of the time it lies in ambush close to reeds and weedbeds, where its mottled colouring helps it blend with the background.

In rivers pike tend to lie in deeper water, particularly bankside eddies or the slacks formed behind weedbeds. In lakes and ponds they could be anywhere that offers them ambush opportunities. Any area where the bottom shelves or is formed in ridges, as in gravel pits, is well worth a try. Although small pike will often take a maggot or worm-baited hook intended for other species, these are accidental captures and you have to approach pike fishing proper in a completely different way.

The three methods used are baiting with a dead fish (any of the freshwater species, or sea fish such as herrings, sprats and mackerel), artificial bait (metal and wooden creations which imitate a wounded fish and arouse the pike's hunting instinct) and livebaiting (using a small live fish on the hook). Of the three, artificial bait generally catches more fish, while natural deadbait sorts out the bigger specimens. Livebaiting can be effective for both quantity and quality, but this method is falling into disfavour with anglers who feel that some element of cruelty is involved.

Deadbait is normally fished on a special terminal tackle with two treble hooks attached to the bait. This is then cast into a likely pike spot and allowed to sink to the bottom, where the pike, always on the lookout for an easy meal, will come along and pick it up. This can be a waiting game, so rod rests are used and the reel is left with the pickup open, as in carp fishing. The double hook rig means that you can strike when line trickles from the spool, allowing you to hook the pike in the mouth before he has a chance to swallow the bait.

Alternatively, deadbait can be used in a more mobile way, the angler walking along the bank, casting into different spots and reeling in slowly, so that the deadbait moves through the water like a wounded fish.

Movement is the key to success with artificial bait, some spinning through the water, some wobbling and others darting from side to side or up and down. The secret is in the way the line is retrieved and the rod tip used. A fast retrieve will make some artificials work properly, while others need a slow, jerky recovery. Most spinners, lures and plugs (see page 26) are used without weights on the line, and should be attached to a wire trace – as should any pike terminal tackle – to avoid the line being bitten through.

Pike are strong fighters and if hooked near the surface will often leap clear of the water in an effort to shake the hooks loose. A carp rod coupled with 4·50kg (10lb) breaking strain line is generally used. When you have your pike safely netted and on the bank, take care with the unhooking, for your own and the pike's sake. A disgorger and a pair of surgical artery forceps (sold in all tackle shops) are useful aids.

Coarse fishing
Bait

✓ Maggots should be lightly hooked through the blunt end so that they remain lively in the water

To make a small worm look as natural as possible, hook it just once through the middle

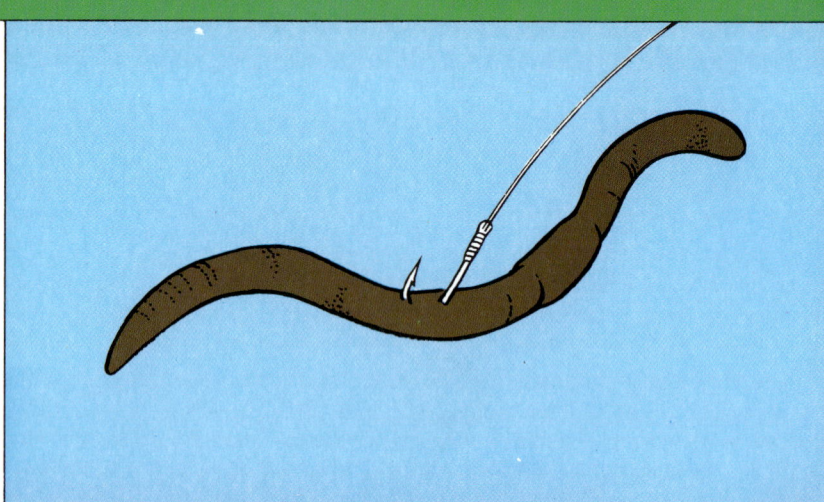

✗ A hook stuck through the middle of a maggot will quickly kill it and make it less attractive to the fish

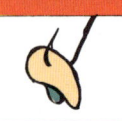

A small worm hooked like this will catch few fish

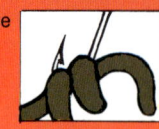

▼ When using flake, bread paste or crust, make sure that the point of the hook is left showing. A pinch of bread from the inside of a fresh loaf, known as flake, makes a good bait when squeezed gently round the shank of the hook. To make the paste, dip the bread from the inside of a stale loaf in water, place it in a clean cloth and squeeze out the excess moisture. Bread crust makes an attractive, buoyant bait which appeals to many species

▼ Cheese is best used grated and mixed with bread paste, in a cloth. Keep the paste in the cloth to prevent it from drying out. If you use cheese straight from a shop, be certain to choose the soft variety. Cheese will harden in water and can obstruct the point of the hook – which might mean a lost fish

Bait is a vitally important part of the angler's equipment, for no matter how expensive the tackle or how good the person using it, few fish will be caught if they are offered the wrong bait or if the right one is presented incorrectly. A little time spent making sure you have the right amount of proper bait before each outing will save a lot of fishless hours. Remember that, in the normal course of events, fish do not live on a steady diet of the various things that anglers put on hooks. They grow and thrive on a natural diet of all manner of things, such as bloodworms, daphnia, snails, fly larvae, bugs, weeds and vegetable matter found in their watery environment. What the angler has to do is try to persuade the fish to forsake their normal fare and try the succulent morsel he is offering.

The best way to do this is with the careful use of groundbait and free food samples put in the water where you are fishing. Groundbaiting serves two purposes. It weans the fish away from their more natural food on to the angler's hookbait, and it brings them into the fishing area. It has to be done properly, however. Too much will overfeed them so that they do not need the bait on the hook. Too little will not interest them. The aim is to give them just enough to whet their appetites. Groundbait can be many things – stale bread, bran, sausage rusk or proprietary bait bought from the tackle shop. It is usually taken to the waterside dry in a canvas bucket (to save weight) and mixed with water just before you start fishing.

Samples of the hookbait should be mixed in so that when the groundbait itself has been washed away or dissolves, the hook samples remain. The wetter the mixture the quicker it will wash away, so if you are fishing a fast water like the Hampshire Avon, keep the mixture stiff. In that way it gets down to the bottom quickly and stays put until the fish find it. On a slow canal, where the fish are likely to be shy, only a light mix will be needed – something that breaks up as soon as it hits the surface and attracts the fish without spoiling their appetites.

The amount of groundbait you need depends on the kind of fish you want to catch, as well as the different types of water in which you might find them. Bream, for example, are hearty feeders which cannot be given too much groundbait at times. Roach, on the other hand, have relatively light appetites and can easily be overfed. When in doubt, use the 'little and often' principle rather than throwing in all the groundbait at the start of a fishing session.

There are times when fish have to be educated to a bait new to that particular water, and this is where pre-baiting serves a purpose, for the fish have to learn that the special bait you intend to use is good to eat. A typical example is sweetcorn, a modern bait which attracts a lot of fish. To make it effective, the angler visits a water several times before he fishes it and introduces free samples of sweetcorn in a number of different areas. On the day chosen for fishing, some more free samples are thrown in and the same bait is then used on the hook.

Do not be afraid of ringing the changes with bait. It may be that the tench or bream in a particular lake are usually caught on maggot, but there may come a time when the catches slow down. That is the time to try something different, such as bread or worms. Just as important as the right bait is the right way to present it, for fish will avoid anything which they sense is not acting naturally. A single maggot on a small size 18 hook will not look too different from the free samples thrown in, but that same maggot on a bigger size 8 hook will look very unnatural. If you go to the other extreme you could face other difficulties. A walnut-sized lump of cheese paste can be moulded round the shank of a size 6 hook and will stay in place while being cast out. The same sized lump on a size 16 will fly off the hook because of the poorer purchase.

A proper angler's canvas bucket is best for mixing groundbait in, but a small plastic container will also serve ▶

Coarse fishing

Listed here you will find the more common bait, but there are many more. Rice, macaroni and bacon rind have accounted for fish at times. Caddis grubs, freshwater shrimp and caterpillars can also be effective, as they are the type of natural food to which many fish are accustomed.

Hemp, wheat and tares (the latter a form of dried pea sold as pigeon food) belong to a family of bait which needs more preparation than the standard one, but they can be deadly at times. Preparation is the same for all three: they should be soaked in clean water overnight before being gently simmered in a saucepan until they soften, when they are ready for use. They are generally used on float tackle for roach, dace, chub and barbel, and samples should be put in the swim on the 'little and often' principle.

Worms are another common and effective bait for most fish, and three types are normally used. Biggest is the ordinary earthworm, known to anglers as the lobworm. It can be found in the earth of most gardens and on top of the lawn on a damp, warm night. The whole worm is a good bait, as is just the tail section. The much smaller redworm, found under rotting logs and other damp places, is much less lively than the lobworm but is still a very good bait. Brandlings are the thin, red and yellow striped worms found in compost and manure heaps. Whichever type of worm you use, keep them out of the hot sun while fishing or they will quickly die.

Another very good worm, normally used by highly-skilled competition anglers, is the bloodworm, a tiny threadlike creature normally found in mud, though you can buy supplies at the better tackle shops. Because of its small size, it has to be used on tiny hooks, using fine tackle.

Bread, as well as being cheap, is the most versatile of all freshwater bait. A piece of crust torn from the outside of a loaf makes an attractive, buoyant bait which appeals to many species. Its only disadvantage is that it does not stay on the hook very long and constant rebaiting is necessary. A pinch of bread from the inside of a fresh loaf, known as flake, makes a good bait when squeezed gently round the shank of the hook. The interior of a stale loaf should be used to make bread paste. The white bread is dunked quickly in water, then kneaded to remove any lumps until a smooth paste is obtained. To prevent it drying out, it should be kept in a twist of damp cloth.

Maggots are the most popular and widely used of all coarse fishing bait, and will account for almost any fish that swim in British waters. They are sold, usually by the ½ litre (1 pint) measure, in all tackle shops, where you can buy them in their natural white form, or dyed in different colours. You can also buy smaller maggots, known as squatts, and various other specials, but the ordinary white is as good as any in most situations. Maggots can be used singly or in bunches and should be hooked through the blunt end so that they remain lively. Keep them in a special maggot tin, with a perforated lid and always store them in a cool place.

Casters are the pupae of the ordinary maggot and make a first-rate bait for many fish. They can be bought in all tackle shops, or you can get a supply by allowing maggots to get warm and turn into casters. Shop-bought casters will always be at the right stage of development so that they sink. If you turn your own, throw away the floaters which are of little use. To identify the floaters, place the casters in a bucket of water; the floaters are those which remain on the surface. Casters should be used on a fine wire hook, otherwise they will burst.

Cheese is a bait usually associated with chub and barbel, but there are times when it will take other fish too. Do not try to use it in cubes, as the cheese will harden in cold water and could obstruct the hook point. The best method is to grate it and mix it with bread into a smooth paste. Keep the paste in a damp cloth to prevent it from drying out.

Sweetcorn is one of the most recent additions to the bait scene, and has accounted for good fish of all species. It needs no preparation – use it just as it comes out of the tin. Depending on the species, fish will accept a single grain or a number of grains bunched on the hook. Any sweetcorn left at the end of the day's fishing can be taken home in a plastic bag and put into the freezer ready for use on the next outing.

Meat is another popular bait, particularly for fish such as barbel and chub – and carp to a lesser extent. Luncheon meat is the easiest to use, cut into cubes just as it comes from the tin. Sausage meat is usually mixed with breadcrumbs or rusk to form a paste. Tinned cat food mixed with the same type of binding agent has been used successfully for carp.

Making a wormery

Anyone with a garden, no matter how small, can quickly make a wormery that will keep him supplied with bait all year round and will need only the minimum of maintenance.

Start by choosing the site carefully. It needs to be somewhere that does not get the full benefit of the sun all day – behind a coal bunker or beside a shed is ideal. Size is not important, but the bigger it is the more worms it will produce, and about 2m by 1m (6ft by 3ft) would be suitable.

Fence the site round with boards or wire netting to a height of 60cm (2ft). The materials for your wormery will go inside this framework. Cover the base with sheets of newspaper, which will help to retain moisture, then fill in the area with garden and vegetable refuse – cabbage leaves, grass cuttings (providing the lawn has not been sprinkled with fertilizer or weedkiller) and green matter of all types.

Dampen each layer as you put it in and cover it with a sprinkle of earth. Windfallen fruit is an excellent medium for small redworms. Simply spread it in an even layer and crush it down. Leaves from any deciduous trees can also be added, but do not make too thick a layer as they take a long time to rot down. The mixture will be all the better for a bag or two of animal manure, which you can buy from a nursery or stable. The important thing is to keep the heap damp and a piece of old carpet (not the modern foam-backed variety) laid across the top will do this. The carpet itself will eventually rot down and enrich the heap, and when this happens, lay a couple of sheets of dampened newspaper on top.

You do not have to start with a brood stock of any sort; redworms and brandlings have an almost magical way of colonizing a perfect environment. You can add any big lobworms that you come across while digging the garden, but take only those which are undamaged. Once the heap is really rotting down, it should provide you with redworms, brandlings and lobworms as long as you keep adding the right ingredients.

▼ Bait containers clipped to a special stand cannot get trodden on or the contents spilled

Coarse fishing
Casting

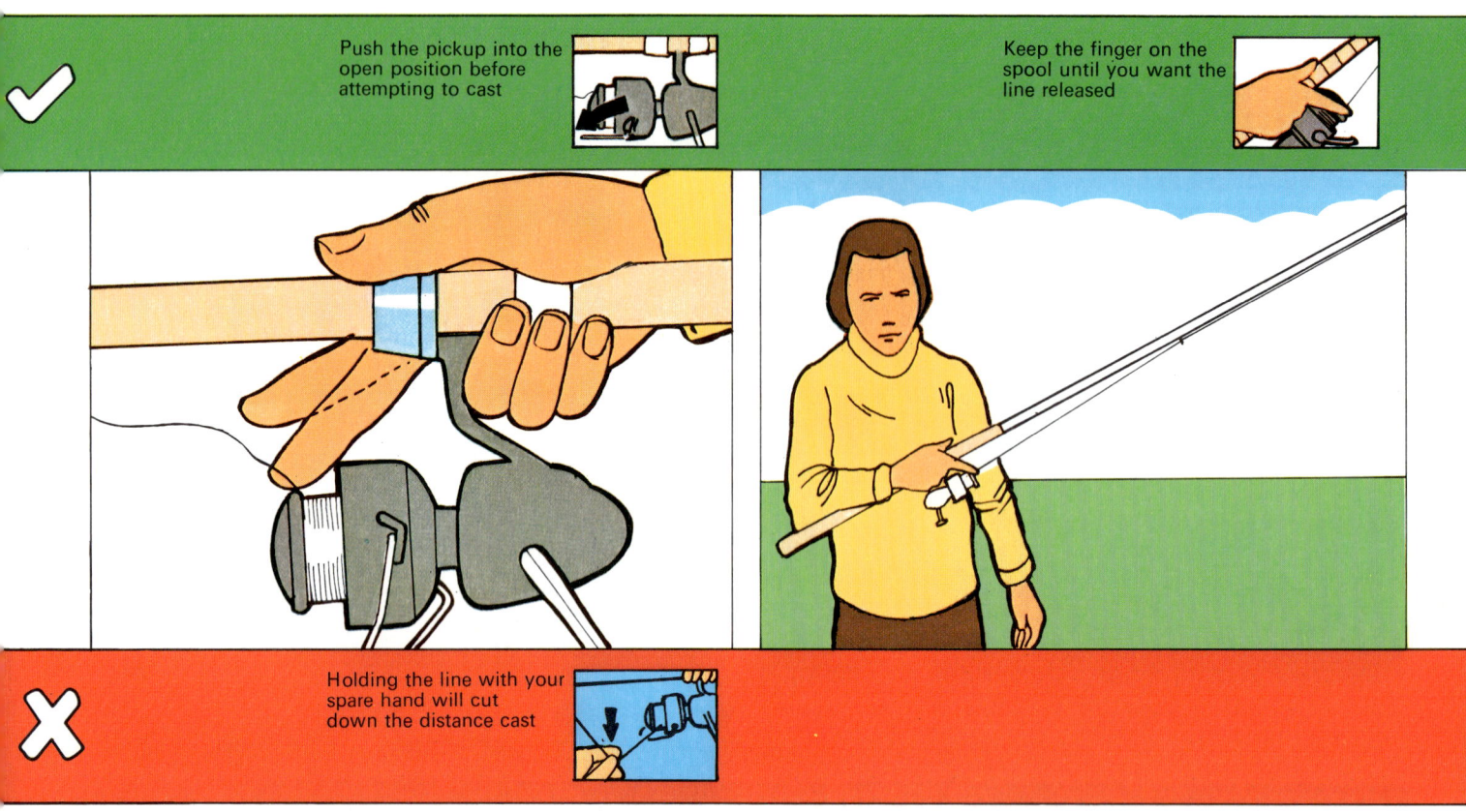

✓ Push the pickup into the open position before attempting to cast

Keep the finger on the spool until you want the line released

✗ Holding the line with your spare hand will cut down the distance cast

▲ Whichever type of cast you make, you must first open the reel pickup and trap the line against the lip of the spool with the forefinger. Keep it there all the time until you want to release the line, then simply lift it off. As soon as the cast is completed and your baited tackle has reached the desired spot, close the pickup by turning the handle

▲ The simple side cast is handy to use when tree branches or similar obstructions above and behind you prevent the use of the overhead cast. With your finger trapping the line against the spool, face the spot on which you want your terminal tackle to land, but make sure there are no bushes or tall rushes on the bank beside you

Once you have decided on a likely-looking spot, considered the fish it might contain and chosen the bait and method most likely to catch them, you then have to present the bait accurately and with as little disturbance as possible. On an open bank you can use the overhead cast. Lay the rod back at an angle of 45 degrees, with the reel pickup open and forefinger holding the line against the spool. Then push the rod forward so that the terminal tackle comes up and over, releasing the line when the rod is just past the top of its swing forward.

Where trees and other obstructions might cause problems, or where long-distance casting is not important, the simple side swing will get any sort of float or ledger tackle out to where it is needed. First, wind in the line. Then, with the reel pickup open and the tip of the forefinger holding the line against the lip of the spool, swing the rod round so that it points at the spot

◀ The overhead cast from a standing position

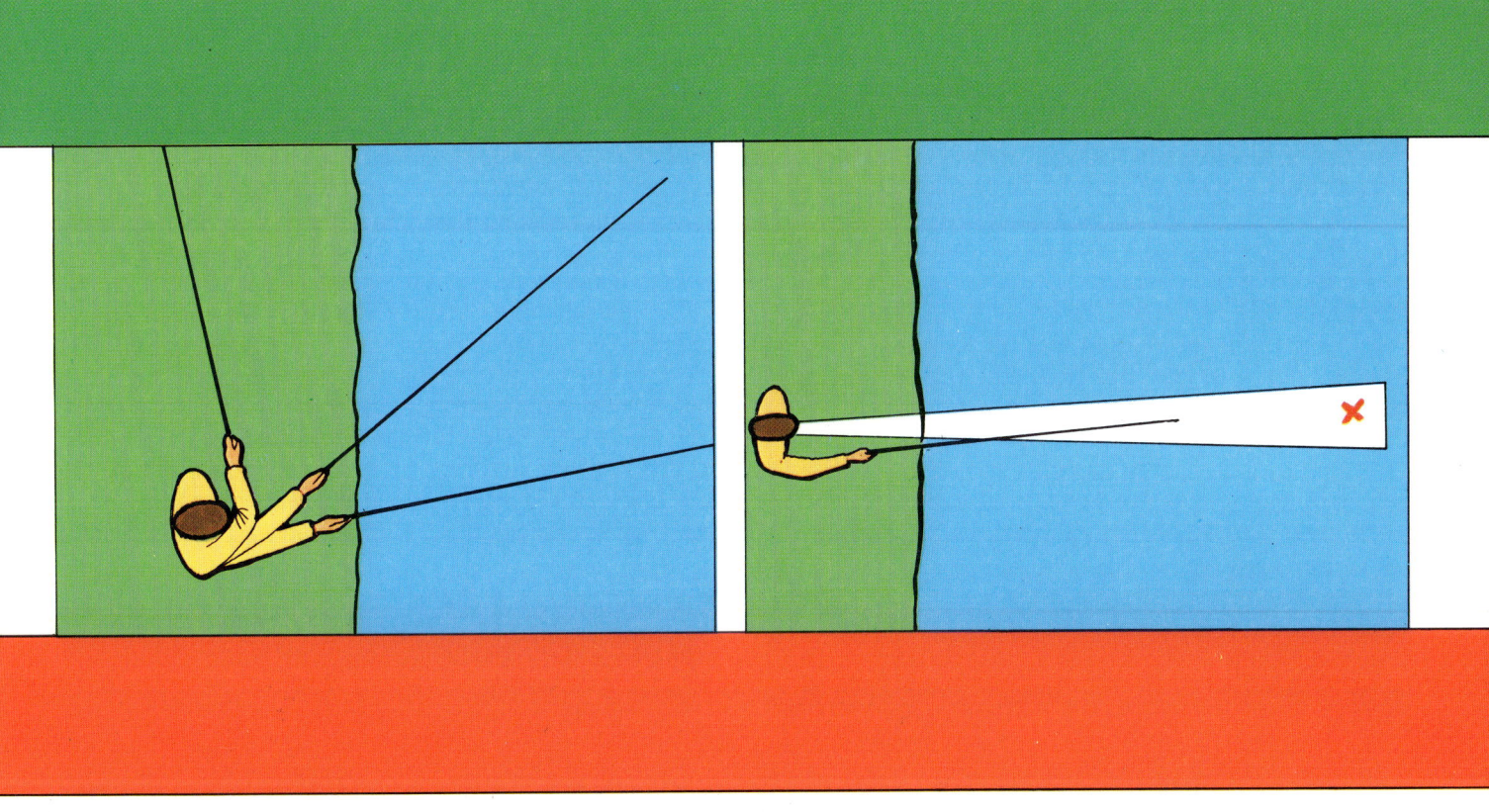

▲ Begin the cast by taking the rod round so that it is parallel to the bank. Then swing it round in one continuous movement, and just before the rod tip points in front of you and at the spot on which you aim to land the tackle, lift your finger so that the line is released

▲ To make sure that the terminal tackle lands exactly where you want it, keep your eyes fixed firmly on the spot you are aiming at. Looking at the reel, rod tip or any other part of the tackle will distract you from the job of casting

on which you aim to land the tackle, removing the finger to release the trapped line just before the rod tip points at the desired spot. Keep your eye on the spot where you want the tackle to land. If you fail to do this, the tackle will land in a different place on each cast, which means the area is not being fished properly.

In most cases accuracy is more important than distance, so concentrate on getting the feel of the tackle until casting becomes second nature. If you consistently fail to reach the spot you are aiming for, it could be because the terminal tackle is too light. In that case, switch to a slightly bigger float which carries more shot, as the more weight there is at the end of the line the easier your casting action will be.

On your first attempts you will find casting much easier if you do it from a standing position. Once you have mastered the action, you will be able to cast without getting up from your stool.

When sitting, the overhead cast is often an easier action than the side cast ▶

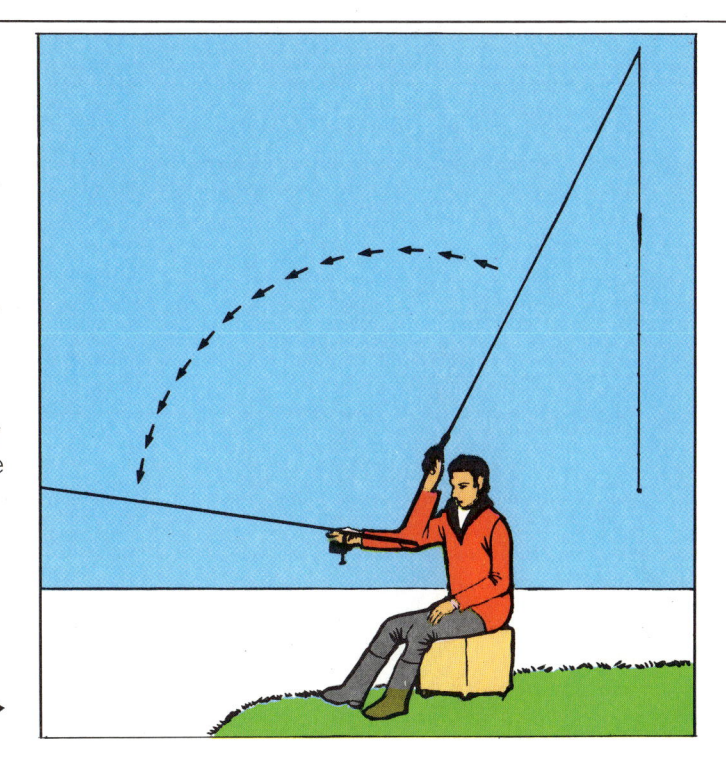

47

Coarse fishing
Striking and landing

The first point of contact between the angler and his quarry is when the fish bites and takes his bait – and recognizing that moment is not always as easy as it sounds. The float vanishing beneath the surface is the most obvious indication of all, but that is not the only way it will show a bite. The float can merely bob, sink just a fraction or even lift slightly, all signs that might go unnoticed by the inexperienced eye, but which are certain indications to a veteran angler. The beginner has to learn how to spot the signs and react accordingly. There are times when a hungry fish will pull the float down with an almost audible plop and there are others when the same fish will give it the merest flicker.

When ledgering there will be no float to help you and this is when you rely on the bite indicator. If you are using a dough bobbin or fold of silver paper, do not always expect it to go up immediately a fish takes the bait. There are plenty of occasions when the angler will receive an early warning by the indicator dropping first, then lifting. There are also times when it will drop and make no other movement.

Whichever type of fishing you are doing, the strike (the movement which gets the hook into the fish) is important. A wild upward slash of the rod will achieve nothing, except possibly a broken line. Make sure that there is not too much loose line between the rod tip and the terminal tackle. If there is, all the strike will do is pick up that loose line and not set the hook. Make sure that the bale arm of the reel is closed, trap the line between your forefinger and the rod and strike with a firm controlled movement of the rod. Once the fish is hooked, do not let it splash on the surface or it will frighten the rest of the shoal. Keep the rod tip in the air so that it can perform its function as a shock absorber. Do not

▼ A sizeable fish has been hooked and beaten and is now ready to be landed. The angler has his landing net sunk below the surface, and he is drawing the fish towards it

drop it so low that it is pointing at the fish.

If the fish is a small one, simply reel in the line until the fish is close enough to be lifted on to the bank and unhooked. If it is a big fish that is putting strain on the line, you will need a landing net, otherwise you risk a line breakage. The golden rule with a landing net is to sink it below the surface and to make sure that the fish is well beaten before drawing it over the net. Do not try to scoop the fish out – you will only frighten it into making another dash for freedom.

If the hook is lodged in the fish's lip you should be able to pull it out with your fingers without trouble, but if it is further back you will need a disgorger. Always wet your hands before handling a coarse fish. Remember that you will release it later and that holding fish with dry hands will remove the protective slime which helps keep disease at bay.

▲ A young angler admires a catch of autumn grayling, hard fighters which nearly always need the use of a landing net

▼ The angler has caught a fish on float tackle. He is not using a landing net, so the fish is obviously small enough to be simply reeled in and lifted on to the bank

Coarse fishing
Clothing

In Britain you can never be certain of the sort of weather to expect when planning a fishing trip. Even in midsummer it is wise to have some form of warm, protective clothing. In winter it is essential if you want to enjoy your fishing. On a dry summer day a showerproof three-quarter-length jacket with plenty of useful pockets is ideal. If the bankside is baked hard by the sun, a pair of light plimsolls will be comfortable and allow you to make a quiet approach to the water's edge.

At any other time of year you should have a pair of rubber boots or proper waders to cope with awkward, marshy banks and for getting to inaccessible places. Wear a pair of thick socks with them for a good fit and to prevent chafing. When the weather is really cold, a piece of polystyrene cut to the shape of your foot and slipped into boots or waders is a great help in keeping your feet warm. Trousers should be heavy enough to withstand the wear and tear caused by bankside bushes and barbed wire fences; they should have provision for a belt if you intend to wear waders.

A proper rainproof three-quarter-length jacket is a good long-term investment, and a pair of waterproof overtrousers is also worth having. Winter gear should include a loose fitting rollneck sweater, a pair of mittens and a long-sleeved woollen shirt. If it is really cold the old-fashioned type of long underwear will do a great deal to keep you warm! An alternative – and one which makes sure that no draughts sneak up your back – is the one-piece suit specially made for anglers. This can be worn over normal clothing and will protect you against the coldest weather conditions.

The best form of weather protection for all forms of static fishing is the angler's umbrella, a familiar sight on every river bank in the country. It will keep out the heaviest rain and is worth its weight in gold when used as a windshield on a cold and breezy day. Buy the largest you can afford so that it covers both you and your tackle comfortably.

▶ The three-quarter-length jacket worn by the angler netting a sizeable roach is an ideal angling garment for most weather conditions. The waders are particularly suitable to cope with the reedy bankside he is fishing, where the margin is likely to be boggy

▼ This angler is wearing a one-piece overall which blends well with the background

▶ A sleeveless jacket with many pockets is ideal for fair-weather fishing

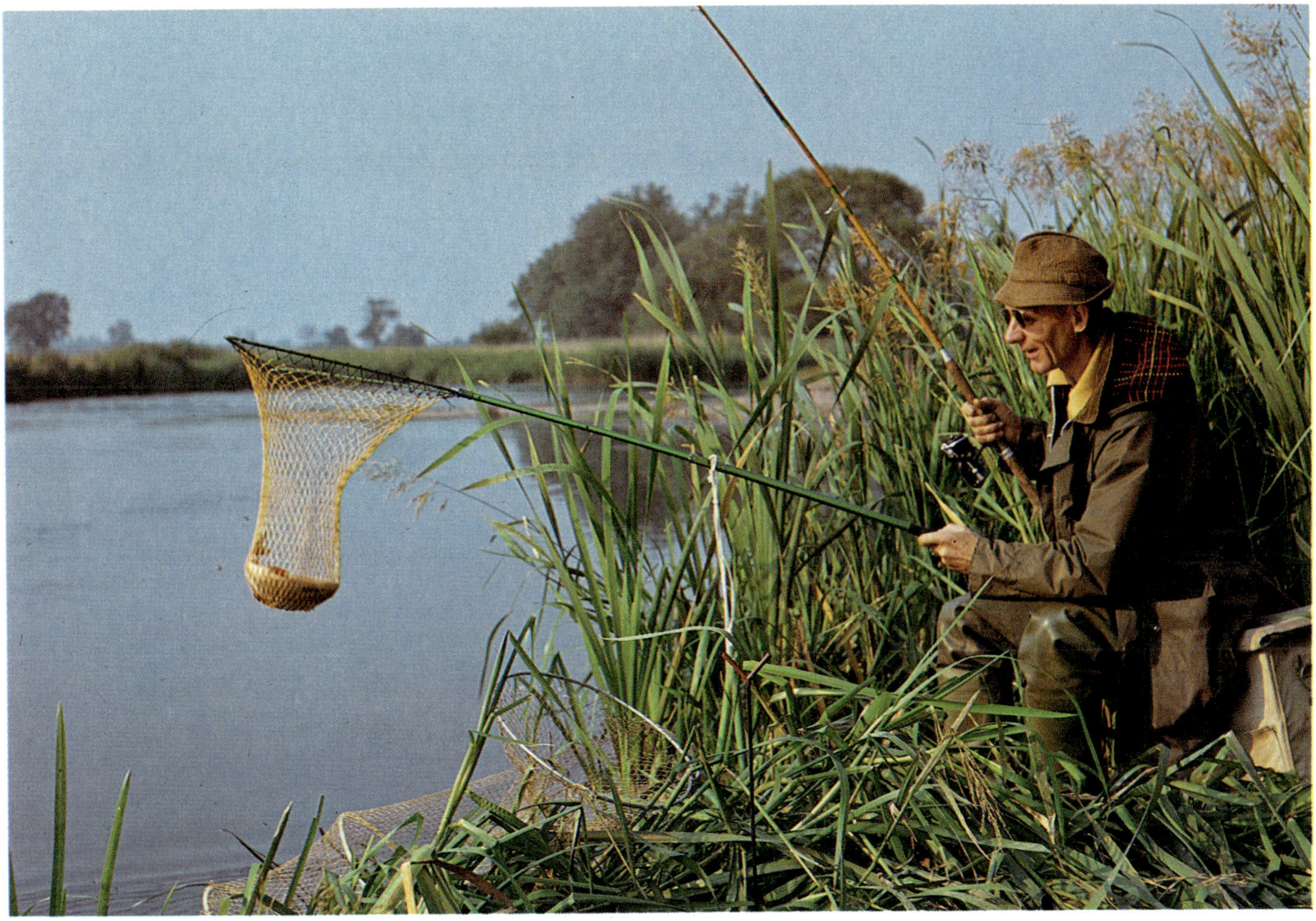

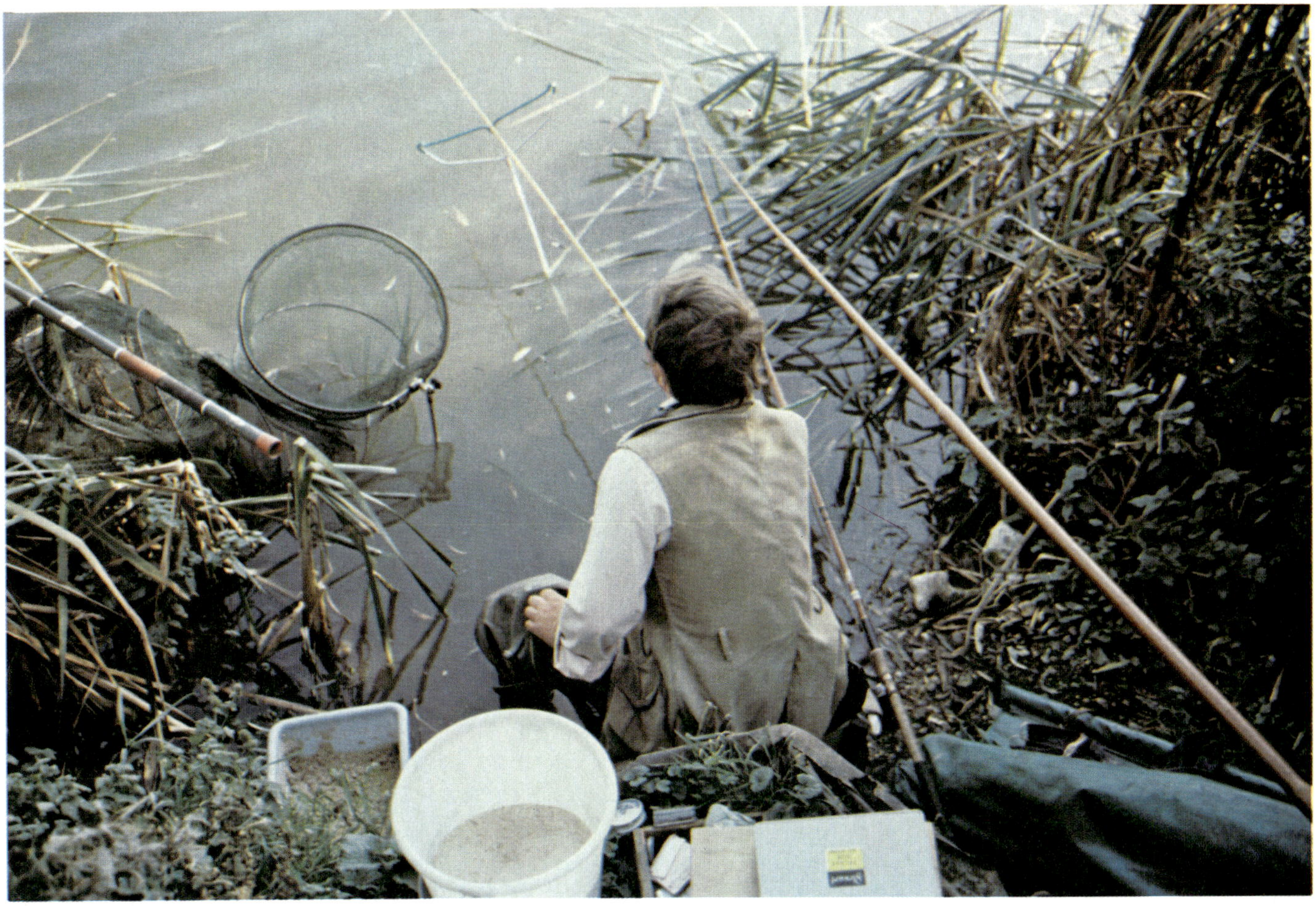

Coarse fishing
Fishing in all weathers

A high temperature and bright sunshine make a perfect combination for many outdoor activities, and such summer days may seem the right time to go fishing, but it is not necessarily so. With the possible exception of carp, which can be seen basking on the surface in hot weather, most fish dislike bright sunshine and will try to seek shelter from it, particularly in shallow waters. On small, shallow waters sheltered from any wind, prolonged bright sunshine will make the fish stick close to the oxygen-giving weedbeds – they will only venture forth and feed when the sun is off the surface and the water temperature drops a degree or two. In those conditions, very early morning or late evening are the most productive times for fishing.

Do not be put off by rain. As long as you are adequately protected against it, you can still catch fish and there are times when it can improve the sport. A sudden heavy rainstorm in the middle of a hot spell can oxygenate a stillwater (such as a lake or pond) enough to quicken the fish's interest in food. A tinge of colour added to a river by floodwater further upstream will also cause fish to feed.

The old saying that 'when the wind is in the east the fish bite least' still holds true, but if it is in any other quarter it rarely affects results. The main problem with wind is that it makes casting and bite indication difficult at times, especially on exposed waters. However, it can be beneficial because of the wave action it causes, bringing food items to an open bank, and so bringing the fish into the angler's range.

Fallen leaves in autumn can cause problems. On stillwaters they have a souring effect, which will put fish off their food. On rivers the slack-water areas will be full of leaves, giving false bite indications each time the angler casts in. Autumn can, however, offer good sport for at that time of year there are generally no wild extremes in weather conditions.

A sudden sharp frost can have a drastic effect on sport in all types of waters, but that does not mean you have to stop fishing once winter arrives. Fish dislike sudden changes, but once winter has set in they become used to the lower temperatures and all but the warm-water lovers, such as carp, tench and barbel, will continue to feed. The best of all winter periods is when the water temperature starts to rise slightly after a week or so of hard frosts. When several mild days cause this slight lift, the fishing can be superb, and cold toes and fingers are soon forgotten!

▼ On bright, summer days early morning and late evening are the most productive times for fishing

▼ Wind makes bite detection difficult on open waters

▲ Fishing can be very good on a mild winter day, especially if it comes after a cold spell

▼ On a frosty morning there is no point in starting early – the best fishing time is around midday

Coarse fishing
At night

The one time you can almost guarantee that you will have the bank to yourself and the choice of any fishing spot you want, with no boats or picnickers to disturb you, is during the hours of darkness. Night fishing is very much a summer pastime, and the rewards often make it well worth the price of a little lost sleep. Tench and carp are the usual quarry of night anglers, but most other species will also feed more readily during a summer night than they will during the bright daylight hours.

Night fishing demands thorough preparation if you are to get the best out of it. The most important thing is to make sure that you are in your chosen spot, with tackle made up and ready, in the last hour or so of daylight. By so doing you will have ample time to observe the surroundings, note any thick weedbeds or snags which could cause problems with hooked fish later on and get the feel of the swim before darkness falls.

Make sure that there are no trees or bushes to get hooked up on when casting, and keep all the accessories you may need close at hand, so that you do not fumble around to find them in the dark. Have a low-powered torch for use with such tricky jobs as unhooking fish, but do not use it more than you have to, otherwise you will destroy your night vision.

Although the day may have been hot, there is a rapid drop in air temperature in the early hours of a summer night, so dress as you would for a winter fishing trip, with warm clothes and a waterproof cover or blanket. For the same reason it is wise to take a flask of warming drink as well.

Remember that the thick weedbeds, which offer fish shelter from bright sunshine during the day, give off carbon dioxide at night, causing the fish to move out into the open water. Note also that, with less bankside disturbance, they will often come close in to the edge to feed, so long casting will not be necessary.

Bite detection can be difficult at night and you will make it easier for yourself if you use a ledger rig rather than float tackle. In this situation one of the electric bite alarms, in which the slightest of line movements triggers off a buzzer, is an enormous help. Using your ears is far less tiring than straining your eyes trying to watch an indicator in moonlight, and should you doze off briefly, the sound of the buzzer will bring you back to reality!

This angler fishes into sunset – but there could be great sport after dark ▶

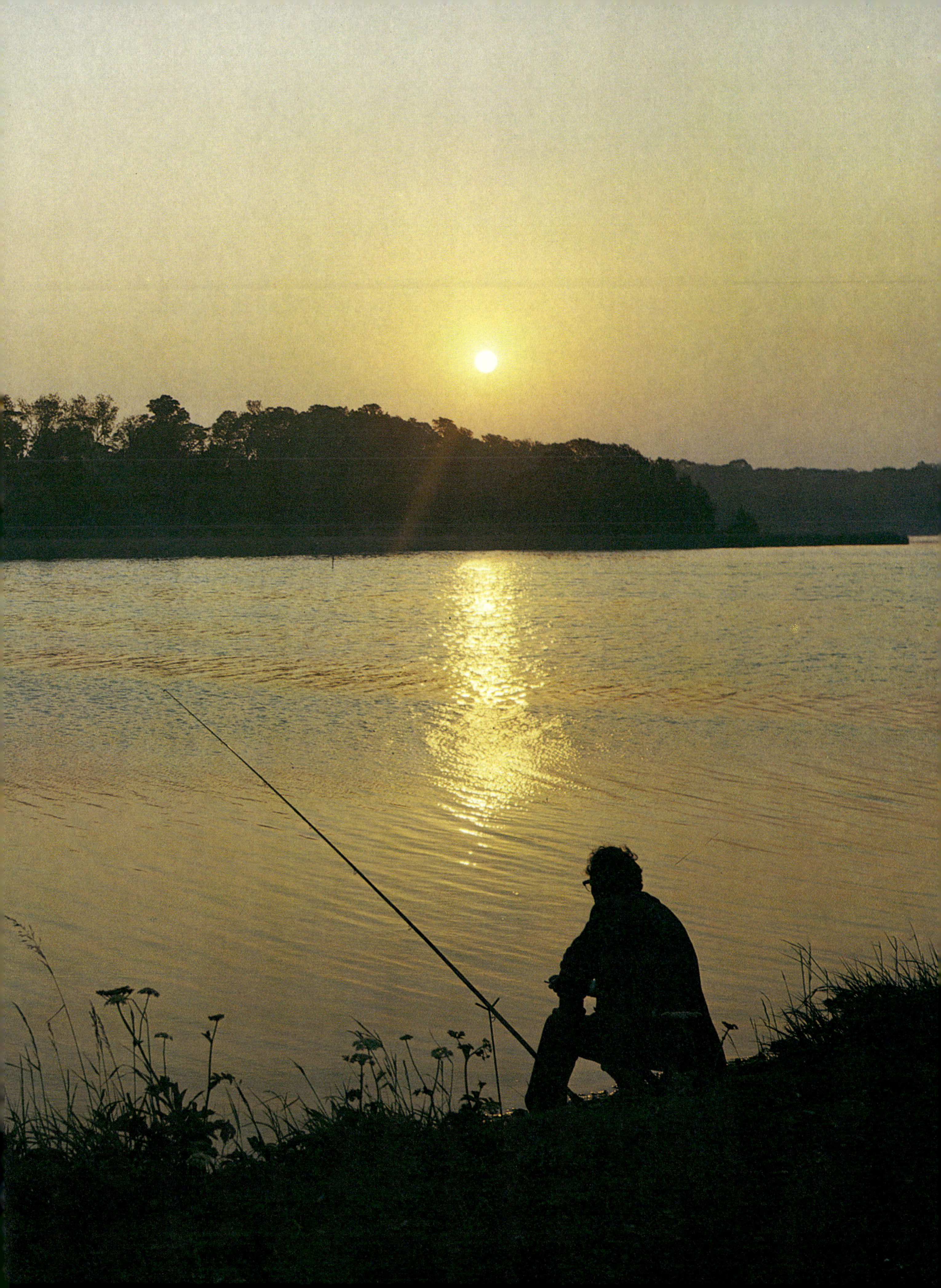

Coarse fishing
Basic knots

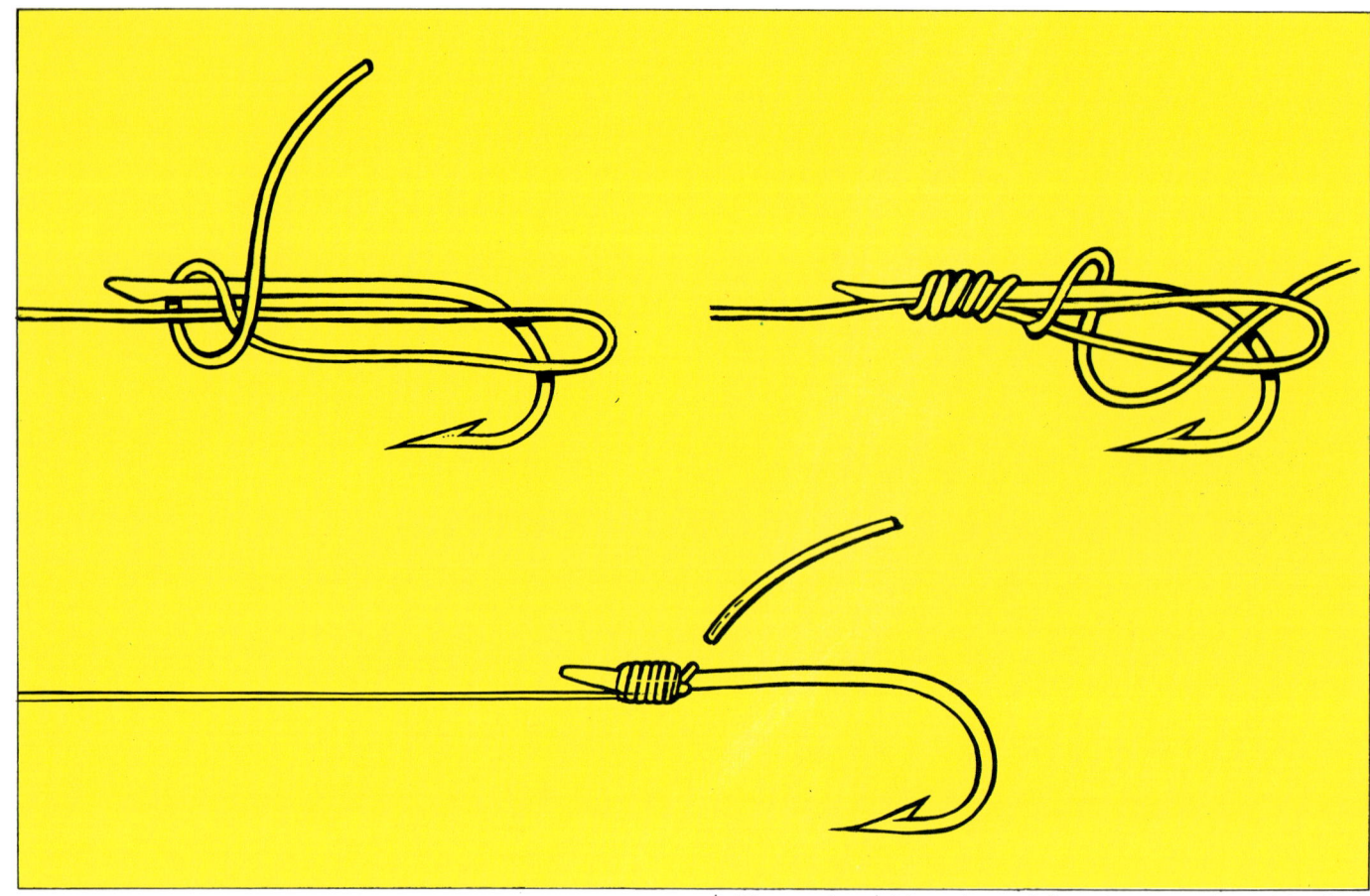

▲ The spade-end knot is used for tying a spade-end hook to a length of nylon

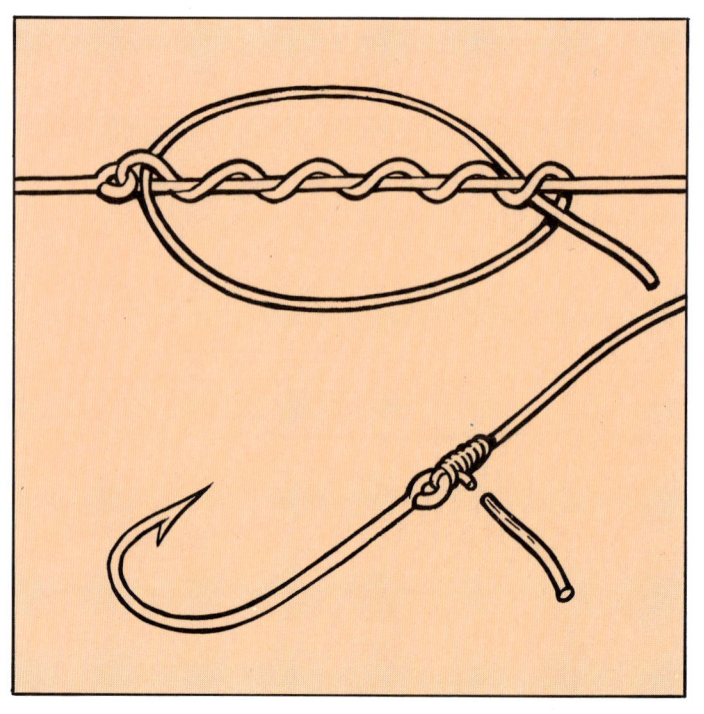

The simple – and clumsy – granny knot used to tie a piece of string round a parcel has no place in angling, nor do any of the other quick lash-ups used for odd jobs. The angler needs to know the special knots used for tying a hook, joining two lengths of line, forming a loop, attaching a swivel and a number of other tasks. Not only must he know them, he must learn to execute them properly, so that he can tie them in the dark if necessary without wasting time.

The importance of proper knot-tying cannot be over-emphasized. Any knot can form a weak point in the link between angler and fish, and it is heartbreaking to see a big fish – maybe the fish of a lifetime – gain its freedom at the last minute simply because a knot gives way at a crucial moment. You do not need to know each and every one of the special knots used in angling, but you must know at least the basic ones. Practise with a bit of spare line at home until you have got the hang of them. Test every knot when you have tied it – far better for the angler to discover any weakness before a fish does! A pair of nail clippers is a very useful gadget for snipping off loose ends and making a tidy job. The knots shown here are the basic ones needed when angling.

▼ The clinch knot, also known as the half blood knot, is used when attaching an eyed hook or a swivel to the line

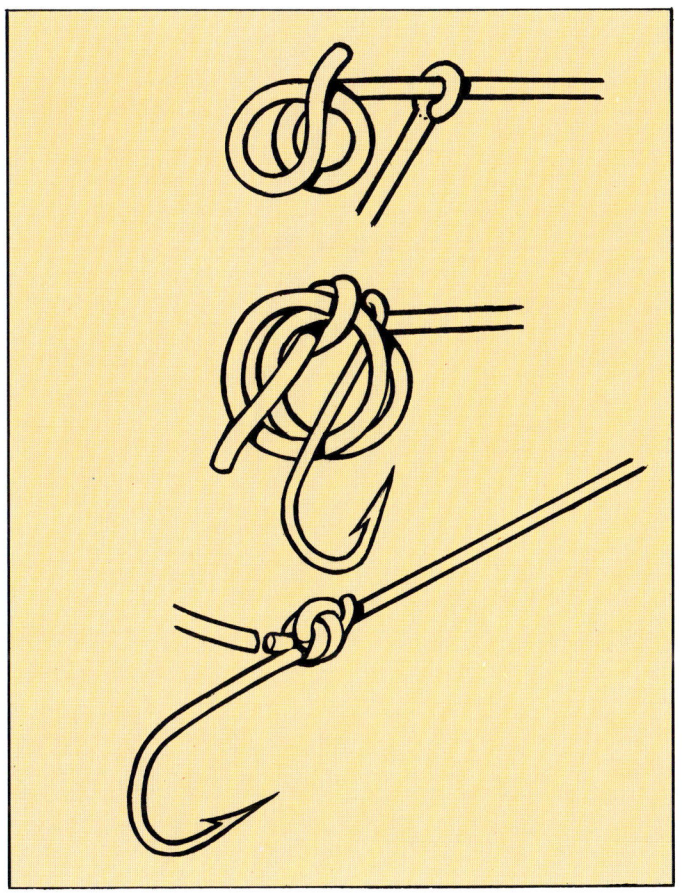

▲ The two circle turle knot is used for attaching a fly or other eyed hook to the line

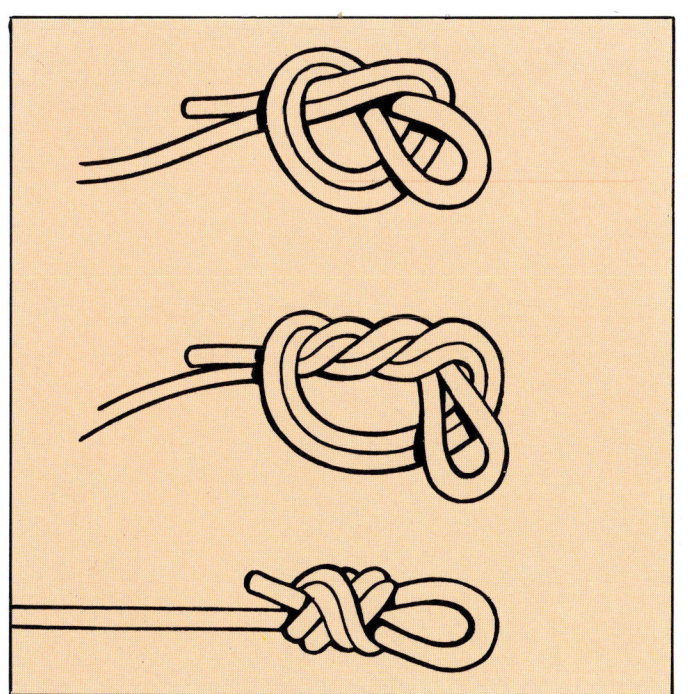

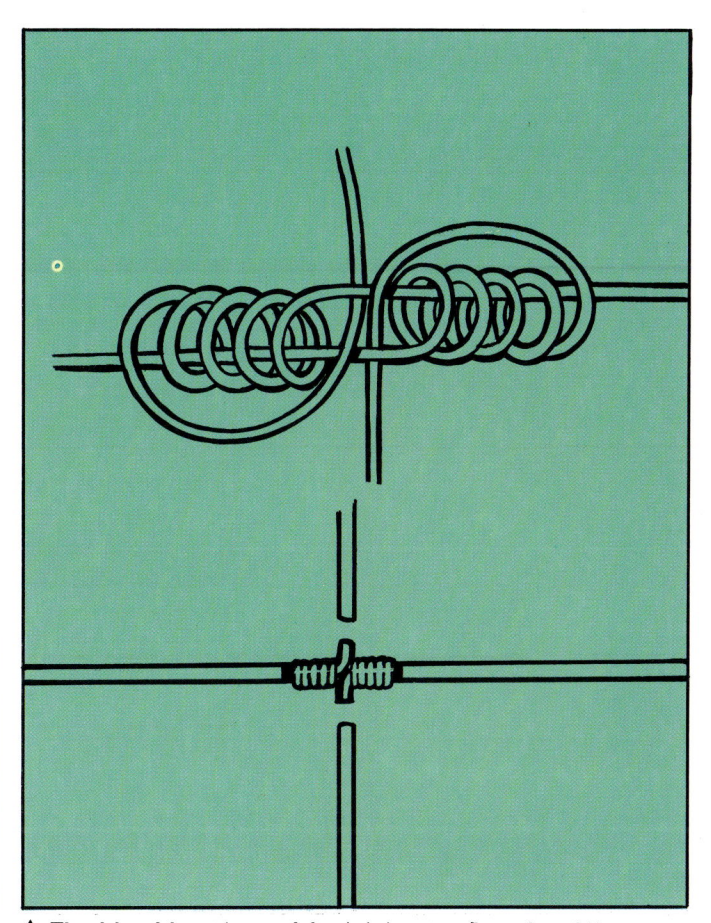

▲ The blood knot is used for joining two lengths of line

▼ The double overhand loop or figure of eight makes a neat loop in the end of a piece of line

▼ The nail knot is used for joining the leader or backing to a fly line (see page 62). An empty ballpoint refill tube is laid alongside the thicker fly line and the thinner monofilament backing passed through it. The tube is then removed

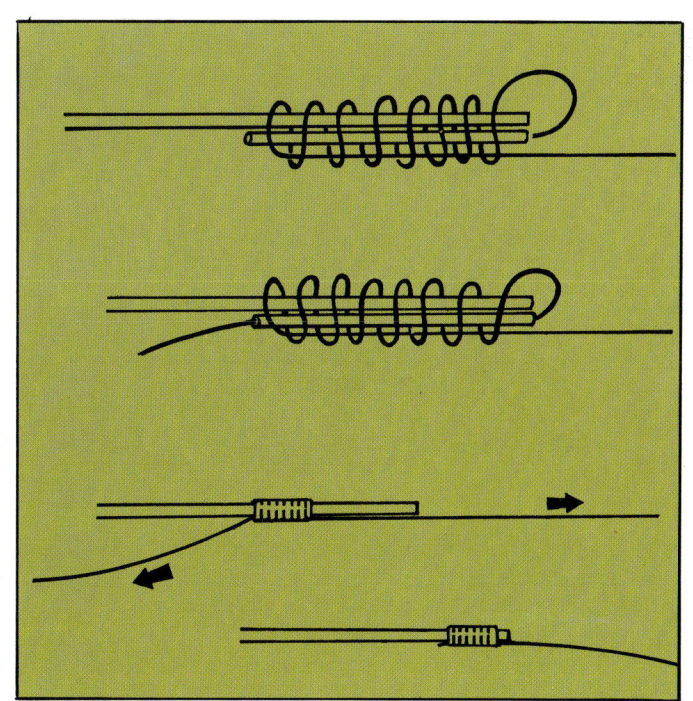

57

The best on the bank

The star performers of the angling world, the men whose names and faces are as well known among their fellow fishermen as television personalities are to the rest of the population, are the cream of the country's competition anglers. Like everyone else, they fish for enjoyment, but they also reap rich rewards in money and national prestige. Top-line performers are often sponsored by tackle firms, and their fishing can take them to all parts of the country for championship competitions and big-money events.

Match-fishing began in the north of England when a group of anglers got together for a day out and a small prize was given to the man with the heaviest weight of fish in his keepnet at the end of the day. The rules applied then are still basically the same, but match-fishing has now spread so that competitions are held all over the country every weekend of the season. These open events – so called because they are open to everyone – are divided

▼ World match-fishing champion Pierre Michiels, from France, in action with the roach pole. Europeans are experts at this style of match-fishing and have won nearly all the world team events

into sections, each with its own small cash prize, but most of the winner's earnings come from the optional sweepstakes. Every match has a range of these, the angler entering for as few or as many as he chooses. Should he pay into the 25p, 50p and £1 sweepstakes and get top weight on the day, he could end up £1,000 the richer!

The big prize matches attract the better quality matchmen and this, in turn, draws the spectators who want to see the stars in action. Top names, such as those of Kevin Ashurst of Lancashire, Ivan Marks of Leicester, London's Ray Mumford, and Clive Smith and Ken Giles, both from Birmingham, are guaranteed to attract big crowds.

Matches can vary in size from those attracting 100 anglers to the country's biggest, the Birmingham Anglers Association's Annual match, which has an entry of nearly 5,000. The nationwide Embassy Challenge, fished in regional qualifying heats, is worth more than £2,000 to the winner. The finalists are taken to Denmark, where the last leg is fished on the River Guden.

The prestige event of the year, however, is the National Federation of Anglers Championships, run in four separate divisions, each of which has a bookmaker in attendance. While matchmen anywhere need a little luck at the draw – which nominates the exact spot on the river they will be fishing – success calls for skill of a very high order – the sort of skill which can catch big bream from one river, small bleak from another and a mixed net of chub and barbel from a third. Top matchmen have to be well versed in every variation of float and ledger fishing, and must be able to cope with every sort of water and weather condition. These high standards have led to three Englishmen winning the individual World Championship: Billy Lane of Coventry in 1963, Robin Harris of Peterborough in 1969 and Ian Heaps of Stockport in 1975.

▼ Inset: Ray Mumford, one of Britain's most successful match anglers; competitors lined up for a big match; at the end of the match the catch is returned to the water

Trout fishing

No branch of English angling has changed quite so dramatically in the last decade as fly fishing for trout. Twenty years ago, the comparatively few anglers who trout-fished regularly did so on streams and rivers, most of which were club controlled or privately owned. In many parts of the country trout waters were scarce and the handful open to the general public tended to be poorly stocked. Then stillwater trout fishing, which had been a minority sport catering for a small band of enthusiasts, became popular and the whole scene changed. It was the opening of Grafham Water, the reservoir in Huntingdon, which heralded the dawn of the new age and opened the eyes of the country's anglers to a brand new and exciting sport.

Built in the early 1960s at a cost of £12,000,000 to supply drinking water to five Midlands counties, Grafham was stocked with trout which thrived and grew fat in their new home. The fishing was opened to anyone on a first-come first-served basis. Anglers simply paid £1 for a day's fishing and were allowed to catch and take away eight trout each, the one strict rule being that only fly-fishing tackle was permitted. Grafham hit the headlines in a big way, and anglers realized that here was a branch of trout fishing which offered excitement and value for money – and they did not have to be a member of a club or association to enjoy it.

In the last ten years this style of trout fishing has become so popular that new waters are opened every season. Ten years ago there were some half-dozen. Today there are more than 180 in England and Wales. They range in size from the huge flooded valleys which form public water supplies, waters so big that you need a boat to cover them properly, to quite small, privately-owned fisheries. Whatever their size, however, the one important thing they have in common is that they are open to all. Addresses of the bigger or better-known trout waters are given on page 118. On the big reservoirs you can buy your ticket on the spot. On some of the smaller waters you may have to buy it in advance. A Water Authority rod licence for trout fishing is also needed.

Prices vary, but the rules are generally the same. On the big reservoirs it costs about £3 for a day's bank fishing, with an extra charge for the hire of a rowing or motor boat. You will be allowed to take away the first eight trout you catch. After that you must either stop fishing or buy another ticket and start again. Fishing is normally allowed from dawn to dusk.

On the smaller, privately-owned waters the cost of a day ticket is generally higher and the catch limit smaller. The cost varies greatly from fishery to fishery, but it comes to an average of £6 per ticket for a four-fish limit.

All fisheries are stocked regularly, and at the end of a day's fishing you will have to fill in a catch return form, which tells the management exactly how many trout you have caught. These returns are vital if a proper balance of stock is to be kept and a good level of sport maintained. Stocking policies vary, but as a general rule the big waters have a massive introduction of fish just before the start of the season, with several big 'topping up' operations later on, while the smaller fisheries put in fewer – and bigger – trout at more regular intervals, often weekly.

◀ Typical of the new style of stillwater trout fisheries is the Drift Reservoir near Penzance, Cornwall

The more traditional style of river fishing is giving way to stillwater fishing in England ▶

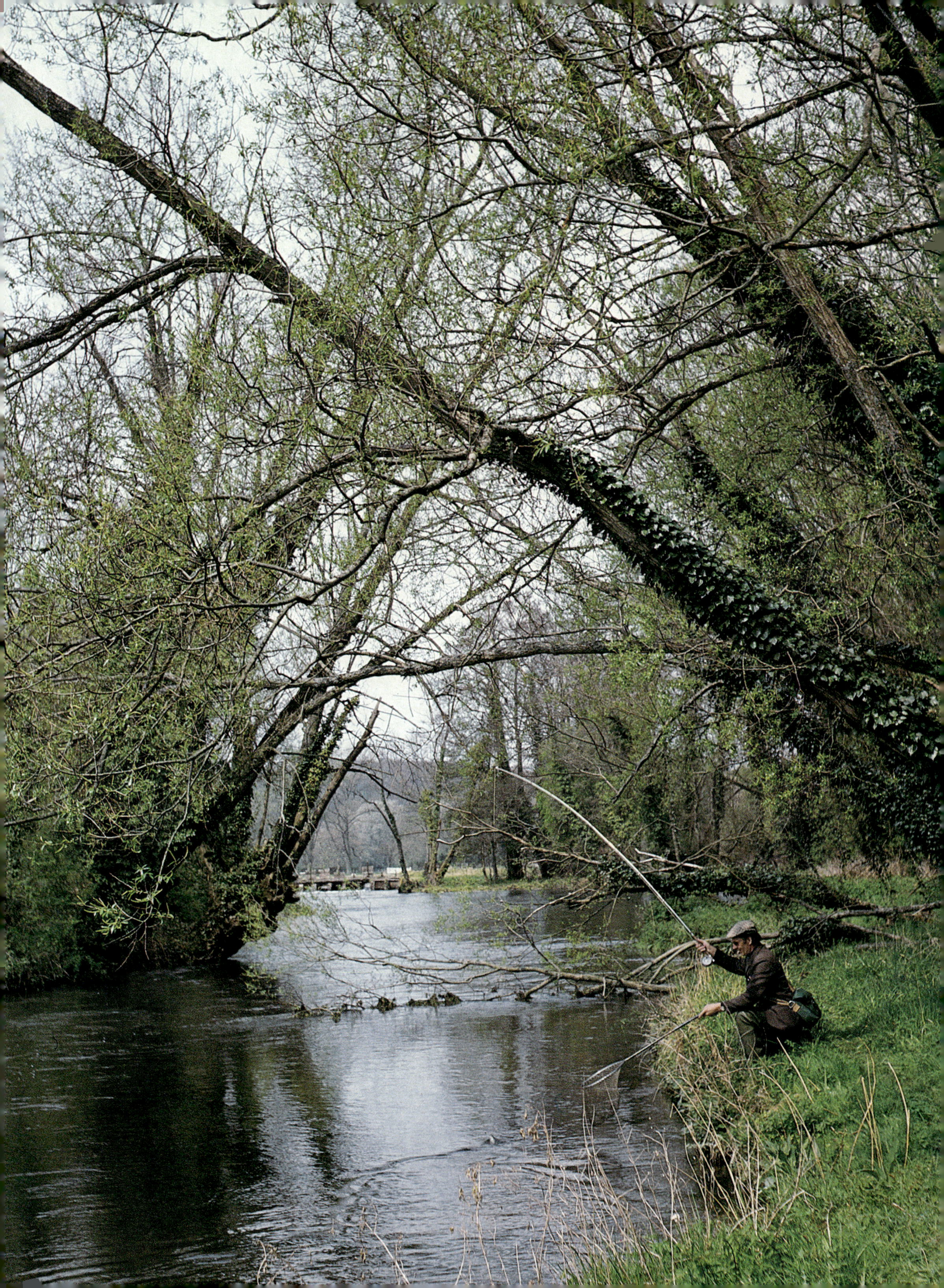

Trout fishing
Fly-fishing tackle

One of the attractions of trout fishing is that the angler does not need to burden himself with a lot of tackle. It is essentially a mobile form of fishing and the less he carries, the more he will be able to move about and enjoy the freedom that trout fishing offers.

The important item of tackle is the rod, which must be light enough to be used all day without tiring the user, but capable of casting a long line when necessary. Although there are some incredibly light and strong carbon fibre rods on the market, they tend to be expensive and the beginner will be better suited by a glass fibre model. Trout rods come in various lengths, but if most of the fishing is to be done from the banks of the new stillwater fisheries you will need one 3m (9ft) long. You will also need a reel with two spools, a floating line, a sinking line, some casts (also known as leaders), a selection of flies and a landing net.

Matching the line to the rod is vitally important. If the balance is wrong, the rod will not cast the line properly and the beginner will find himself flailing his arm about and getting nowhere at all. The certain way of getting the match right first time is to follow the coding system now marked on all rods and lines. This system, devised by the Association of Fishing Tackle Manufacturers, is known as the AFTM rating. A rod marked with the code number AFTM 7-9 on the butt means that it was designed to cast a number 7, 8 or 9 line. The number describes the weight of the line, and the smaller the number is, the lighter the line. They range from a size 4, used for dry fly fishing on rivers where long casting is not needed, to a size 9, which is intended for distance casting on bigger waters.

Fly lines are very different from the kinds of line used in any other form of fishing. Compared to the normal monofilament, they look like clothes lines. Usually 27m (30yd) in length, they vary in colour, shape, density, weight and thickness. Some are designed to float on the water surface and others to sink at different speeds. Colour is very much a matter of personal choice. A double taper line – thinner at each end than it is in the middle – is designed principally for medium-distance fishing, and has the advantage that, when the 'business' end shows signs of wear, it can be reversed on the reel and the other end used. A size 7 floating double taper line will be marked AFTM 7 DT F. The forward taper line is thicker at one end than it is at the other and is designed for long-distance casting, the thinner end being put on the reel first, so that the extra weight helps give distance on the cast. Such a line is also known as a weight forward and a size 8 floater would be marked AFTM 8 WF F. You can also buy a sinktip line which, as the name implies, floats for the greater part of its length but the tip section sinks.

Do not worry too much about the various types of line and their specialist uses. To begin with, one weight forward floating line, for use when trout are feeding near the surface, and a medium sinktip line, for searching them out when they are feeding lower down, will be good enough. You can save money by buying just half a line, known as a shooting head. This gives extra casting distance, because its weight is concentrated in a shorter area. When using a shooting head, the normal practice is to step up

▼ This picture captures the spirit of trout fishing – a hatful of flies flanked by two glass fibre trout rods

▲ The trout reel is a simple piece of equipment. The important thing is to make sure that it is big enough to carry a full-length line plus backing

Springtime at a day-ticket trout fishery, and this angler wading the margin has something to show for his efforts ▶

the line weight. Thus a rod designed to cast a full number 7 line would comfortably manage a number 8 shooting head. All fly lines have to be spliced to a monofilament or level backing line (see diagram bottom right on page 57), which goes on the reel first.

The cast is a length – usually 3m (3yd) – of specially tapered monofilament nylon which forms the link between the fly line and the fly itself. In its simplest form it is knotless and meant for use with just one fly, but you can also buy casts with short lengths of line knotted to the main length which offer the facility of fishing three flies at once, known as a team of flies. My advice to the beginner is to ignore the latter until he has become proficient with the single fly – the more hooks there are swinging about when casting, the greater the chance of one of them getting caught up!

Casts come in different breaking strains, and you will need a selection according to the water conditions. In rough, windy weather on a big reservoir, when the water is coloured, a 3kg (7lb) cast can be used. On a smaller fishery where the water is clear and presentation crucial, you may need to drop down to a 2kg (4lb) line, or even lower.

The flies for stillwater fishing are not the strict floating imitations of the natural insect that the dry fly fisherman of the chalk stream uses, although there are occasions when they will be successful. The stillwater trout angler's armoury is composed of wet flies, designed to be fished below the surface. Some are tied to represent small fish, and some are copies of tiny natural creatures, such as shrimps, beetles and aquatic insects. Others represent no particular food item – their colouring and movement are enough to arouse the trout's hunting instinct.

All trout reels are of the drum type, some with a geared action, some with an automatic retrieve and some with a simple single action. The latter type is perfectly adequate and the cheapest of all. Buy a spare spool, so that you can have one loaded with a floating line and the other with a sinking line. The important thing is size – an 8·8cm (3½in) model will hold a full line plus backing without the line snarling up.

Among the useful odds and ends needed are a pair of nail scissors or clippers, for cutting off the protruding ends of knots, forceps for removing the fly from the trout's jaw, a tin of line grease to help the cast to float when needed, and a small weighted club (known as a priest) for killing the trout quickly and cleanly.

On the reservoirs a long-handled landing net, as used by most coarse fishermen, is easier to use than the small, folding type sold as trout nets. Any sort of pocket-sized tin will do to carry your flies in, providing that they do not rattle around and so blunt the points of the hooks. Alternatively, you can buy a purpose-made wallet or container.

Do not be too worried about the job of splicing the nylon backings to the fly lines. Any big tackle shop will do this for you, either free or for a very nominal charge.

Trout fishing
Choice of stillwaters

Faced with such a wide choice of waters, the main problem for the newcomer to stillwater trout fishing is which one he should select for his initial outing, when he can try his new tackle for the first time. Large reservoir or small lake? Boat fishing or bank fishing? Each offers its own particular form of enjoyment and each has its special rewards.

My advice is to try a small water first, even though the cost of a day ticket will be slightly higher than at a bigger fishery, for the smaller area will offer fewer problems and give the angler a better chance of a fish. Success on the first trip will also boost a beginner's confidence. On the large reservoirs, their sheer size poses a problem for the beginner who has yet to learn about the trout's behaviour pattern and how to read a water. Variation of the underwater contours, the make-up of the bottom and the wind direction make some areas more productive than others – but which ones? Where will most of the fish be in a water of this size? The best casting technique and the right fly pattern will not work if you are fishing in the wrong place. Most bank anglers tend to wade out as far as they can on big reservoirs to cover more water, so the trout are driven further out by the disturbance. This means that the beginner will have to become an accomplished distance caster if he is to reach the fish. Reservoirs also often have exposed banks, where a stiff wind is common, which further inhibits casting.

On a small fishery many of these problems do not exist, leaving the angler free to concentrate on other essentials. Locating fish should not be difficult. Most of the small, privately-owned fisheries maintain a stocking density of about 100 trout per 4,000 sq m (1 acre) and because competition exists between the various fishery owners, each likes to put in as many big fish as he can. These fish do not have much space in which to roam and hide. They may have a preference for a certain part of the lake, because of a particularly thick weedbed or other food source, but they should be found fairly easily. As wading is not necessary, and may often be banned on such fisheries, the trout will not be driven out into the centre of the water, so long-distance casting is not called for. Wind, too, will be much less of a problem, for the small lakes are not generally situated in such exposed positions as the big reservoirs.

Having decided where to go, the next question is when, and the answer here is as early in the season as possible. The open season for trout varies from area to area, but April 1 is regarded as the starting day in most places. The beginner's best chance of a productive trip comes early in the season because the underwater life, which forms the trout's food, is in short supply following the cold days of winter. Insect life does not flourish and multiply until the water warms up in summer, so early season trout are hungry fish anxious for an easy meal.

◀ Well-known trout-angling writer and tackle shop owner Geoffrey Bucknall casts a fly at Peckham's Copse, Sussex

▲ Blagdon Lake, near Bristol, is one of the oldest stillwater trout fisheries in Britain. It is famous for its beautiful surroundings and good stock of trout, and anglers come from all parts of the country to fish it

▼ Three anglers find plenty of room on the banks of Tottiford Reservoir in Devon, one of the West Country fisheries run by the local Water Authority

Trout fishing
Trout in rivers

While stillwater trouting has been the big growth area in the sport, traditional river fishing for trout should not be overlooked, for in those parts of the country blessed with many rivers and a native stock of trout – notably Scotland, Wales and some northern areas of England – the modern type of stillwater fishery is a rarity.

Because there is no need for long-distance casting, and also because river fish tend to be smaller, there is no need for the heavy rods, lines and casts used on the big stillwaters. The heaviest line likely to be needed is an AFTM 6 matched to a suitable rod, with a 1·40kg (3lb) cast. On crystal clear streams, where trout are shy and can spot every move the angler makes, much finer tackle will be the order of the day.

There are two basic styles of river trout fishing: the upstream dry fly and the wet fly. In the former the angler aims to catch a trout he can actually see. He does this by watching the fish, identifying the type of fly on which it is feeding, then casting an imitation of that fly upstream so that it drifts down, copying the natural ones. The dry fly is always fished upstream – nearly all fishery rules ban its use any other way – and as the fly is presented on the surface a floating line is used. Among the problems the angler must solve are the correct identification of the natural fly, how to stalk the fish without frightening it and how to put the line and fly on the water without alarming the fish.

Wet fly fishing is less rigid as far as the rules go. The flies are normally fished in a team of three and can be cast up or downstream. It is a method which can be used on a trout that can be seen actively feeding on a form of insect life just below the surface, and also in situations in which the angler is fishing a likely-looking spot but cannot actually see the trout.

In both dry and wet fly fishing the actual fly used depends on the area and time of year. A pattern which is deadly on a southern chalk stream would be useless on a northern river and vice versa.

Early spring on a Welsh river, and the angler sorts through his box to find the right fly to use ▶

▼ A shorter rod, lighter line and smaller flies are used when fishing a small stream. When using a dry fly, the angler usually casts to a visible fish

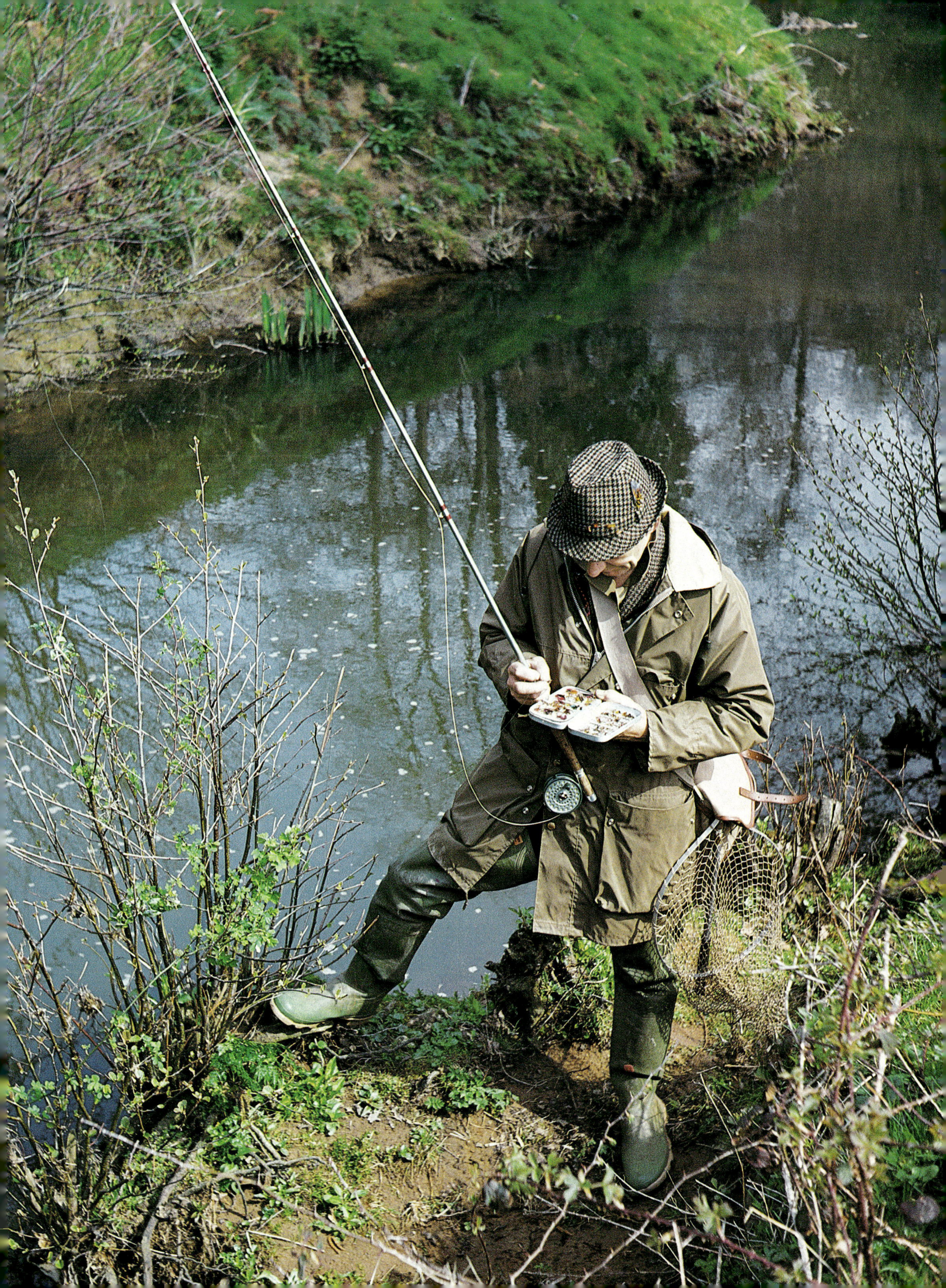

Trout fishing
On the bank

When trying to catch river trout, the angler has the advantage of fishing for trout he can actually see – as in the case of dry fly fishing – or else of trying certain fairly obvious holding spots. A big stillwater does not have the fast glides and deep holes so instantly recognizable on a running water, so the angler has to work out where the fish may be and at what depth they may be feeding. If they can be seen feeding on the surface, then half the battle is won. A floating line will put the fly in the right place.

If there are no such obvious signs, he has to try other tactics. Fortunately, big reservoirs are not the featureless expanses they seem to be at first sight, for nearly all were made by building a dam and then flooding low-lying farmland. Down on the bed of the reservoir there will still be traces of the former ditches, roads and hedges, all of which will be areas that trout like.

Get a map from the fishery office and study it – ten minutes spent plotting the shallows, deeps and other features will be time well spent. Walk around and look for a promontory which allows you to cast into deeper water. Make a note of which way the wind is blowing, for the shore which receives the wind will always have a good share of fish.

Until you are a proficient caster, you have to be careful of the wind. Not only will it throw your line about, it can also blow a fly dangerously close to your face. Choose a bank where the wind is blowing from left to right if you are right-handed. In that way the line will always blow away from you.

A slow-sinking line gives the angler a chance to search all depths of water from the surface down to the bed. The longer the time between the completion of the cast and the retrieve, the deeper the line will sink. Early in the season, when there is little insect life near the surface, most trout will be seeking their food fairly deeply. They will also be near the bottom on bright, hot, sunny days.

Once the fly is in the water, only its action and movement attracts the trout sufficiently for it to make a grab at what it thinks is a tasty mouthful of underwater life. This movement is provided by the angler who, after casting out, has to retrieve the fly in an attractive manner. This is done by holding the line just below the bottom rod ring and tugging it back. Larger lures, which imitate small fish, are generally pulled back in fairly long, steady movements, while the smaller nymphs are twitched back slowly to imitate the movements of the natural insect.

The first thing that becomes obvious is that the line being retrieved has to be put somewhere, and this is where fly fishing differs from coarse and sea fishing. In the latter two sports line should never be anywhere except on the reel, and when a fish is hooked the line is straight between fish and reel. In trout fishing there is a difficulty, for one hand (usually the right) is holding the rod and the other pulling in line – so those loops of line either fall on the ground by the angler's feet or are dropped into a special line tray which fits round the waist. When a trout hits the fly and is hooked, you don't have to wind in the slack before you can play the fish. You play it by simply controlling the line with the left hand, letting it out as the fish runs and pulling it in as the fish is beaten and gets nearer the bank. The rod should be held high all the time, so that its power beats the fish.

◀ A small water with a big reputation is Avington Trout Fishery near Winchester, Hampshire, where this successful angler gets ready to net a fish

A calm corner may look attractive, but on a big water choose the shore that receives the wind, as it will have a good share of fish ▶

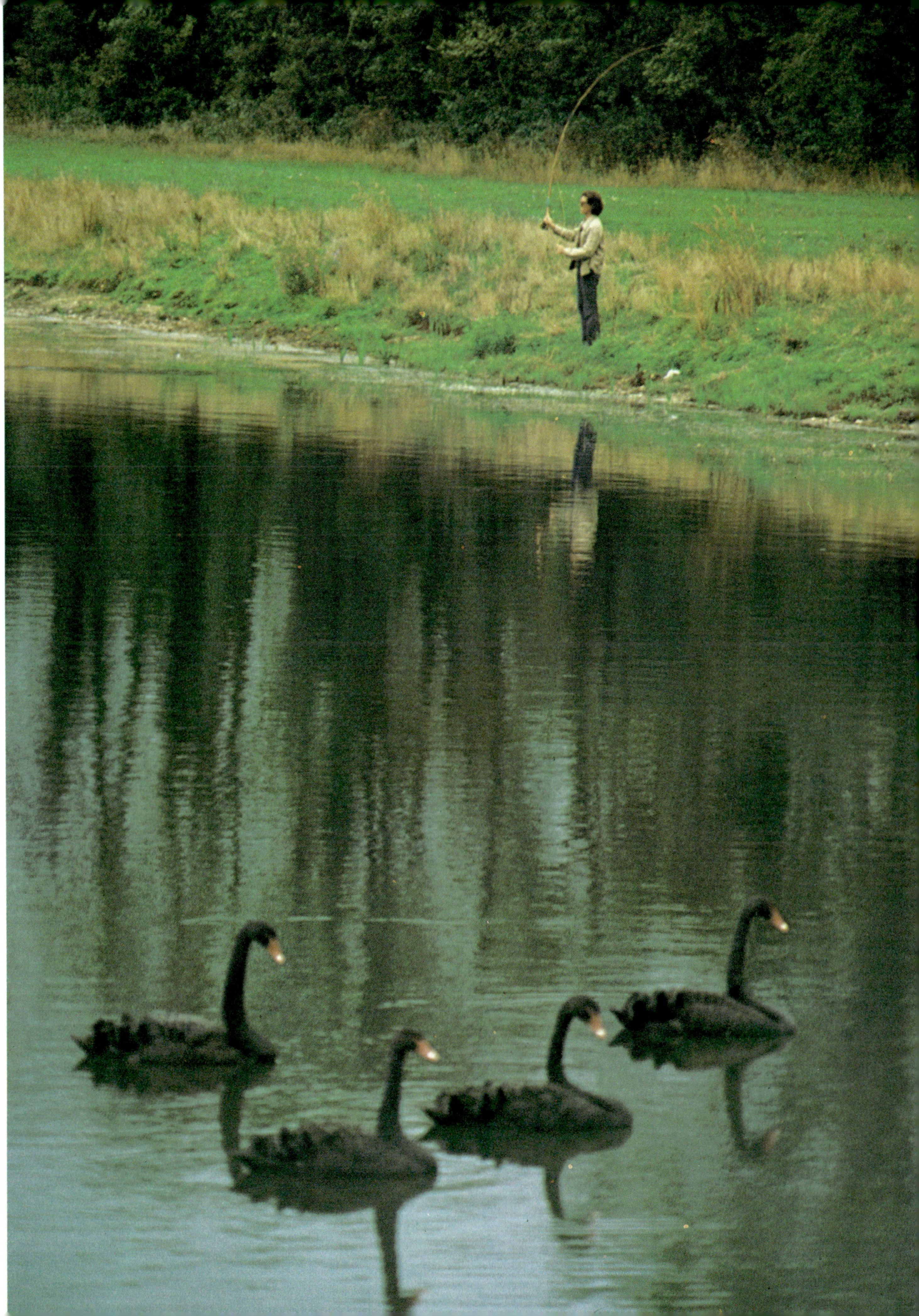

Trout fishing
Casting

This plan view shows how to hold the rod in relation to the body

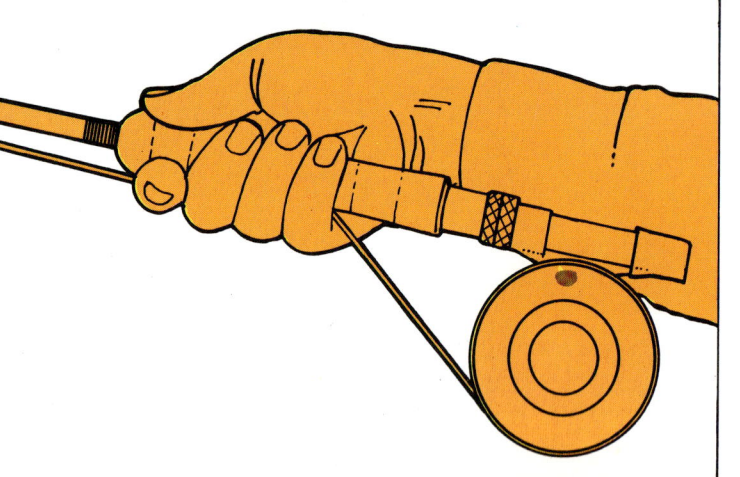

Holding a fly rod in this way will soon make the wrist ache

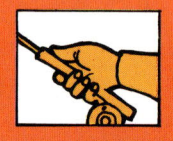

▲ Every type of cast should be started with a proper grip on the rod handle, firm but not so tight as to give you cramp in the fingers. The thumb is kept pressed down on the top of the handle, while the butt is kept tucked against the forearm. If the wrist waggles it will affect the cast

▲ The sequence shown in these diagrams is for the basic overhead cast. With the fly line laid out in front of the rod – and remember that the rod will not work unless there is sufficient line to give it action – the rod is lifted towards the angler's shoulder to get the line in the air

▼ Cast accurately when you see fish near the surface

Casting a fly looks far more difficult than it really is. Complicated though it may seem to anyone trying for the first time, it is in fact nothing more than a sequence of simple movements which, once you have learned them, will be as easy as riding a bicycle. You do not even have to go fishing to perfect the technique, for your local park offers all the space needed for a little practice. A few evening sessions will soon have you casting well enough to catch trout.

You can in due course learn the various casts designed for different situations, such as the side, roll, steeple and double haul casts, but the simple overhead cast is the one that the beginner must master. The thing that makes fly casting so different from the styles used in other forms of casting is that there is no weight on the end of the line which can be simply swung out. It is the weight of the line itself, coupled with the action of the rod, which punches the fly out to where you want to put it. In the overhead cast the action is rather like cracking a whip. It has two separate

If the rod is brought back too far, the line will fall to the ground behind the angler

▲ The line is thrown up and back in one continuous movement, the rod being stopped when it is pointing straight up at the sky. At this stage the line will stream out behind the angler, and it must be straight before the forward part of the cast is begun. When the rod is vertical, the angler pauses for a second for the line to straighten out

▲ The power for the cast comes from the line stretched out in the air behind the angler. This back cast pulls the supple rod back rather like a spring

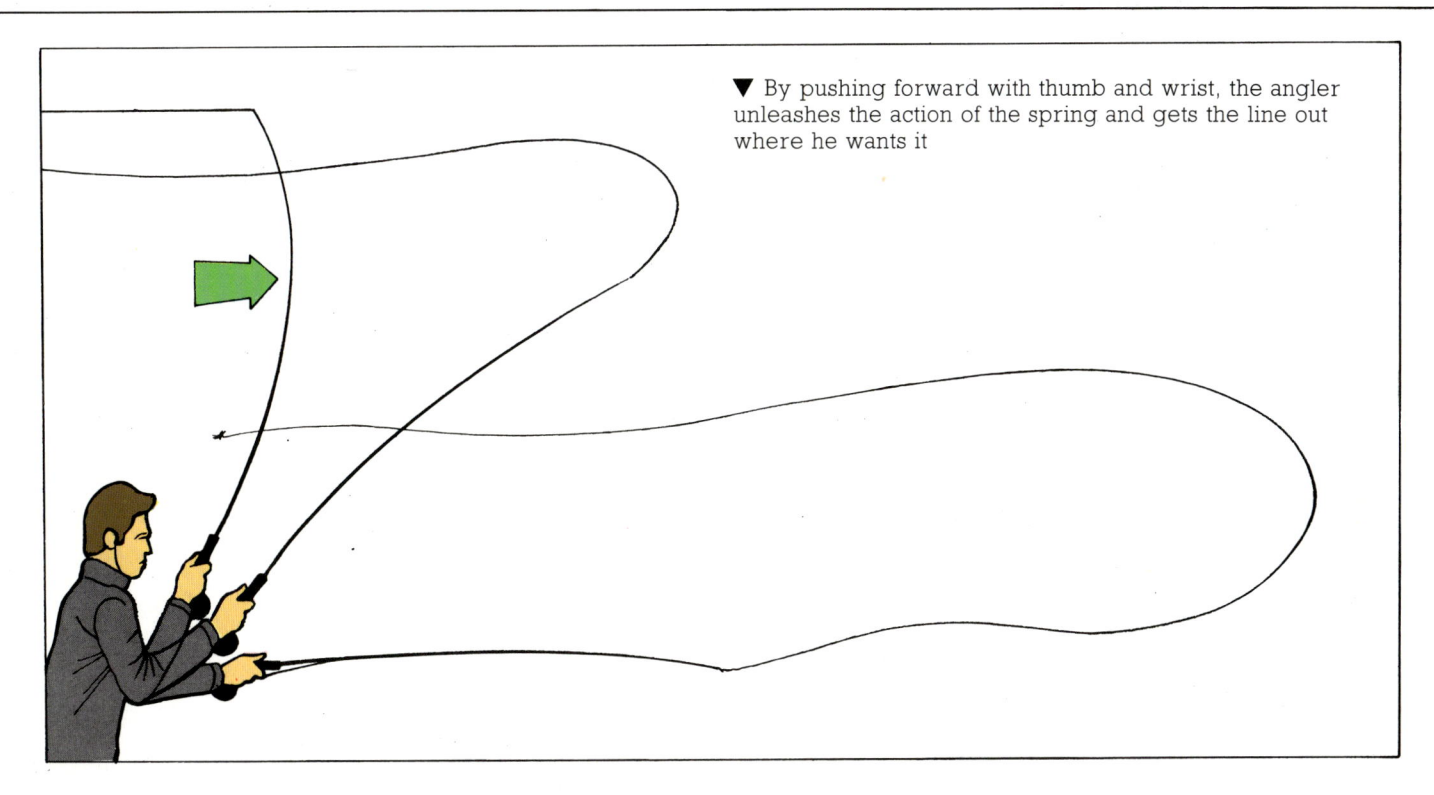

▼ By pushing forward with thumb and wrist, the angler unleashes the action of the spring and gets the line out where he wants it

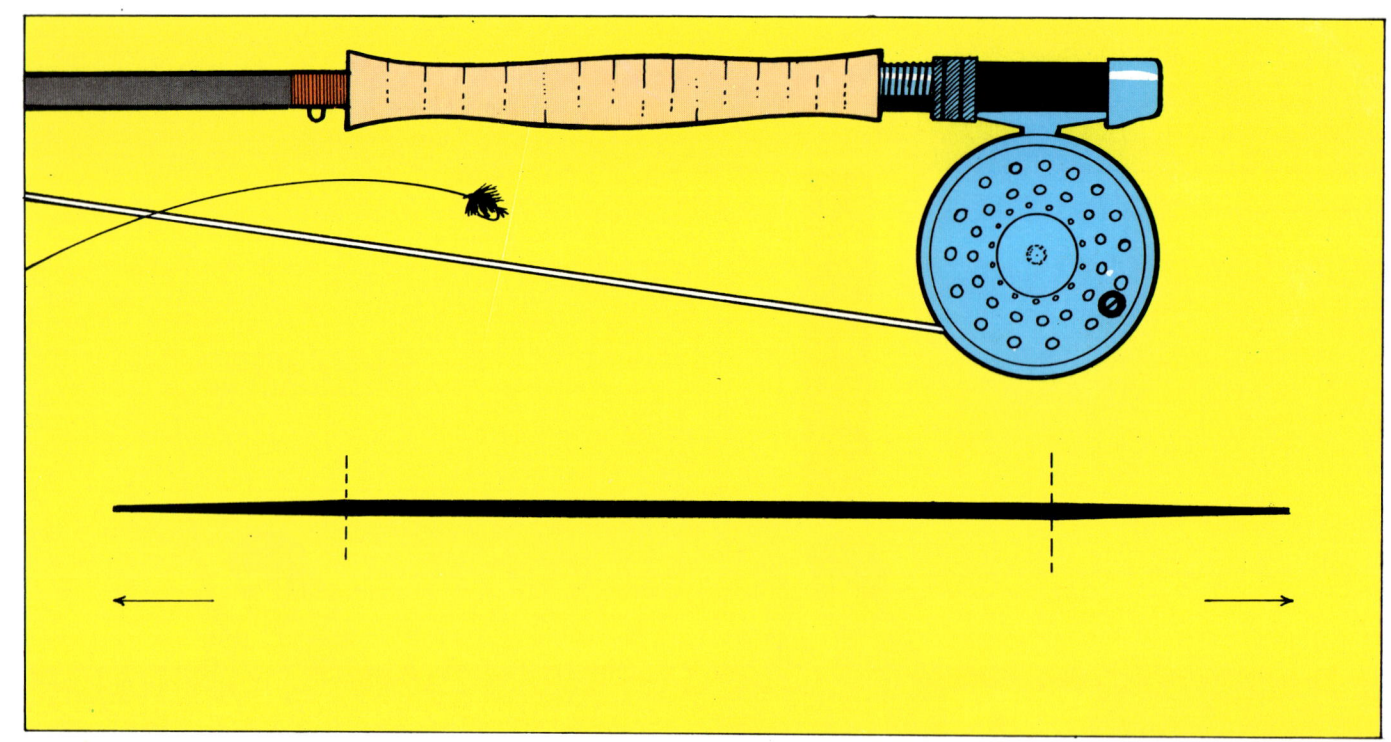

Trout fishing

▲ On a fly rod the reel-seating is always at the extreme end of the handle. You can get some idea of the thickness of a fly line when it is compared to the tapered monofilament cast to which the fly is tied. The profile view of a double taper fly line, also illustrated above, shows how it tapers almost to a point at each end

A fish is landed from Driffield Beck in Yorkshire. ▶ Everything the angler needs for a day's fishing is carried in his shoulder bag

▼ Kempton Park Reservoir, shown here, offers day-ticket trout fishing within easy reach of London

movements, with a distinct pause between them – one when the line is thrown back behind the angler and the other when it is propelled forward, using the power of the rod.

Grip is important. Hold the rod firmly but not too tightly, grasping it by the handle just above the reel-seating, with the thumb on top. Start with the rod pointing out straight in front, with several metres of line laid out on the ground. The first movement is when the rod is lifted smartly, to finish in a vertical position by the angler's shoulder, this action lifting the line and flicking it back behind him. Pause until it straightens, then use the thumb and wrist to push the rod forward so that the line flies straight out in front of you. Try this a few times until you get the feel of it and the action comes easily.

Then try the next step, which is to lengthen the amount of line cast. To do this, hold a loop of line taken straight from the reel with the left hand and release it as you make the back cast. On the forward movement, the extra line will slide through the rings and give you the extra distance. You gain more distance still by letting out more line all the time. Try to get the line to alight on the water as quietly as you can, and keep it straight. Trout feeding on or near the surface can be frightened away by a line which hits the water with a splash. If it lands in a heap or concertina shape, you risk tangles.

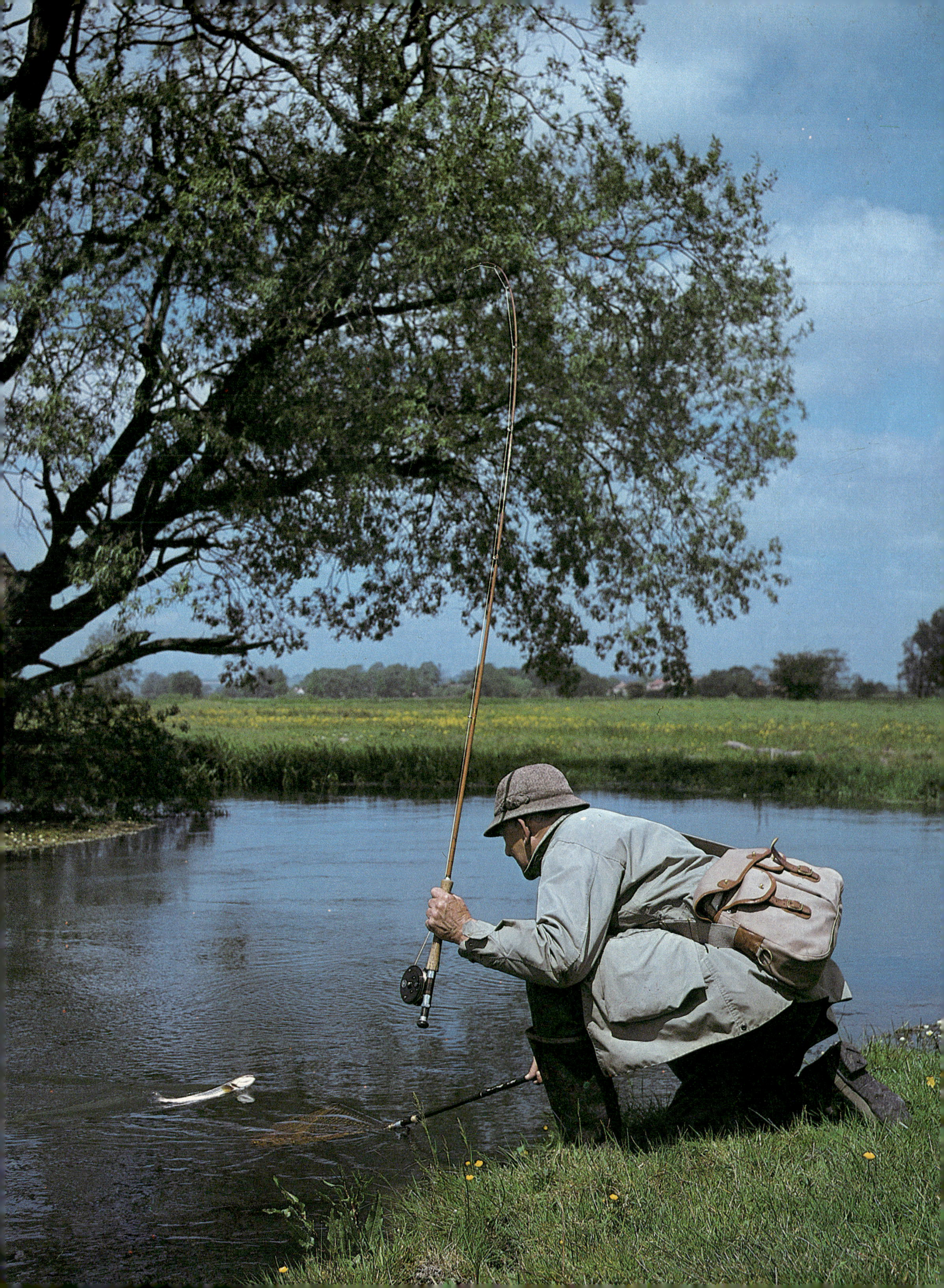

Trout fishing
Recognize the species

▲ The brown trout, Britain's native species, has clearly defined spots on the body only

Three other types of trout: a handsome pair of rainbow trout, a species originally from North America (top); the tiger trout (centre), which is a hybrid from the brown and the American brook trout (below) ▶

The brown trout is Britain's native species. It is very common in Scotland and Wales and in many northern English rivers and lakes. It is now being artificially reared and stocked in stillwater fisheries, although the rainbow trout, a North American import, is farmed in far larger numbers because of its fast growth-rate. In reservoirs and other stillwaters brown trout tend to stay deeper than rainbows. They are highly territory-conscious and have marked predatory tendencies.

Brown trout have a very wide colour variation. On some waters they will be dark brown on top with a buttery yellow stomach, but they can also be as silver as a salmon. The markings include much more definite spots than the rainbow and are generally fewer in number, but the main difference between the two species is that in the brown trout the spots are on the body only.

Browns in rivers weigh on average 680g (1½lb), but they can grow much bigger. Specimens of 2-2·30kg (4-5lb) are caught from stillwater fisheries every season.

Rainbow trout are handsome fish. Their colouring can vary, depending on the time of year and their habitat. Easy means of identification are the star-shaped markings all over the body, including the fins, and the mauve stripe which is often seen down the flank.

They are shoal fish and great roamers, preferring to spend much of their time in the surface layer of water. They cannot spawn 'in the wild' in Britain, so there are times when you may catch sexually mature fish filled with milt or eggs (usually at the beginning of the season). When they are in this condition, they do not have the culinary qualities of a fully fit fish. Rainbows can vary widely in size. In waters with plenty of natural food, fish put in at 450g-1kg (1-2lb) can reach 3·50kg (8lb) or more.

In the last few years several fisheries have experimented on a small scale with different types of trout, all of them crossbreeds. The only other trout which has become quite common is another transatlantic import, the American brook trout. It has a very distinctive red underside and is much smaller than either the rainbow or the brown trout.

75

The fascination of fly-tying

To many anglers, a trout – no matter how big – caught on a shop-bought fly is not prized as highly as one caught on a home-tied creation

Much of an angler's pleasure comes from fooling the fish with a fly he has tied himself during a quiet evening at home, making up either a standard pattern or a variation in which he has included an idea of his own. Fly-tying is not difficult, particularly if you stick to the simple stillwater patterns, but it is addictive and many anglers find it so fascinating that they devote all their spare time to it.

To join the ranks of the ever-growing army of these enthusiastic do-it-yourself fans, you do not need the nimble fingers of a needlewoman or a

▲ These four wet flies are all proven killers. Their names are as follows: (top left) Alexandra; (top right) Peter Ross; (bottom left) Muddler Minnow; (bottom right) Butcher

▲ A foam-lined fly box will keep your collection of flies safe, secure and dry

▲ Wet flies are also known as lures, and these three are typical of those used by stillwater trout anglers. They are designed to be fished below the surface of the water, and are huge in comparison to dry flies

▲ Between the egg and the fully developed fly comes the stage of the nymph, an underwater creature which forms a staple part of the trout's diet. These artificials are the angler's copy of various nymphs

great deal of patience. The only requirements are the proper tools – a fly vice, hackle pliers, a dubbing needle and a scalpel or pair of sharp scissors – and the appropriate materials. These include most sorts of fur and feather, either natural or artificially coloured, plus nylon and other man-made materials. You can buy all these items singly from any of the bigger tackle shops which specialize in equipment for game fishing, or order a beginner's kit that is made up of the basic requirements for tying simple flies.

Not only is fly-tying a perfect way of spending otherwise dull evenings during the trout close season, but it will make you more familiar with the names of the scores of different patterns that the trout angler uses, and give you useful knowledge while you are doing a practical job.

The art of fly-tying is fully explained in a number of specialist books on the subject. Details of two such books are given in the Bibliography on page 124.

▲ The tools and materials needed to tie your own flies are illustrated above and include a fly vice, hackle pliers, a dubbing needle and a scalpel or pair of scissors, plus fur, feather, nylon and other man-made materials, all of which are available from tackle shops

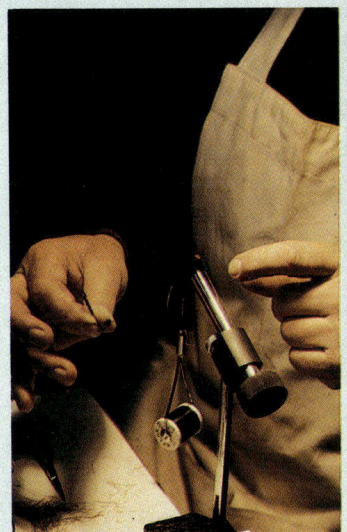

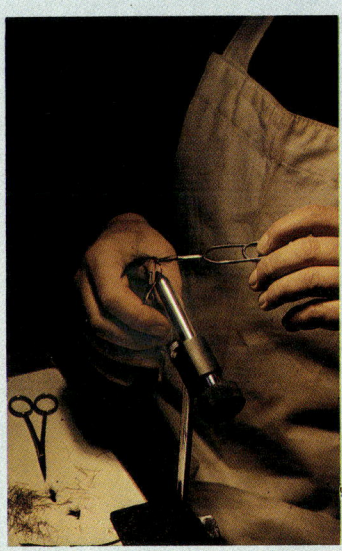

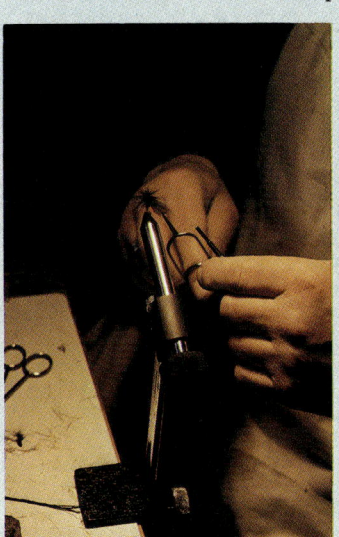

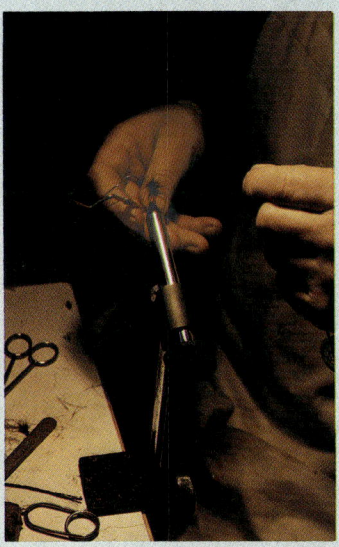

▲ The expert hands of fly dresser Donald Downs fashion a Zulu wet fly. The tail is tied in first with a length of tinsel which will be ribbed around the body of the fly, and the black hackle completes it

▲ These life-like copies of flies are fished on the surface, and are generally used by river trout anglers

▲ A variety of dry flies and nymphs. Knowing which fly to choose and when to use it is part of the art of fly fishing

Salmon and sea trout

Salmon and sea trout are among the hardest fighting fish in the country, as well as providing the tastiest eating. Unfortunately for the beginner, they are also the most inaccessible. Any river which has a good run of either fish – and they are often found together – is generally strictly preserved by the owner. In England there is very little salmon and sea trout fishing available to the casual, unattached angler. The situation is better in Wales but Scotland, with its wealth of suitable rivers, offers the visiting angler the best chance of all. However, even with access to the right water, salmon and sea trout fishing is not easy, for much depends on the state of the rivers. If the level is too low, the fish will not run up-river, and if it is too coloured (by flooding or heavy rain), they will not take the angler's offering.

The two species have similar life-cycles. The eggs are laid in the gravelly headwaters of rivers and the resultant fry develop into small fish, which stay in the rivers for two or three years before migrating downstream to the sea.

The salmon caught in British rivers are all of the Atlantic variety. Once in the sea, the fish head for the rich feeding grounds off Denmark, where they grow to over 27kg (60lb).

Sea trout (which grow slightly bigger than brown trout) also take up a saltwater existence but stay closer to the shoreline. It is when both species return to the rivers of their birth, to spawn and start the life-cycle once again, that they become of interest to the angler and can be caught with rod and line. The season varies, depending on the area of the country in which you intend to fish, but, generally speaking, it runs from early spring to the autumn. The two basic methods of catching them are fly fishing and spinning, and which you should use depends on the time of year and the water conditions.

The type of tackle used for catching reservoir trout is adequate when fly fishing for sea trout, though the flies themselves will be of a different pattern. For the spinning method, all you need is a light spinning rod, fixed-spool reel and a selection of bar-spoons, spinners and artificial minnows. Sea trout also have a liking for worms and maggots, and can often be taken on those bait where their use is permitted. However, on many game rivers only fly fishing or spinning are allowed.

When spinning for salmon, a powerful rod and a multiplier reel filled with 9kg (20lb) line are generally used, with preserved spinning bait, such as sprats or prawns, or artificials, such as Devon minnows.

Fly fishing for salmon is a specialized sport, needing a big, powerful rod and other items of tackle to match. It is always done wet-fly style. The flies themselves are big, colourful creations that imitate no specific form of life, but are designed to attract the salmon's attention and spark off its aggressive instinct.

The British record weights for game fish are as follows: salmon, 29kg (64lb); American brook trout, 2·05kg (4lb 8oz 8dr); brown trout, 8·87kg (19lb 9oz 4dr); rainbow trout, 8·84kg (19lb 8oz). The sea trout record is open at present.

◀ Scotland is the place to go if you want to catch a spring salmon like the one shown in this photograph

Many experienced anglers rate fly fishing for sea trout as ▶ the finest sport of all. These sportsmen are at Christchurch in Hampshire

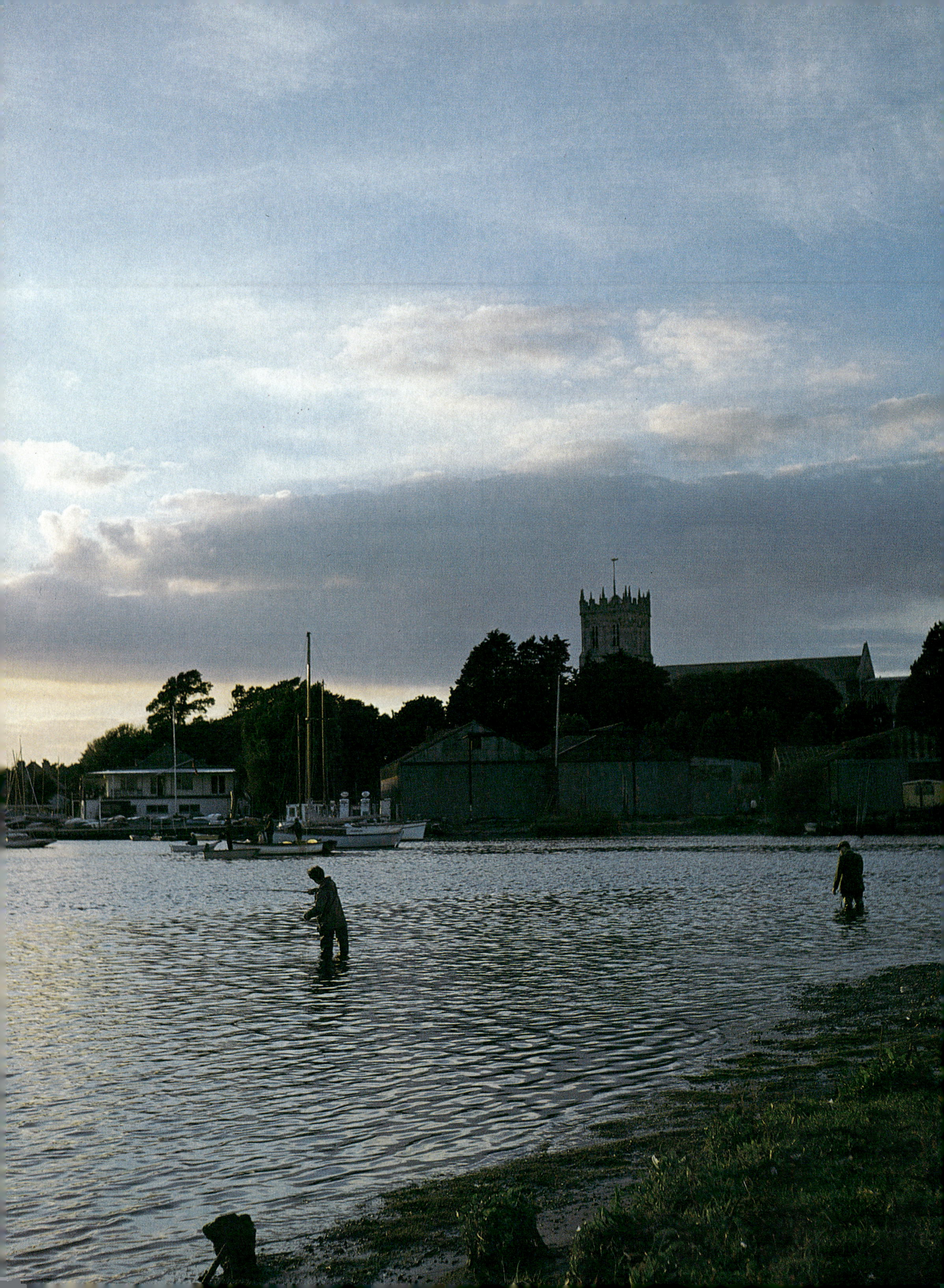

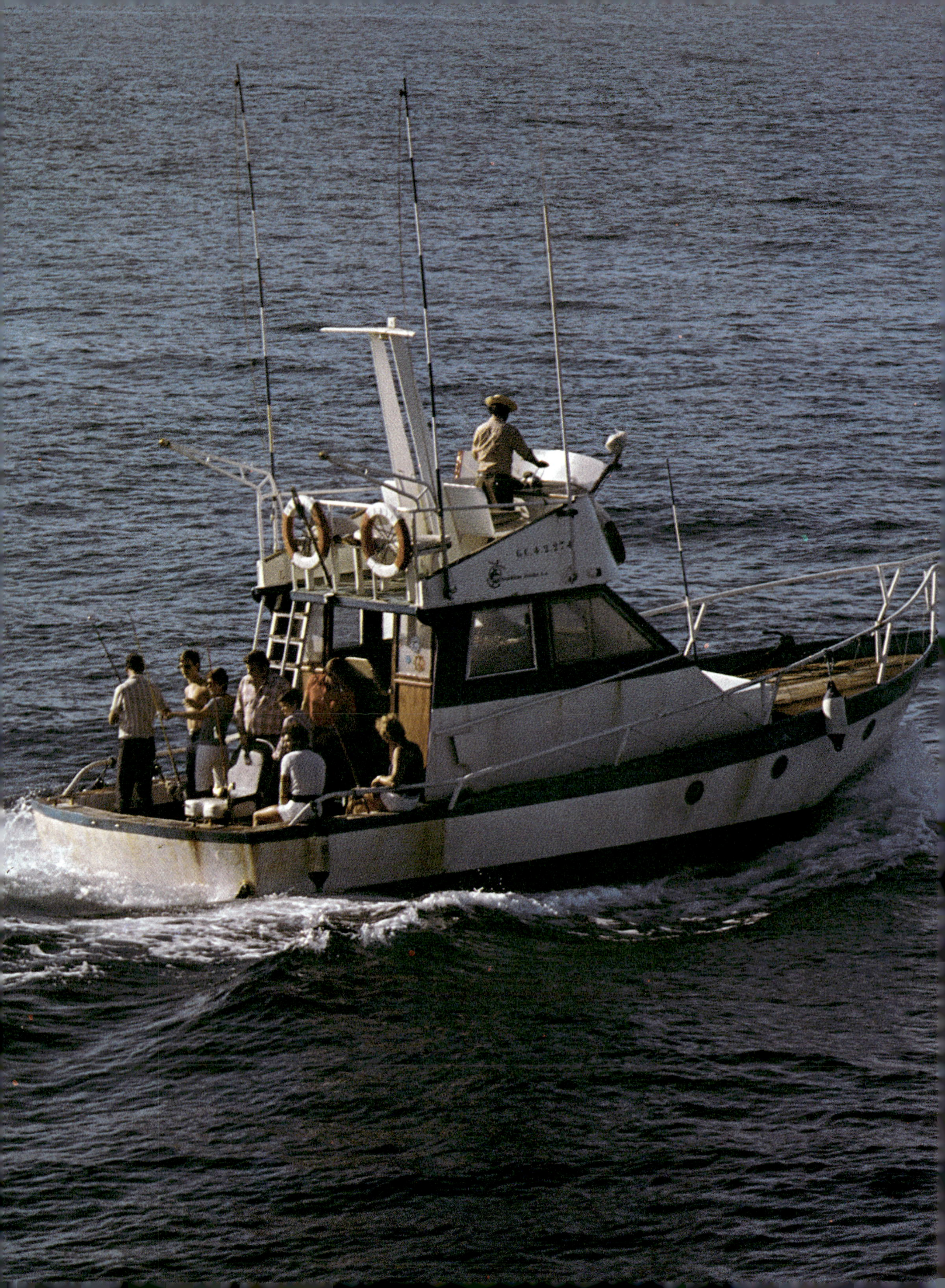

Battling with the big ones

Sleek launches search blue tropical seas to do battle with mighty bluefins, swordfish and man-eating sharks. That's big-game fishing

To most of us big-game fishing means far-away places with romantic names that make the sport sound so exciting: Cabo Blanca, the Great Barrier Reef, Santa Cruz, Catalina, Iquique, Bimini . . .

Bimini, one of the smaller Bahamas Islands and the one nearest to the United States, attracts hundreds of American big-game anglers. Here Ernest Hemingway once lived, wrote about the sea, and fished. Here you can sit in the Game Fishing Club sipping your rum punch sundowner, watching the boats glide home to anchor . . . and see, too, the cruising black triangular fins that herald tomorrow's sport.

And fierce sport it is when you are harnessed into the fighting chair, heavy rod slammed into the chair's socket to leave your hands free to pit your skills against giant bluefin tunny, ferocious sharks and the fighting broadbill swordfish, considered by many to be the gamest fish of all, though it is not always the biggest.

However, not all big-game fishing is in warm tropical seas. For many years the world's heaviest tunny was one taken in the cold, grey North Sea, off Whitby in Yorkshire. That was in the 1930s, when the Scarborough Tunny Club was world famous. Tunny are still in the North Sea, but too far out for economic fishing. Today's big-game fish in British waters is the shark. There are four species – the mako, porbeagle, thresher and blue – and they are fished for off the Isle of Wight, Cornwall and South West Ireland.

Age or sex is no bar to success in big-game fishing. The world record catch of barracuda is one weighing 37·65kg (83lb), taken off Lagos, Nigeria, in 1952 by an 11-year-old boy. The British record for a shark is a 226·80kg (500lb) mako hooked by a 61-year-old grandmother, Mrs Jessie Yallop, of Norwich, off the Eddystone lighthouse in May 1971.

Far away or just offshore, battling with the big ones really is angling for thrills.

Anglers relax (far left), as their boat heads for the fishing grounds, but there's no relaxing once a fish is hooked. Barracuda (above left), small members of the shark family, fight like furies, and giant tunny (left), weighing up to 550kg (1200lb), have been known to struggle for over two hours

81

Sea fishing

One of the advantages of living in Britain is that the sea is never far away, and this is one reason for the popularity of sea fishing.

For most people – and beginners particularly – fishing means having something to show for the day's effort, fish that can be taken home, admired and then eaten! Sea fishing is the perfect sport for them, for every kind of saltwater fish is edible, though some are not as tasty as others. Disposing of the catch at the end of the day is no longer a problem, thanks to inflation and restrictions on trawling fleets. Nowadays, fish is an expensive item in the family budget and a catch of fresh cod, whiting or dogfish is a very welcome addition to the larder or freezer.

There is variety both in the fish themselves and in the style of approach. More than 110 different species are shown on the British Record Fish Committee's latest list and each year one or two more are added. Much of the list is made up of the common fish caught all round the coast; others are migrants that drift into our seas from warmer climates.

The style of approach to sea fishing depends entirely on the angler's preference. He and his family can enjoy a day's pier fishing, relaxing in the sun. They can fish from beaches or rocky cliffs, either in popular seaside resorts or from more remote shores. They can join a charter boat party to catch flatfish or cod, or head out to the deep-water marks (sea fishing spots, such as wrecks, patches of sandy ground or rocks), where giant conger have their homes.

Another advantage for the sea angler is that his sport is free from the restrictions which, of necessity, apply to most forms of freshwater fishing. There is no fixed season and no licence is needed. If he wants to spend all night on the beach – and many do – he is free to do so. He can take away as many fish as he wishes and there is little pressure from other water-users, except perhaps in popular seaside resorts.

Once landed, sea fish should be killed quickly and cleanly by a sharp rap on the head with a heavy object. Never take away more fish than you want, as this creates unnecessary waste, and never kill fish too small to eat.

The Ministry of Agriculture, Fisheries and Food has published a list of size limits for some sea fish. Cod and turbot must be over 30cm (11·8in), plaice and whiting over 25cm (9·8in), sole over 24cm (9·4in) and dabs over 15cm (5·9in). These rules were laid down with commercial net fishermen in mind, but should also be noted by anglers.

▼ These young lads are fishing for flounder at the mouth of Christchurch Harbour, Hampshire, while the boat angler tries a spot just offshore

This angler has found a stretch of quiet beach at Mount's Bay, Cornwall and is trying his hand for bass ▶

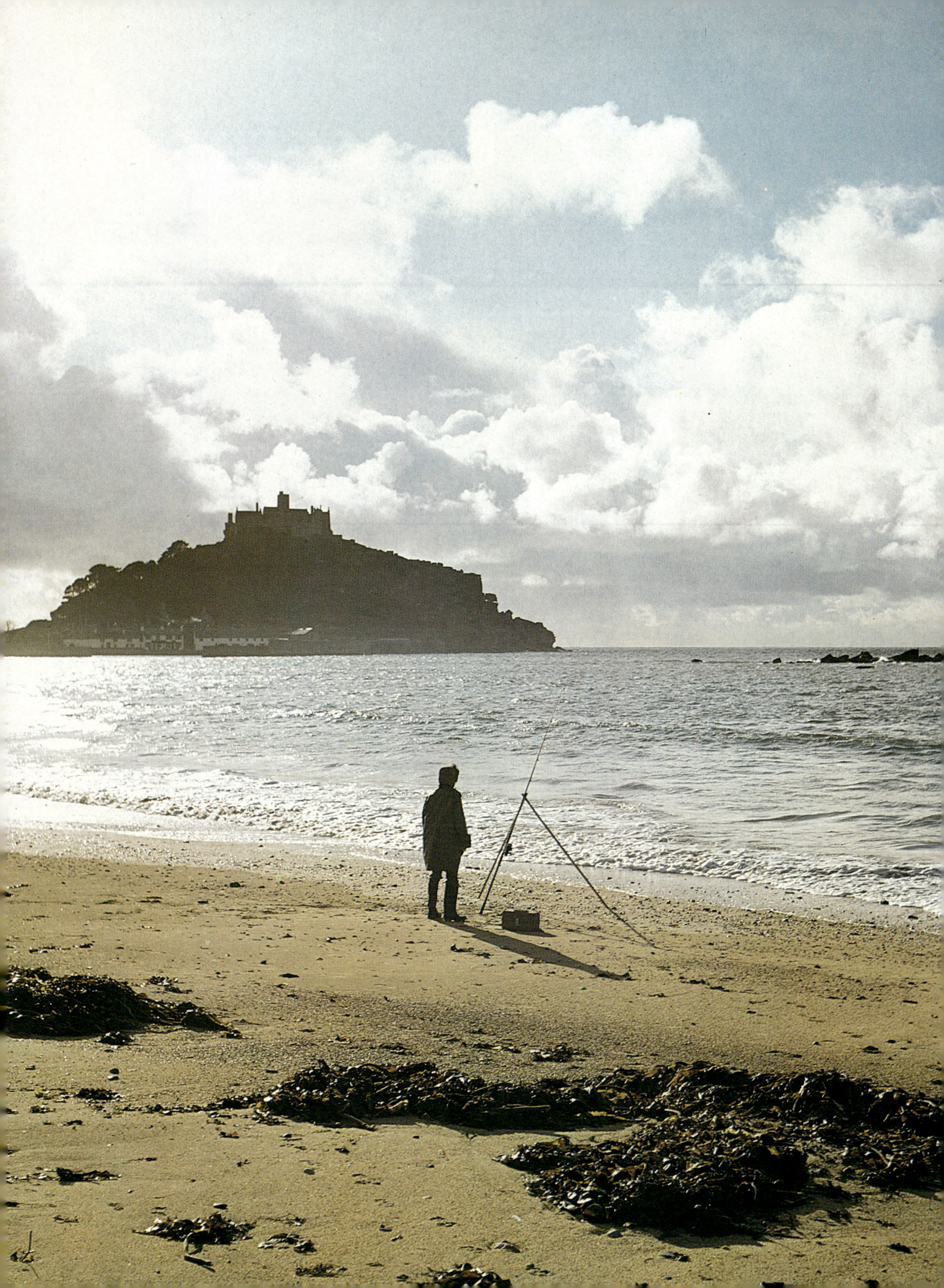

Sea fishing
Tackle

As in any other branch of the sport, no single rod and reel will cope with every saltwater species in every situation. The outfit which gives the angler the most fun when fishing for flounder is totally unsuitable for deep-sea fishing.

There are two basic types of sea tackle, designed for shore and boat fishing. The main differences are in the length of the rod and in the gearing and line capacity of the reel.

Nearly all sea rods are made of glass fibre. Those used for shore fishing – known as beach casters – are available in lengths in the 3-4m (10-13ft) range, and with a slow, fast or medium action. For most people a rod of about 4m (12ft) is suitable, and as the action is not particularly important for the beginner, the medium-action model is adequate. Beach casters are marked with weight signs, which are nothing to do with the weight of the rod itself but indicate the range of lead weights that the rod is designed to cast. Thus, a rod marked 2-4oz (about 50-100g, though rods are not yet marked in metric terms) will be designed principally for light beach work, when you hope to catch flatfish and small species. When long-casting for bigger fish such as cod, the rod should be heavier and capable of handling up to 170g (6oz) of lead.

For the beginner, a saltwater version of the fixed-spool reel is a good choice for beach casting. It is easy to cast with and the gearing makes line recovery simple.

Many experienced beach anglers choose the multiplier reel, which is more complicated than the fixed-spool reel but, in the right hands, gives extra distance. It, too, is geared for rapid line recovery but, unlike other reels, it is designed to be used on top of the rod.

Boat rods are shorter than those designed for shore fishing, and normally measure 1·50-2m (5-7ft). They are usually coupled with a multiplier reel, or a big centrepin made of wood, plastic or metal. Casting is unimportant from a boat, as the bait is simply lowered over the side and allowed to drift downtide. The reel's most important asset is the amount of line it can carry and the ease with which the line can be recovered.

Although several types of line are used for sea fishing, monofilament nylon is still the most popular and should always be used for shore fishing. Braided Terylene is used for heavier boat work, and wire lines – which are used when boat fishing in very strong tides – are best left to the experts.

Lead weights come in many different shapes and sizes. Shore-casting leads are generally bomb- or torpedo-shaped, to minimize air resistance when casting. Those used for boat work are usually heavier (because of the stronger currents found offshore), and are shaped so that the tide helps to keep them in place.

Any seaside tackle shop will have a range of hooks designed for sea fishing. It is a good idea to buy a wide selection, as you can never be certain of the type of fish that will come along. Buy a few Kilmore and Clement's booms, metal devices which carry the leads and are attached to the main line (see photograph on page 109). If you are beach fishing, you will also need a rod rest. A pair of pliers and a sharp knife will be useful for every type of sea fishing.

▼ Light tackle can be used for inshore work, but heavier gear – and a very much bigger boat than this one – will be needed for deep-water fishing

▲ For beach fishing, the angler can choose either a multiplier reel (left) or a fixed-spool reel, although the latter is easier to use

The boat fishing multiplier reel has a deeper and narrower spool than the one used for shore fishing ▶

▼ Torpedo-shaped leads designed for beach casting. Some have spikes to grip the sea bottom

▼ A good, sharp knife is useful for all types of sea fishing

85

Sea fishing
Natural bait

With a few exceptions, sea fish are not the dainty feeders that most of their freshwater cousins are, and will take most kinds of bait when they are hungry. The angler who is fortunate enough to live in a coastal town can collect his own bait – as long as he has ample time – but most anglers who live inland have to buy bait from their local tackle shop.

However, there is always the problem of the effectiveness of the bait, for what is a good bait in one area may be unsuccessful in another. Along the Essex coast, lugworms, more than any other bait, attract cod most successfully, but on the south coast strips of squid are more effective. Similarly, mussels will catch fish in one place but not another. The wise angler will always ask around to discover the most effective bait before fishing a new area.

The beginner should certainly not attempt to catch or dig his own bait before a day's fishing. Unless he has special local knowledge, it can be a time-wasting and often fruitless exercise. It is far better to arrange an on-the-spot supply, either by telephoning a seaside tackle shop before your visit if you are beach fishing, or by asking the skipper to provide bait if you are boat fishing.

The most widely used of all bait is the lugworm, which looks like a bigger and fatter version of the large garden earthworm and lives in sand or in the mixture of sand and mud found on most shores. The other effective marine worm is the ragworm, which can measure up to 30cm (12in) in length. Beginners can sometimes be put off by its appearance, for it resembles a huge flattened centipede, orange in colour and with a pair of pincers at the head end that can nip the unwary finger. There is also a smaller version known as the white ragworm.

Crabs are a first-class bait for most sea fish, but you cannot use them in their normal hard-shelled state. They are most effective when they are just about to shed their old shell as part of the normal growing process, at which stage they are known as peelers. As the new shell begins to grow, the crab is known as a softback and is almost as effective as a peeler.

Mussels, clams, cockles, limpets and razorfish can all be used as hookbait, but they work best when used in the areas in which they are found. The shells should be removed and the fleshy inside used on the hook.

Live sand-eels are difficult to obtain and even harder to keep alive, but they make first-class bait. Tackle shops do not sell them, so you will either have to find a professional bait collector or catch your own. Prawns and shrimps make good bait when fished on light tackle but these, too, will have to be picked up on the spot. The best place to look for them is in rock pools left by a receding tide.

▼ If you live close to the coast you can dig for your bait, but most anglers find it easier to buy their bait at a local tackle shop

Squid, the small ones used whole and the bigger ones cut into strips, is another very good bait, as is its close relative the cuttlefish. Small fish of all sorts are excellent bait to catch their bigger brothers and can be used dead or alive. Larger fish also make effective bait. A strip cut from the side of a freshly-caught mackerel is particularly good.

▲ Two ways of hooking sand-eels, a bait which is most effective but often difficult to obtain in many places

▼ The king ragworm is a good bait, especially for bass. It can measure up to 30cm (12in) in length

▼ The lugworm, which looks like a large garden earthworm, is probably the most widely used of all sea bait

▼ Limpets are a good bait for wrasse. They work best when used in the areas in which they are found

▼ The peeler crab is reckoned to be the finest bait of all

Sea fishing
Artificial bait

▲ Artificial sand-eels, which can be used as spinners or on a weighted trace, come in all shapes and sizes

Although the vast majority of saltwater fish fall to natural bait, such as worms, crabs and molluscs, artificial bait can also be used, particularly for those fish with a predatory nature – and indeed there are times when this type of bait is more effective than any other.

Straightforward metal spinners (see page 26) are normally used in shallow inshore waters and from such vantage points as rocks and jetties. Artificial sand-eels can also be used either as spinners or on a weighted trace (see below), when fishing deeper water from a boat.

The best-known saltwater artificial bait is probably the simple feather, made up of a couple of dyed feathers whipped to a hook. The feathered trace, which consists of a lead weight with a number of feathered hooks tied above it, is commonly used for catching bait fish such as mackerel. The trace is lowered over the side of a boat and jigged up and down in the water to give the feathers movement. Feathers can also be used for bigger fish, such as cod, coalfish and pollack, out in deep water, particularly over wreck marks where fish are often heavily concentrated.

For deep-water feathering, however, the hooks are larger than those used for mackerel fishing and the rest of the tackle will be relatively bigger, for heavier weights are needed to get the feathers down in the stronger tides. The method is similar, the weight being lowered to the bottom and the rod tip raised and lowered as the feathers search the different depths.

Feathered traces are also used in drift fishing, where the boatman takes his craft uptide of a known fish-holding area, such as a wreck or rocky, rough ground. The boat is then allowed to drift downtide over the mark, while the anglers on board jig their feathers as close as they can to the holding area. When the boat reaches the end of the drift, it returns to the beginning and repeats the operation. This type of fishing can be expensive in terms of lost tackle, however, for it can catch in the wreck or rocks.

▲ Big feathers on large hooks are used for wreck fishing

Heavy pirks like these are used for deep-water boat fishing. Other types are simply tubular pieces of metal ▶

Pirks are another very successful artificial bait for deep-water fishing. They are heavy, tubular pieces of metal with hooks attached and, like the feathered trace, are generally used from a drifting boat. They come in a variety of sizes and weights and should be attached direct to the end of the line. No other form of weight is needed.

The key to success with all artificial bait is the clarity of the water. The flash of a spinner or pirk, or the attractive waving movement of a feathered trace, will arouse predatory fish only if they can see them clearly.

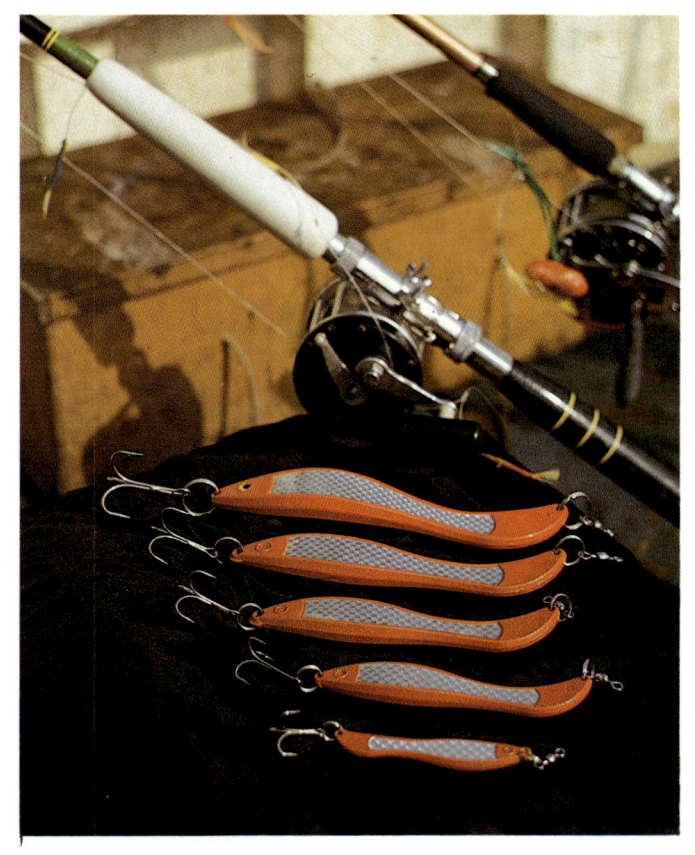

Sea fishing
Understanding the sea

The sea is wide, mysterious and exciting but sometimes it can be dangerous. It washes over jagged underwater reefs, sucks at muddy foreshores, ripples gently up sandy beaches and crashes majestically against rocky outcrops. It can send you home rejoicing with a sackful of fish – but if you treat it lightly, it could injure or kill you.

To get the best results from the sea, the angler should know something of its moods and movements. Most of this knowledge will be gained by experience but, before he wets a line for the first time, the angler should have an understanding of the tides, which have a marked influence on the feeding times of fish.

In each 24-hour period there are two high and two low tides, but their timing does not remain constant. Every year there are 24 spring tides which have nothing to do with that season. They are high and low tides greater than normal, which bring a stronger tide-flow.

There are also 24 annual neap tides, those with the smallest rise and fall which bring a slacker current. Tides are predictable, and local tackle shops can supply you with a tide prediction table for the area, which will tell you exactly when high and low water periods occur. This information can help you plan your fishing. Boat fishing, for example, is hard work on a spring tide. In order to hold the sea bottom in the strong tidal flow, you will need to use heavier amounts of lead. Take local advice about the times to fish. Anglers who fish a particular area regularly can tell you the best state of the tide for fishing.

Understanding the sea also means knowing where the fish are likely to be, for they tend to congregate in certain areas and avoid others. Plaice, for example, like a sandy sea bed, and tope will roam the same sort of terrain. Conger will never stray far from rough ground or the sunken wrecks which are often their home. Some fish – mullet, bass and flounder, for example – will often be found in river estuaries, where the salt content of the water is low.

The key to location is either food or shelter, or both. Some large areas of water offer neither, however, and these will invariably be unproductive. The angler has to ask himself constantly why he is fishing a certain area. Is there a rocky outcrop just offshore? Does a local food-processing plant discharge waste into the area? Are there any mussel beds on the bottom?

Some conservation-minded Americans have pointed the way to fish location by experiments carried out in some of their shallow coastal waters, featureless areas where sportfish were in short supply. Their solution was to make artificial reefs from wrecked cars – a method which was successful. The reefs encouraged marine growth and weeds which in turn attracted small fish, and the bigger fish followed.

Understanding the sea means more than knowing where to look for fish, however – it also means knowing how dangerous it can be. On a calm summer day, when holidaymakers are happily sunbathing on the sands, the coast can be a restful, safe place, but in a strong December gale rocks and jetties can become dangerous places from which to fish. Wandering off on an exploratory trip at low tide can also be dangerous – you may find your return cut off when the tide turns and comes racing in. Always follow local advice about tides.

▼ Rocky shores such as this one in Cornwall are likely places for fish, such as conger and bass. A thorough survey at low tide will give the angler a detailed knowledge of the area he intends to fish

Sea fishing
Pier and harbour fishing

Many people – especially youngsters – get their first taste of sea fishing on the pier during the summer holidays, with a simple hand line bought from a seafront kiosk. It is a cheap and easy way of starting, but using a rod and line provides much more enjoyment. Piers, harbours and jetties are natural gathering places for fish, particularly flatfish. On an otherwise featureless stretch of shore they offer the fish's two basic needs – food and shelter – and you need not be an expert angler to take advantage of them.

Look beneath a pier at low tide and you will see its attractions for the fish. The piles on which it stands will be covered in weed growth and molluscs, and that larder may be supplemented by scraps of food thrown in by holidaymakers. If the pier has a café, some of its waste food may also find its way into the water. The angler can take advantage of all this free groundbaiting.

As most of the fish will be fairly close to the pier in search of all this food, it is not necessary to cast your bait a long way out. Light tackle only is needed, as most fish caught from piers are not very big, although there are, of course, exceptions. Heavier tackle should be used in winter, however, when migratory cod come close inshore.

The simplest and most effective terminal rig for pier fishing is the paternoster, a nicely named old favourite which enables the angler to fish two or more hooks at different levels in the water. The lead goes on the very end of the line, and above it, sticking out at right angles, are plastic booms which carry the baited hooks. Any seaside tackle shop will sell paternosters ready made up to be attached directly to the main line.

There should be no problem in landing small fish, which may simply be wound up until you can swing them over the pier rail. If you hook something bigger, you will need the aid of a drop net, which is a weighted circular net on a long rope. It is lowered down the side of the pier and moved underneath the fish, so that the net and its rope take the strain when the fish is lifted out of the water.

Every pier will have its 'hot spots', its most productive areas, and they are not always, as many people suppose, right at the seaward end. The sea bed around the pier may have odd depressions or obstructions which attract fish, so try to find out where they are before you start. Every pier will also have its quota of old hands who fish it regularly and generally catch more fish than anyone else. Observe how and where they fish, and note if they have a favourite terminal tackle or bait.

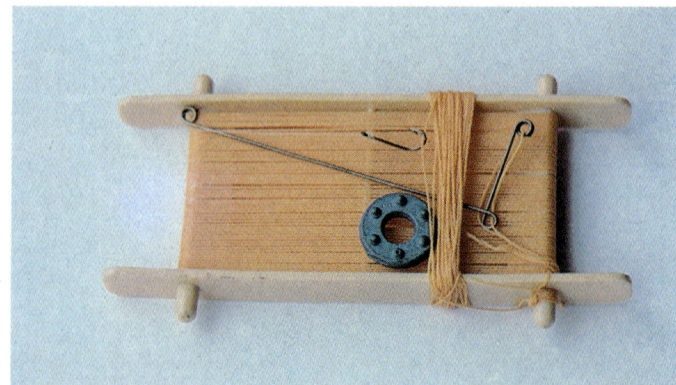

▲ Hand lines can be bought at any seaside tackle shop and, although you may catch fish with them, you will have more enjoyment from using a rod and line

◀ A summer mullet is swung over the pier rails at Douglas, Isle of Man. Although it is only a small fish, it has provided the angler with some fun

Quays and harbour walls are productive spots for fish such as mullet and flounder. These lads are fishing at Newlyn, Cornwall ▶

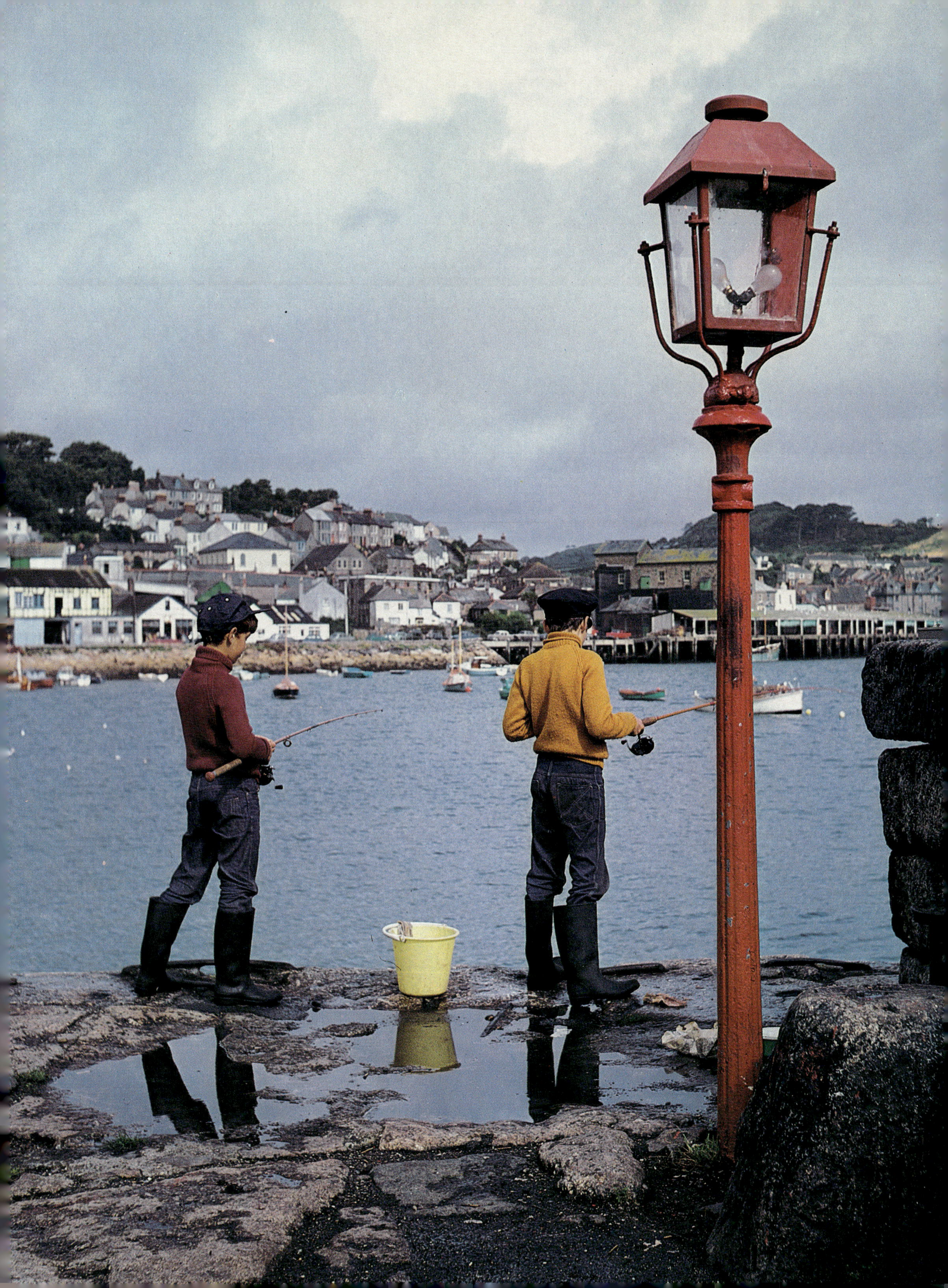

Sea fishing
Beach casting

▲ The casting sequence shown above is an easy one for the beginner to master. With the reel pickup open and the forefinger holding the line firmly against the spool, swing the rod up powerfully with the right hand and arm. Keep the movements smooth – a sudden jerk may snap the line and send the lead hurtling off. Just before the rod tip points at the spot on which you aim to land the tackle, lift your finger so that the line is released

Many beginners visiting a popular beach quickly become disheartened when they see how far the expert can cast. With a seemingly effortless swing, the baited hook goes flying towards the horizon. The beginner, whose own cast seems to go such a short distance beyond the rod tip, feels self-conscious over his weak effort and is almost ready to give up.

There is no need to be disheartened. Long-distance casting is like swinging a golf club or kicking a football – the more you practise, the better you will become. In any case, distance casting is not a vital part of beach fishing. It may look good and it may give a great deal of satisfaction, but often the fish are fairly close inshore and a shorter cast is more effective.

It is more important to make sure that the tackle you have is right for the job and properly put together. Too thick a main line will cut down casting distance because of the air resistance, and you will seldom need a line heavier than 9kg (20lb) breaking strain. In fact, it may often be considerably lighter. The fixed-spool reel should be correctly loaded, and on the business end of the main line you should have 9m (10yd) of a

◀ Dungeness Beach in Kent is one of the best-known shore fishing marks in the south. It attracts top-class casters who fish for bass in summer and cod in winter

heavier line to act as a shock-absorber against sudden casting strains. (Without it, the lead may snap off and become a danger to others.)

The terminal rig should be kept fairly simple. A nylon paternoster with only one hook or a straight ledger rig – both with a bomb-shaped lead – are adequate. Make sure that the reel is fixed firmly to the rod. It is easy to neglect this simple precaution and have the reel fall off at just the wrong moment! Give yourself plenty of room when casting. Do not fish so close to another angler that you are in each other's way.

Practice is essential. On a day when it is clear that very few fish are being caught, use the time to improve your casting technique. Concentrate on getting a good smooth swing until it becomes second nature to you. Once you have mastered this important action, you can begin to increase the length of your cast.

▼ The running ledger rig is often used in shore fishing. The plain bomb-shaped lead aids distance casting and can be used in calm conditions, or when the angler wants his terminal tackle to search out the area. If you want the tackle to stay in one spot, it is best to use the bomb-shaped lead with wire arms which grip the bottom

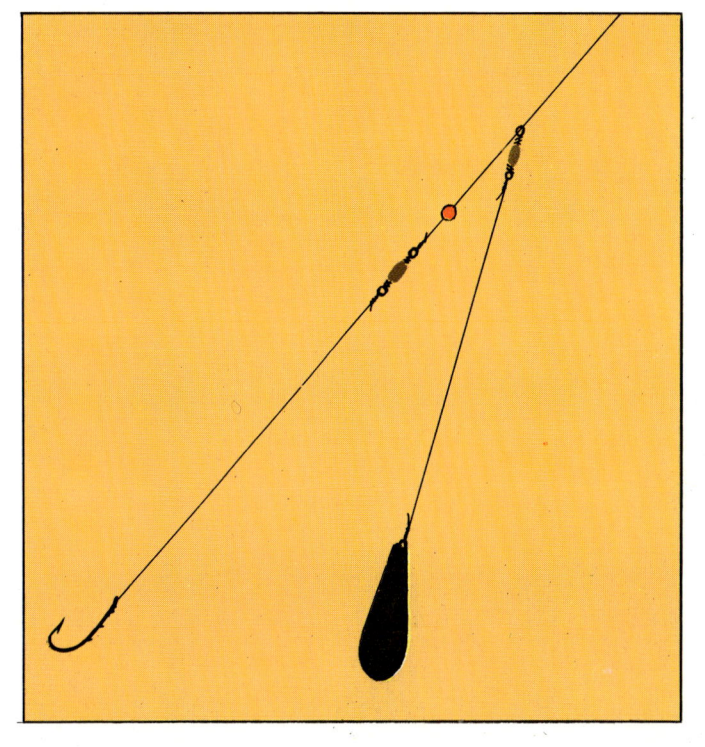

Sea fishing
Rock fishing

Rock fishing is a branch of the sport tailor-made for the more athletic angler who doesn't mind a tough scramble to reach the more inaccessible spots. It may also attract the angler seeking solitude and something different from what the piers and beaches have to offer. Although there are specialists in some parts of the country who fish from their rocky perches for conger and other big species, the beginner is more likely to look for the smaller species, such as wrasse, mullet, pollack or mackerel.

For this type of fishing you need a rod about 3m (10ft) long, matched with a fixed-spool reel. The line strength needed depends on whether there are weedbeds, rocks and other obstructions below the surface, but in most cases 5kg (12lb) is suitable. Standard ledger tackle and conventional bait can be used, but off most rocky shorelines are underwater rocks which can damage such tackle. Where the rocks border deep water, they offer a good opportunity to try spinning or float fishing, both methods that enable the angler to keep his terminal tackle away from underwater snags. A whole variety of spoons and spinners – attached to the main line by means of a swivel – can be used, the angler searching the whole area by fanning out his casts (a method whereby the angler makes successive casts in the pattern of the ribs of a fan).

For float fishing you will need a sliding float, and it is best to use a streamlined model, which has the hole for the line running straight through the centre from top to bottom. This enables the angler to search out water deeper than the length of his rod, a difficult exercise with a standard fixed float because the angler would have too much line between the float and hook to cast properly. The hook is baited with the most effective local bait, such as sand-eel, ragworm or lugworm, and the line has a sliding stop-knot tied above the float at the required depth. If no fish are forthcoming and a change is indicated, try a different depth by moving the stop-knot.

The rock angler may have problems when landing a hooked fish, as he may not be able to reach down and land it by hand. In this situation, he will need the help of a long-handled landing net to bring it ashore.

This angler is float fishing for mackerel and garfish from a typical Cornish rock mark ▶

▼ The water here is too rough for float fishing, but the spot is worth trying for bass with standard ledger tackle

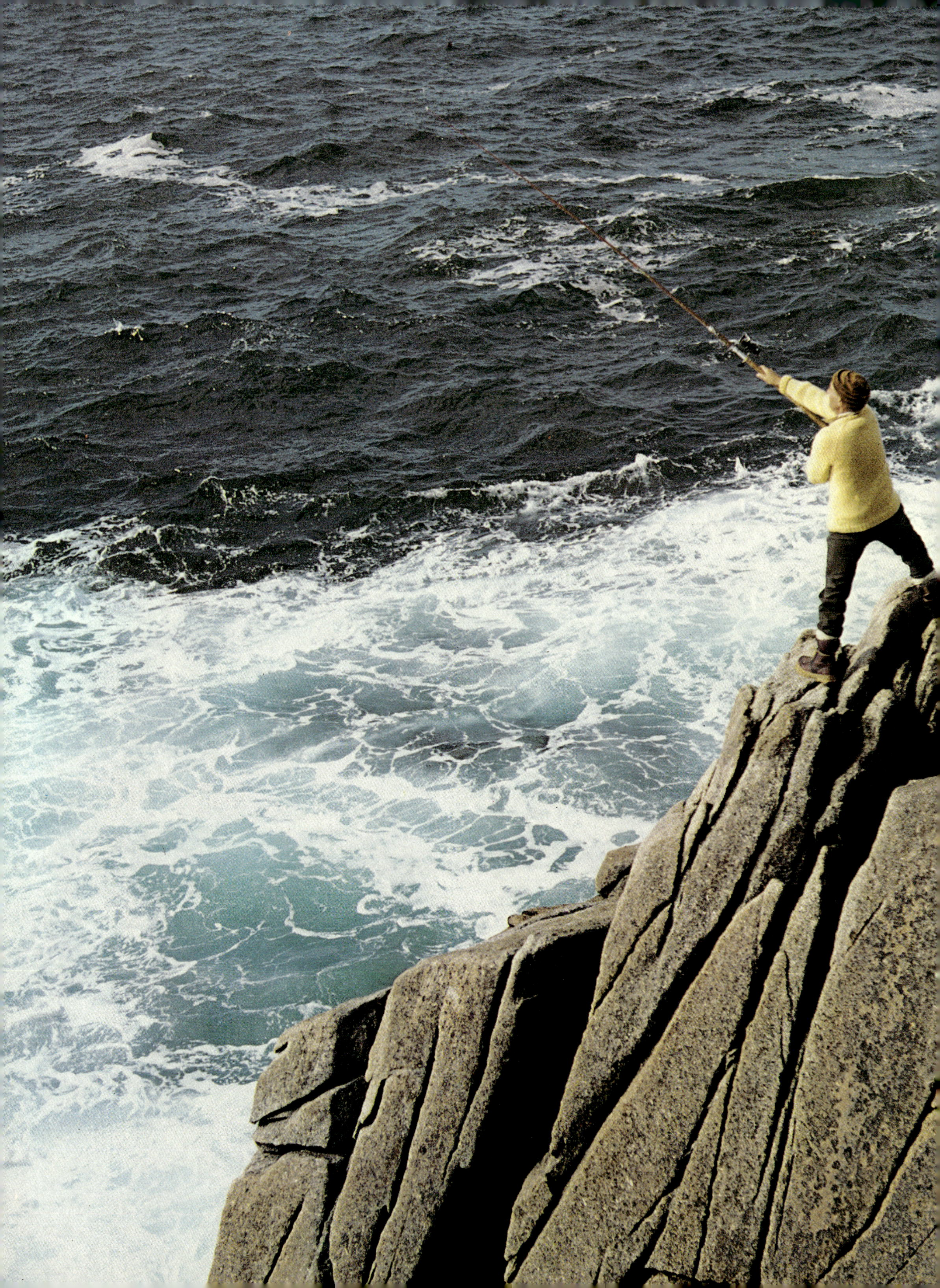

Sea fishing
Recognize the saltwater species

The different species of fish found in Britain's seas are so many that even the most experienced angler could never claim to have caught them all. Distribution governs the species an angler may catch, for fish found in certain areas will be totally absent from others. In Scotland, for example, haddock are common, but very few anglers on the Essex coast will have seen one. Yorkshire anglers can catch cod all the year round, but on the south coast the cod shoals arrive only in winter.

On the following pages you will find descriptions of many of the sea fish that you are likely to catch. The average weight of each fish is given, and the record boat and shore weights are set out on page 105.

The tackle to use for every fish has not been specified, as this depends entirely on the type of sea fishing (whether from a boat, or from the beach or rocks) and also on the weather and sea conditions. For general information on sea tackle, see pages 84 and 108.

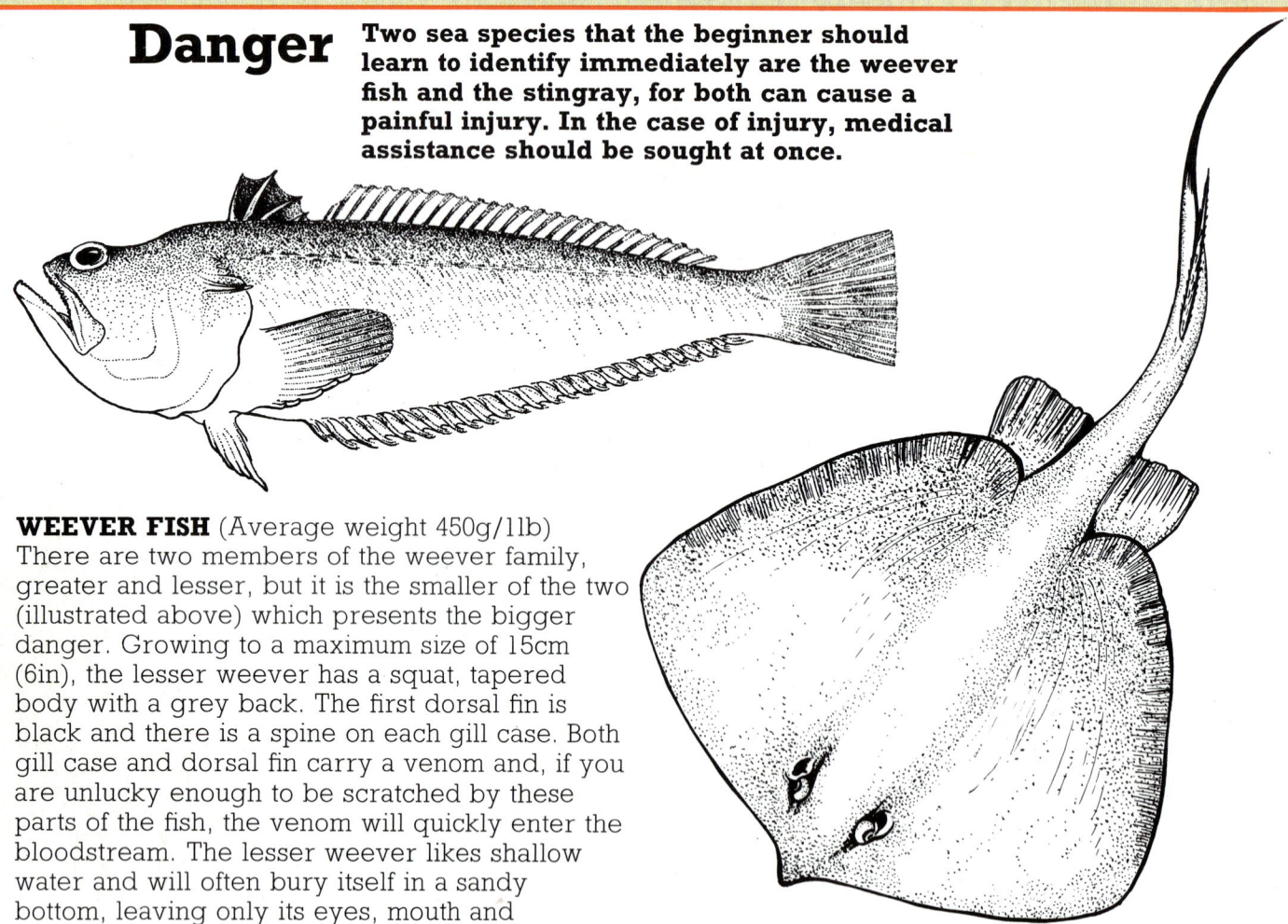

Danger Two sea species that the beginner should learn to identify immediately are the weever fish and the stingray, for both can cause a painful injury. In the case of injury, medical assistance should be sought at once.

WEEVER FISH (Average weight 450g/1lb)
There are two members of the weever family, greater and lesser, but it is the smaller of the two (illustrated above) which presents the bigger danger. Growing to a maximum size of 15cm (6in), the lesser weever has a squat, tapered body with a grey back. The first dorsal fin is black and there is a spine on each gill case. Both gill case and dorsal fin carry a venom and, if you are unlucky enough to be scratched by these parts of the fish, the venom will quickly enter the bloodstream. The lesser weever likes shallow water and will often bury itself in a sandy bottom, leaving only its eyes, mouth and poisonous dorsal fin showing above the surface – a danger to anyone with bare feet.

The greater weever, which grows to about 40cm (16in), is yellow and, though just as venomous, is less of a danger in that it is usually found in deeper water. Neither fish is widely distributed and they are found in the shallower parts of the North Sea.

STINGRAY (Average weight 7kg/15lb)
Like the weever, the stingray is a fish of the summer, but the distribution area is different and you are likely to come across it only on the south and east coasts. It has a strong, serrated, arrow-shaped spine halfway along the whip-like tail which, although not venomous, can cause a painful gash. Stingray like shallow inshore water and are often caught by anglers in the summer on the Essex coast. No special bait is recommended for the stingray or the weever, as they will take almost any food offered.

LING (Average weight 7kg/15lb)
The famous West Country wreck marks, home of big fish of many species, are the best places to try for a big ling, as it likes deep water and an uneven, broken bottom. It has a body shape similar to that of the conger eel, and the two species often share the same habitat. The ling can be caught with most artificial bait, as well as with fish strips.

WHITING (Average weight 450g/1lb)
This is a species which arrives in Britain at the start of winter and in most parts of the country its arrival coincides with that of the cod shoals. Unlike the cod, which gives a slow, deliberate pull at the bait, the whiting gives an unmistakable sharp rap which jerks the rod tip. It has a streamlined shape, distinctive silvery-white flanks and a green back. Whiting are shoal fish that feed on shrimps, crabs, smaller fish and worms, so any of these can be used as bait.

HADDOCK (Average weight 1·40kg/3lb)
Although the haddock is a member of the cod family, it differs from its bigger and more common cousin in that it has a less predatory nature. A good fighter and a very tasty table fish, it is a shoal fish that favours the colder waters off the northern half of the British Isles. Its colour is greyish-brown on the back and there is a small barbule under the chin, but the distinguishing feature, which makes it easy to recognize, is the oval black blotch – known to commercial fishermen as 'St Peter's thumbprint' – on the shoulder. Favoured bait are most types of shellfish and worms.

GURNARD (Average weight 450g/1lb)
The gurnard family, four members of which are commonly found in British waters, are odd-looking creatures with large, almost prehistoric-looking heads, beneath which are three fleshy feelers, and tapering bodies. Colour is not necessarily a guide to identification, for the tub, or yellow, gurnard, the largest of the group, will sometimes have a tinge of red. The red gurnard truly lives up to its name, but the smaller grey gurnard can also have a red tinge. The rarest fish of the group is the streaked gurnard. All are bottom feeders, eating almost anything that comes their way. The best chance of catching gurnard is in summer; best bait are worms and molluscs. Do not be put off by its odd appearance – it makes excellent eating.

Sea fishing

PLAICE (Average weight 680g/1½lb)
The plaice is the best known of the flatfish and, like most of that family, is usually a fish of the warm summer months. It can be identified by the large orange spots dotted along its brown back. Plaice are particularly fond of small shellfish, and any area which contains mussel beds is always worth fishing. Best bait are worms or shellfish, fished hard on the bottom. The plaice needs no introduction as a table fish – it is one of the tastiest dishes the sea has to offer.

MACKEREL (Average weight 450g/1lb)
The mackerel's superbly streamlined body, the top half of which is covered in irregular scribbled lines, is unmistakable. It is a surface feeder that arrives in Britain in great shoals during the summer months and will often come close enough to be caught from beaches, piers and rocks. To most anglers the mackerel's main attraction is as a bait for bigger fish, but it is a magnificent sporting species in its own right and makes good eating. Anyone who abandons the normal heavy sea tackle and uses a freshwater spinning rod with line to match will have a fight to remember. Anything bright, such as a small spinner or coloured feathered lure, will attract a mackerel and, because of its liking for the warmer surface layers, light float tackle baited with worm can also be used.

SKATE and **RAYS** (Average weight 4·50kg/10lb)
The very distinctive flattened kite-shaped skates and rays form a large family group – a group consisting of such members as the blonde, cuckoo, bottle-nosed, eagle, electric, sandy, small-eyed, spotted, undulate and thornback. The vast majority have fairly limited distribution areas in southern and western parts of Britain, but the most common of all – the thornback (illustrated above) – has the widest distribution and is found all round the coast.

Its colouring can vary, but the most distinctive feature is the one from which it gets its name, a series of small spines – rather like the thorns on a rosebush – running down the back and tail and on the wings. Like most of the ray family, it may be found in shallow inshore waters during the summer months.

Thornback have a fondness for fish bait, and a strip cut from the side of a herring or mackerel often attracts them, but they will also take worms. All rays will settle their flat bodies on a bait before taking it in their mouths, so a delayed strike should be made. If you strike at the first indication, you will merely foul-hook the fish (hook the fish in its body rather than its mouth). In a strong tide-run a big thornback can give a steady fight before it is beaten.

DAB (Average weight 340g/12oz)
The dab is the smallest of the flatfish family and has a liking for sandy, shallow bays. It is generally caught in such places during the summer months. When winter approaches, the dab moves out into the deeps. Its colour is a dull brown and its scales feel rough to the touch. The dab is not a fussy feeder – worms are an effective bait.

DOGFISH (Average weight 4·50kg/10lb)
Identifying the various members of the dogfish family can cause problems – except when they are served in a fried fish shop under the general name of rock eel! Some of the family are known by several names. The greater-spotted dogfish, for example, is also called the bull huss or nurse hound, and the lesser-spotted dogfish is also known as the rough hound. Other members of the family are the spurdog (illustrated above), two species of smooth hound and the blackmouthed dogfish, the latter being a rather rare catch.

Identifying the various types is comparatively easy, as their habits are very similar. They are all related to the shark and have the same body shape as that of their more famous cousin. Spurdogs and both types of smooth hound are grey-blue in colour with white spots along the shoulders and flanks. The greater- and lesser-spotted dogfish are brown with black spots. The blackmouthed dogfish is dark grey with black blotches on the side of its body.

Most dogfish will be caught by the boat angler. When a pack of spurdog move in, you will have a lively time, for their greed is legendary. If you boat a spurdog, be careful when handling it. It lives up to its name by having a sharp spur on the leading edge of each dorsal fin. All dogfish do most of their feeding on the bottom and are partial to fish bait, but they will also take worms.

MULLET (Average weight 1kg/2lb)
Of the four types of mullet found in British waters, the thick-lipped grey mullet is the most common. It is a summer species which can be found in the brackish water of estuaries during the warmer months. Shoals are often spotted in the lower reaches of rivers, in harbours and among the supporting pillars of piers and jetties.

However, seeing a shoal of mullet and catching any of them are two different things. It has the reputation of being the most difficult of all saltwater fish to catch. The mullet's natural diet consists of tiny organisms, which makes it almost impossible to catch on normal sea tackle. The only way to succeed is to use tackle and bait suitable for freshwater fish.

Once you have found a shoal of mullet, the normal practice is to introduce groundbait to wean them on to the hookbait. Groundbait may be mashed bread or fish minced into very small pieces. Whatever the mix, make sure that the same is used on the hook, which should be a freshwater size 8 used on float tackle.

Sea fishing

TOPE (Average weight 9kg/20lb)
The graceful, streamlined, fast-moving tope is a member of the shark family, but with a much wider distribution, being found round most parts of the British coastline. A true predator, it hunts its prey in the warm, shallow areas during the summer months – wide, sandy bays are always productive areas – and retires to deeper water in winter. The tope has a reputation as a tough fighter, often making line stream from the reel on its initial run, and it is highly rated as a sporting quarry. Fish strip is the best bait.

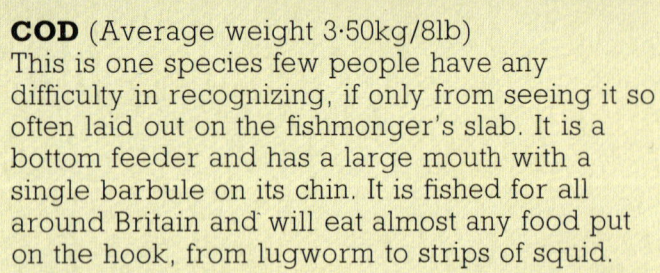

COD (Average weight 3·50kg/8lb)
This is one species few people have any difficulty in recognizing, if only from seeing it so often laid out on the fishmonger's slab. It is a bottom feeder and has a large mouth with a single barbule on its chin. It is fished for all around Britain and will eat almost any food put on the hook, from lugworm to strips of squid.

Apart from the east Yorkshire coastline, which has a resident stock of cod that can be caught all year round, most parts of the country are visited by migratory shoals only from about the end of October. They can be caught through to the end of March from beach, boat and pier, although, as with most other species of sea fish, the bigger cod are caught from boats. During the winter months, when cod fishing is at its height, charter boats will be fully booked every weekend. In terms of sheer numbers, the east and south coasts are the most productive areas; when the cod are biting, some beaches become as crowded as they are in midsummer.

BASS (Average weight 2·30kg/5lb)
The bass has a wide following among those specialist anglers who value it both for its fighting qualities and the challenge it offers. It is a handsome, silver, large-scaled predator with a spiky dorsal fin. It is to be found mainly in southern parts of Britain where, during the summer months, it will often be caught in the brackish water of river estuaries. At one time bass were thought of as a summer-only species, but in the last few years enough big fish have been caught during the winter months to show that the angler need not turn his attention to other species once the cold weather sets in.

The bass is a slow-growing species, and immature fish weighing up to 450g (1lb) will often swim in shoals, when they are known as school bass. As they grow bigger, they become more solitary. They can be caught from boat, beach and around piers and jetties with most types of artificial bait and also worms, small fish, crab and squid strip. To the specialist, beach fishing is the most enjoyable way of taking bass.

SOLE (Average weight 450g/1lb)
Beach fishing during the hours of darkness in summer is the best time to catch a sole, for it is a nocturnal feeder found close inshore when the water is warm. Considered by many to be the best flavoured of all Britain's saltwater species, it is certainly among the most expensive to buy at the fishmonger's. That is because it is fairly rare, so if you catch one, treat it as a bonus fish. Small worm bait will attract it.

GARFISH (Average weight 230g/8oz)
One of the oddest-looking of all Britain's sea fish, the garfish is a summer visitor which causes great interest when a holidaymaker hauls it on to the pier. It is a long, slender, eel-shaped creature with elongated, beak-like jaws, a brilliant green back and silvery sides. Like the mackerel, it is a lover of the sea surface, where it lives on minute forms of plankton and tiny fish. When the shoals are on the move, fish can often be seen breaking the surface. The type of light freshwater tackle used for mackerel should also be used for garfish, with either small spoons, spinners, feathers or tiny pieces of bait on float tackle.

When cooked, the bones of a garfish turn green, but this odd colour does not affect the taste in any way.

POUTING (Average weight 450g/1lb)
Pouting is one of Britain's most common sea fish. It has a deep, striped body and a barbule on its chin. Opinions about this species differ widely among anglers. Those after more sporting species will complain when yet another pouting takes the bait meant for something better, while those taking part in the many angling competitions held round the coast will praise it, for a large bag of pouting can add up to a winning catch. Although it is not regarded as a sporting species, it often saves an otherwise blank day when no other fish are being caught, and will take almost any bait.

It does not rate very highly as a table fish, as it deteriorates quickly once dead but, if gutted and washed immediately after capture and eaten soon afterwards, it can make a tasty meal.

WRASSE (Average weight 1kg/2lb)
This species is the most brightly coloured of all Britain's sea fish but, of the five types found in British waters, only one, the ballan (illustrated above), is of interest to the angler, as the others are too small. Wrasse are very much a rock angler's fish, for they are found, on the warmer coasts, inshore among the weeds and boulders, where they live on shellfish and crabs of all kinds. They are a summer species as far as shore fishing is concerned – very few are caught during the colder months.

The ideal way to attract wrasse is with float tackle, which can be used to search out the deeper gullies among the rocks. Bait may be any sort of shellfish, such as limpet or marine worm. Wrasse are generally considered to be one of the very few sea fish not worth eating, so if you catch one, return it alive to fight another day.

103

BREAM (Average weight 680g/1½lb)
The two types of bream which most interest the angler are the black and the red, though he will have to fish in the southern part of Britain if he is to find them. Both are summer visitors, the red being found mainly in deep water off the south-west coast, while the more common black arrives in large shoals off the south coast. The photograph above shows the current record red bream. The black bream is a hard-fighting fish, which gives of its best only when light tackle is used. There should be no confusing its deep shape, small head and dark blue colouring with any other fish. Although bream can be taken from the shore, far more are caught by boat anglers. Small strips of fish, worms or feathers can be used as bait.

POLLACK and **COALFISH** (Average weight 4·50kg/10lb)
The similarities of the pollack (illustrated above) and coalfish (illustrated top) make it easy to confuse the two species when trying to identify them. Both have the same general body shape and colouring and are found in similar areas. However, they may be told apart by remembering that only the coalfish has a white lateral line. The coalfish is found in greater numbers in the northern part of Britain, while the pollack has a more southerly distribution.

Both fish like rough ground, and the smaller ones offer great sport to the rock angler. The really big fish of both species are wreck-dwellers, often found in deep water, where they are usually caught on artificial eels or any bait with an attractive flashing movement.

FLOUNDER (Average weight 450g/1lb)
The flounder, the most common of all Britain's flatfish, is found all round the coast and is often the mainstay of sport when other species are absent or not in a feeding mood. It likes shallow water over a sandy or muddy bottom, and tidal estuaries are one of its favourite haunts. It is an avid feeder and will take almost any type of bait.

One unique method, the baited spoon, was designed solely for flounder and is often used by boat anglers. This consists of a baited hook, with a plastic or metal blade mounted so that it revolves, fixed uptrace (above the baited hook). The tackle is spun or rolled slowly along the bottom, where the blade acts as an attractor, luring the flounder to the baited hook.

Sea fishing
Some British sea fish records

		Boat records		Shore records	
Angler fish	37·53kg	82lb 12oz	30·90kg	68lb 2oz	Angler fish
Bass	8·33kg	18lb 6oz	8·22kg	18lb 2oz	Bass
Bream, Black	3·13kg	6lb 14oz 4dr	2·22kg	4lb 14oz 4dr	Bream, Black
Bream, Gilthead	2·27kg	5lb	3·14kg	6lb 15oz	Bream, Gilthead
Bream, Ray's	2·80kg	6lb 3oz 13dr	3·60kg	7lb 15oz 12dr	Bream, Ray's
Bream, Red	4·31kg	9lb 8oz 12dr	1·36kg	3lb	Bream, Red
Brill	7·26kg	16lb	2·61kg	5lb 12oz 4dr	Brill
Bull Huss	9·61kg	21lb 3oz	8·14kg	17lb 15oz	Bull Huss
Catfish	7·14kg	15lb 12oz	5·78kg	12lb 12oz 8dr	Catfish
Coalfish	13·95kg	30lb 12oz	7·49kg	16lb 8oz 8dr	Coalfish
Cod	24·04kg	53lb	20·18kg	44lb 8oz	Cod
Conger	49·61kg	109lb 6oz	30·42kg	67lb 1oz	Conger
Dab	1·25kg	2lb 12oz 4dr	1·17kg	2lb 9oz 8dr	Dab
Dogfish, Blackmouthed	1·28kg	2lb 13oz 8dr	454g	1lb*	Dogfish, Blackmouthed
Dogfish, Lesser-spotted	1·84kg	4lb 1oz 13dr	2·04kg	4lb 8oz	Dogfish, Lesser-spotted
Flounder	2·58kg	5lb 11oz 8dr	2·01kg	4lb 7oz	Flounder
Garfish	1·27kg	2lb 13oz 14dr	1·13kg	2lb 8oz	Garfish
Gurnard, Grey	1·10kg	2lb 7oz	680g	1lb 8oz	Gurnard, Grey
Gurnard, Red	2·27kg	5lb	1·19kg	2lb 10oz 11dr	Gurnard, Red
Gurnard, Streaked	454g	1lb*	637g	1lb 6oz 8dr	Gurnard, Streaked
Gurnard, Yellow	5·19kg	11lb 7oz 4dr	5·53kg	12lb 3oz	Gurnard, Yellow
Haddock	6·21kg	13lb 11oz 4dr	3·06kg	6lb 12oz	Haddock
Hake	11·48kg	25lb 5oz 8dr	2·27kg	5lb*	Hake
Halibut	96·27kg	212lb 4oz	6·35kg	14lb*	Halibut
Herring	481g	1lb 1oz	454g	1lb*	Herring
Ling	25·91kg	57lb 2oz 8dr	6·94kg	15lb 5oz 11dr	Ling
Mackerel	2·44kg	5lb 6oz 8dr	1·82kg	4lb 8dr	Mackerel
Monkfish	29·94kg	66lb	22·68kg	50lb	Monkfish
Mullet, Golden-grey	737g	1lb 9oz 15dr	1·19kg	2lb 10oz	Mullet, Golden-grey
Mullet, Red	1·59kg	3lb 8oz*	1·64kg	3lb 10oz	Mullet, Red
Mullet, Thick-lipped	4·56kg	10lb 1oz	4·54kg	10lb 12dr	Mullet, Thick-lipped
Mullet, Thin-lipped	1·81kg	4lb*	2·58kg	5lb 11oz	Mullet, Thin-lipped
Plaice	4·62kg	10lb 3oz 8dr	3·66kg	8lb 1oz 4dr	Plaice
Pollack	11·34kg	25lb	7·60kg	16lb 12oz	Pollack
Pouting	2·49kg	5lb 8oz	1·47kg	3lb 4oz	Pouting
Ray, Blonde	17·12kg	37lb 12oz	11·45kg	25lb 4oz	Ray, Blonde
Ray, Small-eyed	7·37kg	16lb 4oz	6·15kg	13lb 8oz 15dr	Ray, Small-eyed
Ray, Sting	26·76kg	59lb	23·24kg	51lb 4oz	Ray, Sting
Ray, Thornback	17·24kg	38lb	8·62kg	19lb	Ray, Thornback
Ray, Undulate	8·80kg	19lb 6oz 13dr	4·82kg	10lb 10oz 4dr	Ray, Undulate
Rockling, Three-bearded	1·42kg	3lb 2oz	1·31kg	2lb 14oz 8dr	Rockling, Three-bearded
Scad	1·50kg	3lb 5oz 3dr	1·05kg	2lb 5oz 13dr	Scad
Shark, Blue	98·88kg	218lb	34·02kg	75lb*	Shark, Blue
Shark, Mako	226·80kg	500lb	34·02kg	75lb*	Shark, Mako
Shark, Porbeagle	210·91kg	465lb	34·02kg	75lb*	Shark, Porbeagle
Shark, Thresher	133·81kg	295lb	34·02kg	75lb*	Shark, Thresher
Skate, Common	102·74kg	226lb 8oz	68·04kg	150lb*	Skate, Common
Smooth Hound	12·70kg	28lb	6·75kg	14lb 14oz 12dr	Smooth Hound
Smooth Hound, Starry	9·49kg	20lb 15oz 12dr	10·48kg	23lb 2oz	Smooth Hound, Starry
Sole	1·81kg	4lb*	2·04kg	4lb 8oz	Sole
Sole, Lemon	966g	2lb 2oz	990g	2lb 2oz 15dr	Sole, Lemon
Spurdog	9·61kg	21lb 3oz 7dr	7·60kg	16lb 12oz 8dr	Spurdog
Tope	33·88kg	74lb 11oz	24·60kg	54lb 4oz	Tope
Tunny	386·01kg	851lb	45·36kg	100lb*	Tunny
Turbot	14·60kg	32lb 3oz	12·92kg	28lb 8oz	Turbot
Whiting	2·83kg	6lb 4oz	1·42kg	3lb 2oz	Whiting
Wrasse, Ballan	3·40kg	7lb 8oz 5dr	3·80kg	8lb 6oz 6dr	Wrasse, Ballan
Wrasse, Cuckoo	908g	2lb 8dr	568g	1lb 4oz 8dr	Wrasse, Cuckoo

*This weight is the minimum required to qualify. There is no record held at the time of publication

Sea fishing
Boat fishing

▲ This charter party is fishing an inshore mark in Scotland in a boat typical of the sort used for fishing trips

While you can have a great deal of enjoyment fishing from piers, beaches and rocks, there is also a lot to be said for boat fishing, which can take you several miles offshore, beyond the sight of land. The boat angler's mobility gives him an advantage over his shorebound counterpart.

The first boat trip is critical. If you have a good, productive day out, you will be an enthusiast for life, but a bad day can make you vow never to go afloat again. So start on the right foot by going out on a regular charter party with an experienced skipper. He will know all the best areas and how they will fish at different states of the tide.

Make sure also that you know the basic rule of boat fishing, which is that if you become seasick you will just have to make the best of it. The skipper will not return halfway through the day just because one member of the party is feeling unwell. To guard against this, take a travel pill before setting out, and have a good breakfast (but avoid too much greasy food), as seasickness is worse on an empty stomach.

Charter parties vary in size, as do the boats of course. On some parts of the coast, large boats cater for a dozen or more anglers; in other places there will be smaller craft taking no more than six. In general, the smaller the party, the more it will cost each angler. In the coastal towns which have a fairly big fleet of angling boats, the local tackle shop often runs a booking service for anglers seeking a boat trip, so telephone the shop in advance to ensure your place. At the same time, you can discover if bait is included in the service or whether you must supply your own. You may also check whether boat tackle can be hired, for many coastal tackle shops offer this service as well. Food is rarely provided for your meals on the boat, so make sure you take along enough for the day's outing.

Once aboard the boat, you will almost certainly be in the company of more experienced anglers and you can learn a lot by watching them. Tell the skipper that you are a beginner and he will keep an eye on you, making up the tackle, baiting your hook and making sure that your first important fish is safely boated. Do not be frightened to ask questions – in the comradeship on a boat you will find other anglers more than willing to help.

One way to make yourself unpopular on a boat is to stand up and attempt to hurl your terminal tackle as far as possible. Casting is not

▲ Ready with a gaff to secure the catch

An attractively-marked undulate ray is admired by its young captor ▶

necessary. More than that, it is frowned upon because of the potential danger of flying leads and hooks in such a confined space. Most charter parties fish at anchor, the skipper trying different known spots – or marks – until the feeding fish are found. You will normally fish with your bait hard on the bottom.

You will need a variety of lead weights, for, as the tide changes, you must alter the weight to cope with the varying run of water. If you are in doubt about the size to use, it is best to err on the heavy side. Too light a lead will not hold the sea bottom, and terminal tackle may be swept along and become entangled with other lines on the boat.

Keep your spare tackle and other odds and ends tidy and out of the way of others. Above all, remember that at sea the skipper is in charge and that you must always follow his advice.

Sea fishing
Boat tackle

Boat anglers not only have the advantage of being able to move fairly quickly from one mark to another, they have the other bonuses that they can catch bigger fish and a wider variety of them. Tackle used depends on the fish being sought, of course. For instance, conger eels need much tougher tackle than that used for cod, and cod demand stronger tackle than the light outfit which can be used for flatfish.

As no casting is needed, long rods are more of a handicap than a help, and the average boat rod normally measures about 2m (6ft) in length. Fixed-spool reels are not usually favoured for boat work; multiplier and centrepin are the reels more often used. Line strength depends on the likely size of fish, the amount of lead needed to hold the sea bottom and the type of bottom itself. Every area has a favourite end tackle, but the running ledger is probably the most widely used of all. The hook length is connected to a link swivel which in turn is attached to another swivel at the end of the main line. A Clement's or Kilmore boom, which carries the lead, goes on the main line and a bead stops it sliding down on to the swivel.

Once the hook is baited, the tackle is lowered over the side and the line released until the lead hits the bottom. The tide will keep the trace out behind the lead and prevent any tangles. Bites vary according to the type of fish which has taken the bait, but there is rarely any need to strike in the same way as the coarse fish angler does. At the first sign of a bite, the angler should lower the rod tip and allow the fish a bit more slack line, lifting the rod tip only when a good pull shows that the fish is firmly hooked.

The combined weight of fish and lead makes hauling up the catch difficult at times, particularly if there is a strong tide running. When this happens, the angler 'pumps' his fish to the surface: this is done by dropping the rod tip, winding the reel to recover the line gained, lifting the rod tip and then repeating the process. Once the fish is on the surface, the skipper will use either a net or gaff (a hook attached to a handle, as shown in the picture above right),

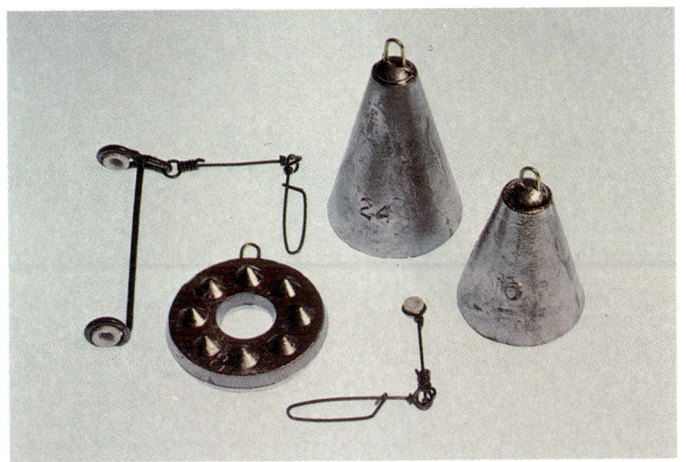

▲ Three different types of lead – two pyramids and a grip – used for pier and boat fishing, together with Clement's and Kilmore booms to which the leads are attached

◄ A not-so-warm day afloat and the anglers aboard this charter boat are dressed for the occasion. In such conditions, good windproof clothing is essential

The average boat rod is about 2m (6ft) in length. As no casting is needed, a longer rod is a handicap ▶

▼ The gaff, a large barbless hook attached to a handle, is used for lifting heavy fish on board

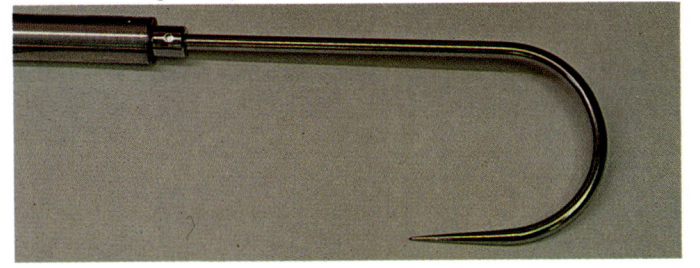

depending on its size, to bring it on board. Trying to lift a heavy fish over the side of a boat may well result in the hook being pulled out and the fish escaping.

Protective clothing makes fishing more comfortable no matter what kind you do, but it is a vital part of a boat angler's equipment. However warm the weather is on land, there is always a breeze at sea, and normally a cold one, so that even in summer you need some sort of protection. In winter the right clothing can mean the difference between a day spent shivering in the bottom of the boat in a vain effort to keep warm and a day when you are warm enough to concentrate on catching fish.

A winter's day on an open boat demands really warm clothes: long underwear, a pair of thick trousers and a pair of windproof overtrousers, plus two pairs of thick socks, rubber-soled boots, a long shirt, heavy woollen long-sleeved jumper, loose jacket and windproof storm-coat. Alternatively, a heavy one-piece suit can be worn over thick clothes. A snug-fitting fabric hat, which pulls down over the ears, provides protection against the wind. Remember that on a boat you will be sitting in one position all day, with no chance to walk about and restore the circulation when you feel cold. You will not be rebaiting, casting and hook-tying as often as the freshwater angler does, so you can wear thick gloves, removing them only when it is necessary to play a fish, reel in or to do other jobs requiring dexterity.

You will also need to keep the inner man warm. Take along with you a nourishing curry, stew or soup in a wide-necked vacuum flask, and a few thick slices of bread. This type of meal will do you much more good than sandwiches and tea.

Catch a conger

The conger eel is the roughest, toughest, hardest-fighting adversary that the average angler is ever likely to catch on the end of rod and line. The current record is a fish well in excess of 45kg (100lb)

Congers are creatures of the sea bed. They make their homes in the wrecks of sunken ships, and in rocky and broken ground. Tough tackle is needed if the angler is to succeed in bringing one aboard a boat, as they have strong jaws and sharp teeth. A wire trace has to be used as a hook link because they can quickly bite their way through any other material. As soon as the conger feels the hook, its favourite trick is to wrap its tail round the nearest obstruction and hang on grimly, a tactic which can lead to a muscle-pulling fight for the angler at the other end of the rod!

The waters around Devon and Cornwall – an area which produces big fish of many species – is the best place for really big conger. The wartime wrecks which lie out in deep water there act as a magnet for enthusiastic conger anglers from all over the country.

The conger eel is a hard-fighting adversary and tough tackle is needed if the angler is to succeed in bringing one aboard. West Country waters provide the best conger fishing in Britain. The picture on the far left shows a conger caught off the Cornish coast. The conger on the left, caught off Plymouth, weighed 36·30kg (80lb), but the biggest one on record is shown above. Weighing 49·61kg (109lb 6oz), it was caught by Robin Potter of Bristol in 1976 off a wreck mark south of the Eddystone Reef

111

The mighty sharks

In recent years shark fishing has increased tremendously in popularity and is now a big tourist attraction. Every year holidaymakers sample this exciting and exhilarating sport – often with considerable success

It is a strange paradox that some of the biggest fish Britain's seas have to offer, fish which dwarf ordinary run-of-the-mill catches, are often caught by people who have never handled a rod and line before. Shark fishing is the name of the game, a sport which has grown into a big tourist attraction. Four species of shark are found in British waters: the mako, porbeagle, thresher and blue. The West Country is the best place to find them; the tiny port of Looe in Cornwall is the main centre.

The blue is the most common of the four species and also the smallest, the record being 98·88kg (218lb). Rarest is the thresher with a record weight of 133·81kg (295lb) and biggest the mako at 226·80kg (500lb), although the porbeagle comes a close second with a record weight of 210·91kg (465lb). With the exception of the thresher, all those record fish came from the West Country, an area which owes its shark population to the warm water of the North Atlantic drift which runs near that coastline.

Shark fishing is now very much part of the summer holiday scene in that part of the country and, although Looe is the main centre (and headquarters of the Shark Angling Club of Great Britain), a number of other coastal towns run charter boats for the sport.

The charter fee normally includes the use of all tackle, and bait is caught on the way out to the shark grounds, which may take several hours to reach. Charter trips for shark fishing differ from most others in that those on board usually take turns to fish; there are rarely more than three rods used at the same time.

Groundbaiting is an important part of sharking. On the way out to the shark grounds, the skipper prepares the groundbait mixture by chopping and mincing several bucketfuls of fish, such as mackerel and pilchards. Once the fishing area has been reached, this mixture (called rubby dubby) is placed in a net bag and hung over the side of the boat so that it leaves a trail of scales and pieces of fish in a long slick behind the boat. As the boat drifts with the current – and sharking

Shark fishing provides the angler with exhilarating sport. The blue shark on the left, about to be hauled aboard, was caught off Tenerife in the Canary Islands, and weighed 54·40kg (120lb). The thresher (above), the rarest of the shark species found in Britain, weighed in at 95kg (209lb) on the scales and the porbeagle (inset) at 93kg (205lb)

is always done from a drifting boat – the slick spreads and any shark in the area will home in on it.

Hookbait is fresh mackerel and the tackle will be arranged so that each rod has its bait set at a different depth, making it easier for the shark to find. The floats used for such fishing range from rubber balloons to pieces of polystyrene and there is no doubt when a shark has taken the bait – the floats vanish under the water immediately!

As soon as a shark is hooked, the other lines are reeled in to avoid the risk of tangles. Once the shark is beaten, the skipper gaffs it and brings it aboard. Finally, the weighing ceremony takes place back on the quay with a special set of clock scales.

Safety and courtesy

Angling is one of the safest of sports but, like any other, it has its share of dangers and accidents, and it is essential to be aware of the potentially tricky situations so that you can avoid them.

The person most at risk is the sea angler, and each year the angling papers carry stories of accidents at sea, most of which could have been avoided. No professional skipper would risk his clients' lives and his reputation by putting to sea in hazardous conditions, so when he tells you that a trip has been cancelled because of the weather, believe him. Do not look around for someone else to take you out; and beware the enthusiastic boating friend whose proud boast is that he knows enough about the sea not to worry about the weather – he is likely to lead you into danger.

On any boat, and particularly a small one, do not move about more than necessary. Make sure that your footwear has the type of sole which offers a good grip on a wet deck. Before you go out, check that the craft has enough lifejackets and distress flares – professional skippers will always have the proper equipment, but the odd 'cowboy' operator may not. If you go out on a private boat, tell someone where you are going and when you expect to return.

When shore fishing, if you see notices on a stretch of cliff or pier indicating that a certain section is unsafe, respect them. Do not take chances by finding out the truth the hard way.

On an unfamiliar beach, particularly one where the tide goes out a long way, take care when exploring at low tide and keep a weather eye open for when it turns. A shallow gully that you crossed at low water might well be 2m (6ft) deep – and still rising – on your return. On a crowded beach or pier, take extra care with your casting – flying leads are dangerous, as are the hooks on the trace. Be cautious when walking on muddy estuaries at low tide; there are places where the mud may be deeper than you expect.

Rock anglers can find themselves in dangerous situations if they are not careful. Many stretches of rock are solid enough to climb over, but watch out for places where the rock is loose – you could risk a twisted ankle or a broken leg. Weed-covered rocks are slippery when the tide goes out, leaving them wet. Rubber-soled shoes are dangerous on such surfaces, and it is advisable to wear the type of non-slip footwear favoured by sailors or, better still, stout shoes with steel studs on the soles.

Freshwater anglers do not face the obvious dangers which the sea angler might encounter, but they can still find themselves in trouble on occasions. After flooding there is always an undercut bank or two on any given stretch of river, usually on a bend where the current cuts its way into the soil. Such banks can collapse without warning and are often situated over deep water.

Wading, too, can present problems, particularly on a fast-flowing river. The further out you wade, the harder the push of the current, and if you stumble even slightly, the water will quickly push you off your feet. Many modern trout reservoirs are simply flooded farmland, and the beds of such waters are often criss-crossed with ditches or sunken paths. There are normally notices which warn of such conditions, so take care, and feel your way out gently.

When you are still a novice at fly casting, it pays to wear a pair of glasses of some sort as protection for the eyes. Polaroid-type sunglasses are best, because they also cut out surface glare. A gust of wind catching the line in mid-cast can quickly wrap it round your neck, and even a small hook can do a lot of damage if it hits you in the eye. One of the golden rules of fly fishing is never to walk too close to an angler in the act of casting. If he is a good caster, his back cast will reach behind a long way and you may walk straight into it.

Apart from the dangers that can cause real physical pain or injury, there are a number of minor discomforts you may experience. Wasps, gnats, stinging nettles and brambles are very much part of the country scene, and in high summer it is all too easy to be stung or scratched. The angler should carry a small first-aid kit in his tackle bag to cope with such nuisances.

Most forms of angling are governed by national, club or local rules, and failure to comply with them can get you into trouble. Even when you are not certain of the rules (and ignorance is no defence), there are certain things you should not do.

It goes without saying that freshwater anglers should obey the Country Code. Do not leave litter, especially nylon monofilament line which can maim or even kill animals. In fact, go one better and pick up any litter that others may have left. A dustbin liner bag kept in your fishing holdall is handy for this. Do not take a dog with you – or a portable radio! Dogs chase cattle, and radios upset other water-users who are seeking a little peace and quiet. Do not climb fences, except at a stile, and if you use a gate, make sure you close it after you. Do not light fires. Bankside vegetation forms a useful sight screen between

▲ The rock on which these anglers are enjoying their sport looks safe enough in calm weather, but it could be a potentially dangerous spot

angler and fish, so never tramp it down just because it is in your way. One famous club has a sign beside its most popular fishery which sums up what your attitude should be: 'Leave nothing but your footprint'.

Sea anglers should also be aware of other people using the beaches and piers. Pieces of spare bait and dead fish littering the deck of a pier are offensive and dangerous; so too are lengths of old line left lying around. If you are taking fish home to eat, kill them quickly and cleanly. A luckless flatfish flapping about on the pier deck as it gasps its life away does no good for the public image of angling.

When night fishing – on an inland water or popular beach – do not annoy local residents by slamming car doors late at night or early in the morning, and make sure that the car is parked where it does not cause an obstruction.

Always remember that many forms of wildlife are found in the surroundings that anglers enjoy, so do not disturb them.

The unwritten rules are easy to follow: just treat your favourite fishing spot as if it were your own back garden.

Do-it-yourself rods

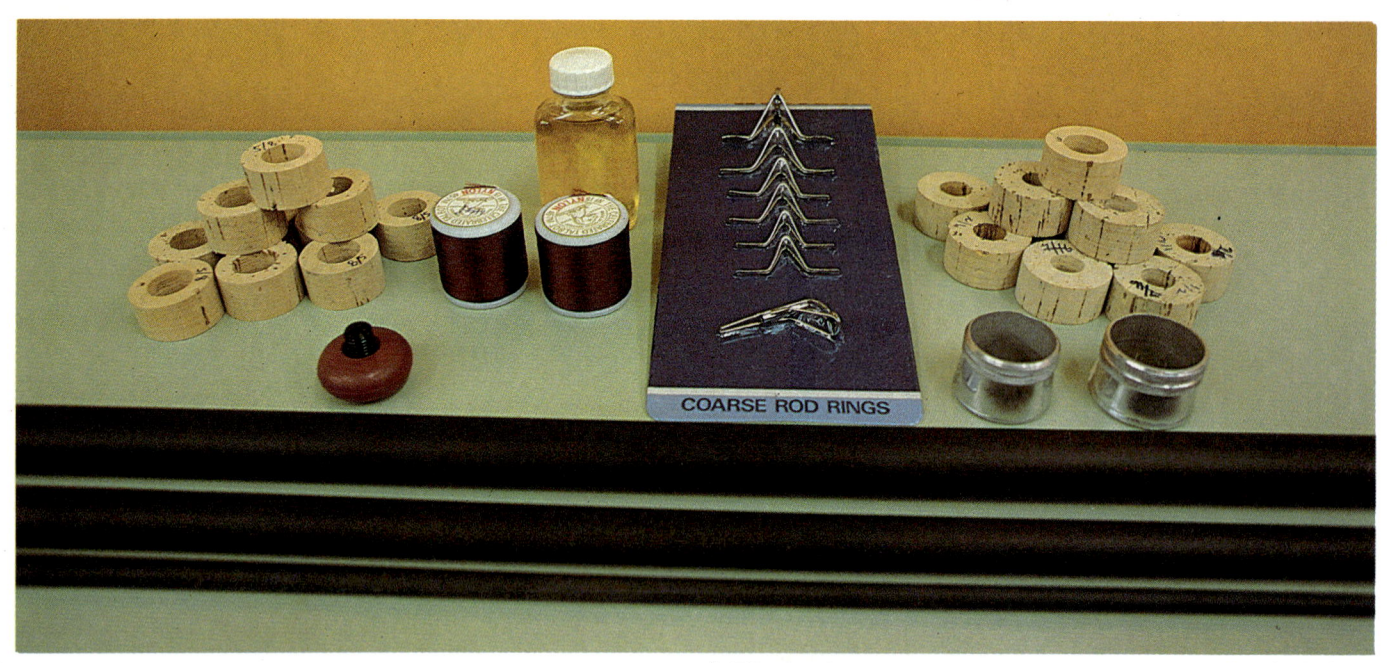

▲ The equipment you need to make your own rod includes the glass fibre blanks, corks, rod rings, reel fittings, varnish, whipping silk and a butt cap

With such a wide variety now available, most anglers can find exactly the rod they need for any specialized purpose, from fly fishing to deep-sea work, by looking no further than their local tackle shop. However, anglers who want something a little different, or want to save money, can always turn to do-it-yourself work.

There are two basic ways of making your own rod, neither of which demands the skill of a craftsman. You may either buy the glass fibre blanks (the basic body of the rod), the corks for the handle, reel fittings and rod rings separately, or opt for a partially finished kit. In the kit all the trickiest parts have already been done and all you have to do is assemble the rod. Prices vary depending on what type of kit you choose.

If you are starting from scratch, you must know exactly how many corks will be needed to make up the handle and the number of rod rings required. The shopkeeper can give you these figures, but you can always check them for yourself by looking at a production model of the same type.

Glue, a sharp knife, a medium file and varying grades of sandpaper are the basic tools needed.

You begin by glueing the spigots, the glass fibre pegs, into the thinner end of each of the bottom two rod lengths, making sure that they fit evenly and do not rock.

Once the spigots are in position and have been left for the glue to harden, the next step is to make the handle. Slide the corks on to the butt and check the fit. Then file the middle section of corks until it is of the right thickness to take the reel fittings. This part takes a little time and patience; sandpaper should be used for the final part of the operation. When this has been done, take the corks off and smear the butt with glue. Then slide the corks and the reel fittings back on to the glued section. Screw the butt cap into the cork at the end of the handle.

Rod rings can be held in position with a small piece of sticky tape to make the job of tying them on with whipping silk that much easier. Keep checking to make sure that they are all in a straight line. Once completed, the whippings should be given a coat of dope, a solution which helps to retain the colour, and then an application of varnish. Put a whipping around the end of each of the female ferrules where they slide over the spigots. This will add strength to the rod and help prevent damage.

You can personalize the rod by marking your initials in Indian ink just above the butt, another job which should be done before the final varnish is applied. Use your finger rather than a brush for varnishing, as in this way you will be able more easily to rub the varnish into the whippings.

Buy a partitioned bag in which to keep the completed rod. This will protect the varnish from chipping and the rod rings from getting knocked, as well as keeping grit out of the blanks and away from the spigots.

You should aim to produce a better rod than this one! ▶

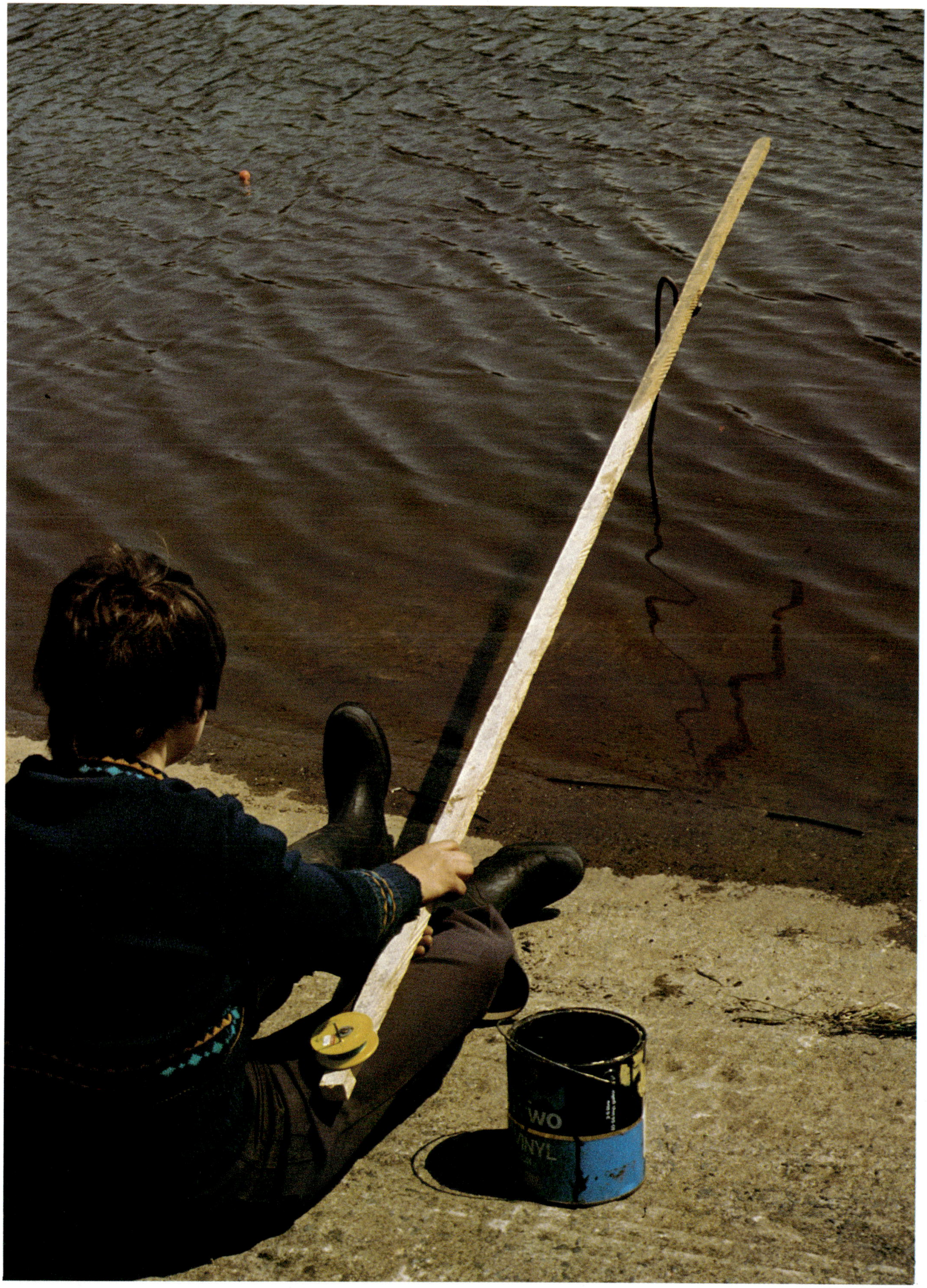
WO
VINYL

Trout waters

While it is impossible to list all the stillwater trout fisheries available on a day-ticket basis, this guide will be useful to anyone wanting to know the location of some of the bigger or better-known ones. Unless otherwise stated, the 'fly fishing only' rule applies. The fisheries are listed under the relevant Water Authority in whose area they are situated.

An acre is equivalent to 4840 square yards or 4046 square metres

ANGLIAN WATER AUTHORITY
Ardleigh Reservoir, nr Colchester, Essex. *130 acres.*
Church Hill Farm, Mursley, nr Milton Keynes, Bucks. *Two lakes totalling 9 acres. Reduced price for evening tickets.*
East Hanningfield Lake, East Hanningfield Hall, nr Chelmsford, Essex. *2 acres.*
Elinor Fishery, Aldwincle, nr Thrapston, Northants. *Two lakes totalling 40 acres.*
Eye Brook Reservoir, Caldecott, Uppingham, Leics. *400 acres. Evening tickets available.*
Grafham Water, West Perry, Hunts. *1,670 acres.*
Pitsford Reservoir, nr Northampton. *739 acres. Reduced price for evening tickets.*
Ravensthorpe Reservoir, nr Northampton. *114 acres. Reduced price for evening tickets.*
Rutland Water, nr Oakham, Leics. *3,100 acres.*
Toft Newton Reservoir, nr Market Rasen, Lincs. *40 acres.*

NORTH WEST WATER AUTHORITY
Bank House Fishery, Low Mill Caton, nr Lancaster. *Lake of 2 acres. Reduced price for evening tickets.*
Lamaload Reservoir, nr Macclesfield, Cheshire. *70 acres.*
Rivington Reservoirs, nr Bolton, Lancs. *Eight waters totalling 601 acres.*
Thurstonfield Lough, nr Carlisle, Cumbria. *37 acres.*
Vale House, Tintwistle, Cheshire. *Reservoir of 62 acres.*

NORTHUMBRIAN WATER AUTHORITY
Derwent Reservoir, Edmundbyers, nr Consett, Durham. *1,100 acres.*
Grassholme and Selset, nr Barnard Castle, Co. Durham. *Two reservoirs totalling 415 acres.*
Lockwood Beck, Teesdale. *Reservoir of 40 acres.*
Tunstall Reservoir, nr Wolsingham, Weardale. *80 acres.*
Whittle Dene, nr Newcastle, Northumberland. *Six reservoirs totalling 120 acres.*

SEVERN/TRENT WATER AUTHORITY
Colewick Park Reservoir, nr Nottingham. *65 acres.*
Cromwell Lake, nr Newark, Notts. *Just over 18 acres.*
Draycote Water, nr Rugby, Warks. *600 acres. Half-day tickets available.*
Foremark Reservoir, nr Derby. *230 acres.*
Hamps Valley Fishery, Winkhill, nr Leek, Staffs. *Two lakes each of 1 acre plus ½ mile of double bank river.*
Higham Farm, nr Alfreton, Derby. *Four lakes totalling 12 acres and 1½ miles of river.*
Ladybower Reservoir, nr Bamford, Derbyshire. *504 acres.*
Lake Vyrnwy, nr Llanwddyn, Powys. *1,100 acres. Half-day tickets available.*
Llyn Clywedog, Llanidloes, Powys. *Reservoir of 600 acres. Evening tickets available.*
Ogston Reservoir, nr Alfreton, Derby. *206 acres.*
Packington Fisheries, Meriden, Warks. *Six lakes totalling 120 acres and 2½ miles of River Blythe. Three lakes and river open to day tickets, remainder members only. Evening tickets available.*
Patshull Park Trout Fishery, Patshull Road, Pattingham, nr Albrighton, Staffs. *Three lakes totalling 100 acres.*
Peatswood Lakes, Market Drayton. *Two lakes totalling 8 acres.*
Shustoke Reservoir, nr Coleshill, Warks. *100 acres.*
Thornton Reservoir, nr Leicester. *76 acres.*
Tittesworth Reservoir, nr Leek, Staffs. *190 acres.*

SOUTH WEST WATER AUTHORITY
Argal Reservoir, nr Penryn, Cornwall. *65 acres.*
Burrator Reservoir, nr Plymouth, Devon. *150 acres.*
Crowdy Reservoir, nr Camelford, Cornwall. *115 acres.*
Darracot, nr Great Torrington, Okehampton, Devon. *2½ acres.*
Dart Raffe Farm, Witheridge, Devon. *Lake of 2 acres. Reduced price for evening tickets.*
Drift Reservoir, nr Penzance, Cornwall. *65 acres. Reduced price for evening tickets.*
Fernworthy Reservoir, nr Moretonhampstead, Devon. *76 acres.*
Gammatons and Jennets Reservoirs, nr Bideford, Devon. *Three waters totalling 2½ acres.*
Kennick, Tottiford and Trenchford, nr Bovey Tracey, Devon. *Three reservoirs totalling 113 acres.*
Little Dart Reservoir, Witheridge, Devon. *2 acres. Reduced price for evening tickets.*
Meldon Reservoir, nr Okehampton, Devon. *50 acres.*
Payhembury Trout Ponds, nr Honiton, Devon. *Two lakes totalling 2½ acres. Reduced price for evening tickets.*
Porth Reservoir, nr Newquay, Cornwall. *40 acres.*
Siblyback Lake, nr Liskeard, Cornwall. *140 acres.*
Slade, nr Ilfracombe, Devon. *Two reservoirs totalling 10 acres.*
Stafford Moor Fishery, Dolton, Winkleigh, Devon. *Lake of 14 acres. Reduced price for evening tickets.*
Stithians, nr Redruth, Cornwall. *Reservoir of 274 acres.*
Trenchcreek Lakes, St Austell, Cornwall. *Two lakes totalling 2 acres.*
Upper Tamar Lake, nr Bude, Cornwall. *81 acres.*
Wistlandpound, nr Barnstaple, Devon. *Reservoir of 41 acres.*

SOUTHERN WATER AUTHORITY
Ardingly Reservoir, nr Haywards Heath, Sussex. *189 acres.*
Avington, Avington, nr Winchester, Hants. *Three lakes plus a stretch of river.*
Bewl Bridge, nr Lamberhurst, Kent. *Reservoir of 777 acres. Half-day tickets available.*
Boringwheel Fishery, nr Nutley, Sussex. *Lake of 6 acres.*
Bossington Lake, Houghton, nr Stockbridge, Hants. *Lake of 2½ acres.*
Darwell Reservoir, nr Mountfield, Sussex. *180 acres.*
Ladywell Lakes, Alresford, nr Winchester, Hants. *Three lakes totalling 2½ acres plus small stretch of chalk stream. Closed on Tuesdays.*
Peckham's Copse, nr Chichester, Sussex. *Two lakes totalling 40 acres.*
Pooh Corner Fishery, Rolvenden, Cranbrook, Kent. *Two pools totalling 1½ acres. Evening tickets available.*
Powdermill Reservoir, Great Sanders, nr Sedlescombe. *57 acres.*
Tenterden Trout Waters, Tenterden, Kent. *Three lakes totalling 4 acres.*

THAMES WATER AUTHORITY
Barn Elms (No. 7), Merthyr Terrace, Barnes. *Reservoir of 23 acres. Part-day tickets available.*
Barn Elms (No. 8), Merthyr Terrace, Barnes. *Reservoir of 20 acres. Part-day tickets available.*
Farmoor ll, nr Oxford. *Reservoir of 240 acres. Part-day tickets available.*
Kempton Park, Sunbury Way, Hanworth, Middx. *Reservoir of 23 acres. Part-day tickets available.*
Latimer Park Lakes, nr Chesham, Bucks. *Two lakes totalling 12 acres. Evening tickets available.*
Lower Moor Fishery, Oaksey, Malmesbury, Wilts. *Lake of 30 acres.*
Netherhall Trout Fishery, Hoddesdon, Herts. *Gravel pit of 5 acres.*
Oughton Fishery, Burford Ray Lodge, Bedford Road, Hitchin, Herts. *Lake of 2 acres. Evening tickets available.*
Queen Mother Reservoir, Horton Road, Colnbrook, Berks. *475 acres. Part-day tickets available. Boat fishing only.*
Stratfield Saye Lake, nr Basingstoke, Hants. *Two lakes totalling 14 acres.*
Walthamstow Reservoir (No. 4), Ferry Lane, Walthamstow. *30 acres. Part-day tickets available.*
Wick Water, South Cerney, Glos. *Two lakes totalling 20 acres.*
Willinghurst Fishery, Shamley Green, Surrey. *Four lakes totalling 6 acres.*
Wroughton, nr Swindon, Wilts. *Reservoir of 3 acres.*

Trout waters

WELSH WATER AUTHORITY
Aberystwyth Lakes, Dyfed. *12 lakes.*
Alwen Reservoir, nr Cerrigydrudion, Corwen, Clwyd. *368 acres.*
Beacons, nr Brecon, Powys. *Reservoir of 52 acres.*
Brenig, nr Denbigh. *Reservoir of 191 acres. Reduced price for evening tickets.*
Cambrian Fisheries, Afonwen, nr Mold, Clwyd. *Lake of 18 acres. Reduced price for evening tickets.*
Cantref, nr Merthyr Tydfil, mid-Glamorgan. *Reservoir of 42 acres.*
Cwmystradllyn, nr Beddgelert, Gwynedd. *Reservoir of 95 acres.*
Dol-y-Gaer, nr Talybont, Powys. *Reservoir of 96 acres.*
Eglwys Nunydd, Margam, Port Talbot. *250 acres.*
Elan Valley Estate, nr Rhayader, Powys. *A complex of rivers and lakes totalling 1,500 acres.*
Ffestiniog Fishery, nr Cynfl, Gwynedd. *Reservoir of 95 acres.*
Llan Alaw, Anglesey. *Reservoir of 77 acres. Reduced price for evening tickets.*
Llandegfedd Reservoir, nr Cardiff, South Glamorgan. *Reservoir of 429 acres.*
Llanishen and Lisvane, nr Cardiff, South Glamorgan. *Two reservoirs totalling 78 acres.*
Llanlawddog Lake, Carmarthen, Dyfed. *2½ acres.*
Llwyn On, nr Brecon, Powys. *Reservoir of 59 acres.*
Llyn Celyn, nr Bala, Gwynedd. *Reservoir of 800 acres. Reduced price for evening tickets.*
Llys-Fran Reservoir, nr Maenclochog, Dyfed. *187 acres.*
Pant-y-Reos, nr Bettws, Gwent. *Reservoir of 16 acres.*
Pontsticill, nr Talybont, Powys. *Reservoir of 253 acres.*
Rheidol, nr Aberystwyth. *Two reservoirs totalling 740 acres.*
Rosebush Reservoir, nr Maenclochog, Dyfed. *Reservoir of 39 acres.*
Talybont Reservoir, Brecon, Powys. *Reservoir of 318 acres.*
Teifi Pools, nr Tregaron, Dyfed. *Four lakes totalling 125 acres.*
Upper Lleidi, nr Llanelli, Dyfed. *Reservoir of 25 acres. Reduced price for evening tickets.*
Upper and Lower Neuadd, nr Talybont, Glamorgan. *Two reservoirs totalling 40 acres.*
Usk Reservoir, nr Trecastle, Powys. *280 acres.*
Wentwood Reservoir, nr Newport, Gwent. *41 acres.*
Ynsfro Reservoirs, Newport, Gwent. *Two reservoirs totalling 26 acres.*

WESSEX WATER AUTHORITY
Allens Farm, Sandleheath, Fordingbridge, Hants. *Five lakes totalling just over 6 acres plus ½ mile of river. Half-day tickets available.*
Barrow 1, 2 and 3 Reservoirs, nr Bristol. *125 acres.*
Blagdon Lake, Blagdon, nr Bristol. *430 acres. Tickets at reduced rate after 3 p.m.*
Breech Valley Trout Fishery, Tweed Farm, Coleford, Bath. *3½ acres.*
Cameley Trout Lakes, Temple Cloud, nr Bristol. *Two lakes totalling 4 acres.*
Chew Valley Lake, Chew Stoke, nr Bristol. *1,210 acres. Tickets at reduced rates after 3 p.m.*
Clatworthy, nr Taunton, Somerset. *130 acres. Half-day tickets available.*
Damerham, nr Fordingbridge, Hants. *Five lakes totalling 14 acres.*
Durleigh, nr Bridgwater, Somerset. *80 acres. Half-day tickets available.*
Hawkridge Reservoir, Spaxton, nr Bridgwater, Somerset. *32 acres.*
John O'Gaunt's Lake, King's Somborne, Hants. *5 acres.*
Leominsted Trout Fishery, Emery Down, nr Lyndhurst. *Lake of 8 acres.*
Martins Trout Lake, Wimborne, Dorset. *2½ acres. Half-day tickets available.*
Otterhead Lake, nr Churchingford, Taunton, Somerset. *Two lakes totalling 4½ acres.*
Sutton Bingham, nr Yeovil, Somerset. *142 acres. Half-day tickets available.*

YORKSHIRE WATER AUTHORITY
Fewston and Swinsty, nr Blubberhouses, Otley, Yorks. *Two reservoirs totalling 410 acres.*
Greenfield Lake and Beck, Buckden, nr Skipton, Yorks. *3 acres.*
Leighton Reservoir, nr Masham, Yorks. *100 acres.*
Linacre Reservoirs, nr Chesterfield, Derbyshire. *Two reservoirs totalling 43 acres.*
Morehall Reservoir, Bolstertone, nr Sheffield, Yorks. *65 acres.*
Thruscross, nr Otley, Yorks. *Reservoir of 360 acres.*

Useful addresses

WATER AUTHORITIES

Anglian Water Authority, Diploma House, Grammar School Walk, Huntingdon PE18 6NZ.
North West Water Authority, Dawson House, Great Sankey, Warrington WA5 3LW.
Northumbrian Water Authority, Northumbria House, Regent Centre, Gosforth, Newcastle upon Tyne NE3 3PX.
Severn/Trent Water Authority, Abelson House, 2297 Coventry Road, Sheldon, Birmingham B26 3PU.
South West Water Authority, 3-5 Barnfield Road, Exeter EX1 1RE.
Southern Water Authority, Guildbourne House, Worthing, Sussex BN11 1LD.
Thames Water Authority, New River Head, Rosebery Avenue, London EC1R 4TP.
Welsh National Water Development Authority, Cambrian Way, Brecon, Powys LD3 7HP.
Wessex Water Authority, Techno House, Redcliffe Way, Bristol BS1 6NY.
Yorkshire Water Authority, West Riding House, 67 Albion Street, Leeds LS1 5AA.

No Water Authority licence is needed to fish in Scotland.

ASSOCIATIONS, CLUBS AND SOCIETIES

Anglers Co-operative Association, Midland Bank Chambers, Westgate, Grantham, Lincs. NG31 6LE.
Angling Foundation, Dick Orton, The Limes, Alvechurch, Worcs.
Barbel Catchers Club, Roger Baker, 153 Langley Hall Road, Olton, Solihull, West Midlands.
Bass Anglers Sport Fishing Society, J. Churchouse, Rishon, Longfield Road, Weymouth, Dorset.
Birmingham Anglers Association, 40 Thorp Street, Birmingham B5 4AY.
British Carp Study Group, Peter Mohan, Heywood House, Pill, Bristol BS20.
British Conger Club, R. Quest, 5 Hill Crest, Mannamead, Plymouth, Devon.
British Light Tackle Club, R. Rush, 10 Southcote Road, Tufnell Park, London N19.
British Waterways Board, Melbury House, Melbury Terrace, London NW1 6JX.
Chub Study Group, B. Woodcock, 707 Sqdn, HMS Heron, Yeovil, Somerset.
European Federation of Sea Anglers, Don Metcalfe, Redlands, High Street, Worle, Weston-super-Mare, Somerset.
Inland Waterways Association, 114 Regents Park Road, London NW1 8UQ.
London Anglers Association, 183 Hoe Street, Walthamstow, London E17.
National Anglers Council, 5 Cowgate, Peterborough PE1 1LR.
National Association of Specimen Groups, Alan Otter, 10 Cope Street, Hyson Green, Nottingham NG7 5AB.
National Federation of Anglers, Haig House, 87 Green Lane, Derby.
National Federation of Sea Anglers, Bob Page, 26 Downsview Crescent, Uckfield, Sussex TN22 1UB.
Pike Anglers Club, Barry Rickards, 4 Willow Crescent, Milton, Cambs.
Salmon and Trout Association, Fishmongers Hall, London Bridge, London EC4R 9EL.
Shark Angling Club of Great Britain, B. Tudor, Jolly Sailor Inn, West Looe, Cornwall.
Sports Council, 70 Brompton Road, London SW3 1EX.
The Tenchfishers, Robin Haywood, 12 Ganders Hill, Haywards Heath, Sussex.

Glossary of terms

Adipose fin: the tiny, fleshy fin just in front of the tail on game fish.
Alevin: recently-hatched salmon and trout which still have the yolk sac attached to their bodies.
Antenna: a float designed to be used with most of the body under water.
Arlesey bomb: a pear-shaped lead with a built-in swivel used for ledgering.
Backing: line put on reel beneath the main line.
Bale arm: a curved metal line pickup on a fixed-spool reel.
Bite alarm: an electronic or battery-operated indicator used for night fishing. When a fish takes the line, the indicator gives an audible warning by bleeping or buzzing and a visual signal by means of a small light.
Blank: the basic glass fibre body of a rod. Also, the term used by the angler when he has caught nothing.
Bloodworms: tiny, thread-like worms found in mud. They are popular bait on hard-fished waters in which the fish are shy.
Bootlace: a slang term for a small eel.
Brandling: a small, lively, striped worm that lives in manure heaps.
Caddis: a small, maggot-sized aquatic grub found on river beds, which makes a good bait when removed from its case.
Cast: the length of line between hook and main line. Also, the term used to describe the act of casting.
Caster: the term now used to describe the chrysalis of a maggot, a good bait for many freshwater species.
Chalk stream: a river that flows from the chalk hills. Found mostly in the south of England, they are very clear and produce big fish.
Closed-face reel: a variation of the fixed-spool but with a cover over the front.
Coarse fish: all freshwater fish which do not belong to the game family.
Crayfish: a small freshwater crustacean which looks like a miniature lobster.
Devon minnow: a fish-shaped spinning bait normally used for salmon.
Disgorger: an instrument used for removing the hook from the fish's mouth.
Drop net: a circular net on a rope used to lift hooked fish up the side of a pier or jetty.
Dry fly: any artificial fly meant to be fished on the surface of the water.
Ferrule: the joint used for connecting rod sections.
Fixed-spool reel: the most popular reel in use today. The spool around which the line is wrapped does not move, and the line is fed out or reeled in over its lip.
Foul-hook: catching a fish by the hook lodging in any part of the body except the mouth.
Free lining: a freshwater method in which no weight or float is used. It is a method normally used in carp fishing.
Fry: baby fish of all types.

Gaff: a large, barbless hook attached to a handle, and used for landing large sea fish.
Gozzer: a special type of soft maggot.
Groundbait: an attractor bait used to bring fish into a certain area.
Kelt: a salmon or sea trout which has spawned and is returning to the sea.
Lateral line: the line of cells along the flank of a fish which is sensitive to vibrations.
Laying on: a form of float fishing where the bait is fished overdepth and allowed to lie on the bottom with the last couple of shot.
Ledgering: fishing with a weight to keep the bait on the bottom. No float is used.
Lobworm: the big common earthworm found in most gardens.
Lure: a general term which describes all artificial bait. In trout fishing it generally means the bigger wet flies tied on large hooks.
Mark: the term used in sea fishing to describe a productive spot, often above a wreck or rocks.
Mona's scale: a weight-for-length table used to estimate the weight of pike.
Multiplier: a geared drum-reel used mostly in sea fishing.
Nymph: the larvae of various aquatic flies.
Parr: young salmon.
Peg: the set area from which a match angler fishes. The peg number is drawn just before the start of the match.
Pirk: a self-weighted artificial bait used in saltwater boat fishing.

Rover: the type of competition, normally held in the southern part of Britain, where the angler chooses his own fishing spot.
Rubby dubby: a mixture of minced or crushed fish hung over the side of a boat to attract shark.
Run: the term used to describe a fish's dash for safety once it has been hooked.
Specimen: a term used to describe a better-than-average fish.
Split shot: small lead weights used in freshwater fishing.
Swim: a term used by coarse anglers to describe the spot they are fishing.
Tailer: a wire loop on a handle used for landing salmon. The tailer is slipped over the tail and the loop pulled tight.
Trotting: a method of float fishing where the tackle is drifted downstream with the current.
Wet fly: any artificial fly meant to be fished below the surface of the water.

Bibliography

Collins Encyclopedia of Fishing in the British Isles edited by Michael Prichard
Billy Lane's Encyclopedia of Float Fishing (Pelham Books)
Geoffrey Bucknall's Book of Fly Fishing (Thomas Nelson)
Fly Tying for Beginners by Geoffrey Bucknall (Ernest Benn)
Fly Tying by R. Sugg, K. Whitehead and A. Vare (Rod and Gun)
Stillwater Angling by Richard Walker (MacGibbon & Kee)
Spinning for Pike by R. C. R. Barder (Arco)
Legering by Peter Stone (Arco)
Carp for Everyone by Peter Mohan (David & Charles)
Complete Guide to Sea Fishing by Hugh Stoker (Benn)
Beginner's Guide to Pike Fishing by Martin Gay (Pelham Books)

Acknowledgments

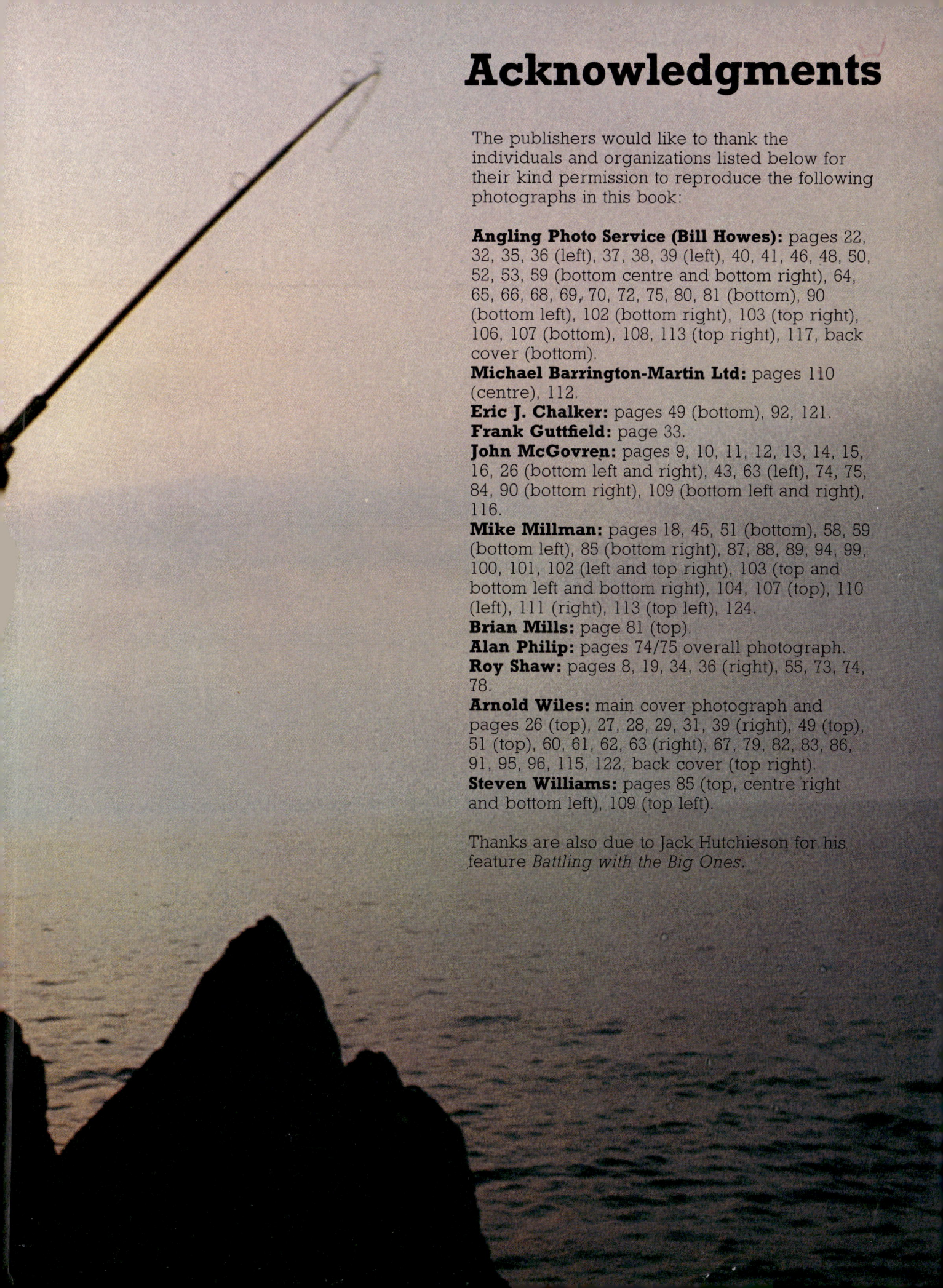

The publishers would like to thank the individuals and organizations listed below for their kind permission to reproduce the following photographs in this book:

Angling Photo Service (Bill Howes): pages 22, 32, 35, 36 (left), 37, 38, 39 (left), 40, 41, 46, 48, 50, 52, 53, 59 (bottom centre and bottom right), 64, 65, 66, 68, 69, 70, 72, 75, 80, 81 (bottom), 90 (bottom left), 102 (bottom right), 103 (top right), 106, 107 (bottom), 108, 113 (top right), 117, back cover (bottom).
Michael Barrington-Martin Ltd: pages 110 (centre), 112.
Eric J. Chalker: pages 49 (bottom), 92, 121.
Frank Guttfield: page 33.
John McGovren: pages 9, 10, 11, 12, 13, 14, 15, 16, 26 (bottom left and right), 43, 63 (left), 74, 75, 84, 90 (bottom right), 109 (bottom left and right), 116.
Mike Millman: pages 18, 45, 51 (bottom), 58, 59 (bottom left), 85 (bottom right), 87, 88, 89, 94, 99, 100, 101, 102 (left and top right), 103 (top and bottom left and bottom right), 104, 107 (top), 110 (left), 111 (right), 113 (top left), 124.
Brian Mills: page 81 (top).
Alan Philip: pages 74/75 overall photograph.
Roy Shaw: pages 8, 19, 34, 36 (right), 55, 73, 74, 78.
Arnold Wiles: main cover photograph and pages 26 (top), 27, 28, 29, 31, 39 (right), 49 (top), 51 (top), 60, 61, 62, 63 (right), 67, 79, 82, 83, 86, 91, 95, 96, 115, 122, back cover (top right).
Steven Williams: pages 85 (top, centre right and bottom left), 109 (top left).

Thanks are also due to Jack Hutchieson for his feature *Battling with the Big Ones*.